Innovations in Career and Technical Education

Strategic Approaches Towards Workforce Competencies Around the Globe

A volume in
Adult Education Special Topics:
Theory, Research, and Practice in Lifelong Learning

Series Editor:
Kathleen P. King, *Fordham University*

Adult Education Special Topics: Theory, Research, and Practice in Lifelong Learning

Kathleen P. King, Series Editor

Innovations in Career and Technical Education:
Strategic Approaches Towards
Workforce Competencies Around the Globe (2008)
edited by Victor C. X. Wang and Kathleen P. King

Innovations in Career and Technical Education

Strategic Approaches Towards Workforce Competencies Around the Globe

edited by

Victor C. X. Wang
California State University

and

Kathleen P. King
Fordham University

Information Age Publishing, Inc.
Charlotte, North Carolina • www.infoagepub.com

Library of Congress Cataloging-in-Publication Data

Innovations in career and technical education strategic approaches toward workforce competencies around the globe / edited by Victor C. X. Wang and Kathleen P. King.
    p. cm. -- (Adult education special topics. Theory, research, and practice in lifelong learning)
 Includes bibliographical references and index.
 ISBN-13: 978-1-59311-839-6 (pbk.)
 ISBN-13: 978-1-59311-840-2 (hardcover)
 1. Occupational training. 2. Vocational education. 3. Technical education. 4. Adult learning.
I. Wang, Victor C.X. II. King, Kathleen P.
 HD5715.I47 2007
 370.113--dc22

                                                                        2007033624

ISBN 13: 978-1-59311-839-6 (pbk.)
        978-1-59311-840-2 (hardcover)
ISBN 10: 1-59311-839-2 (pbk.)
        1-59311-840-6 (hardcover)

Printed in the United States of America

DEDICATION

To Katie, Anni, Anthony, and Dr. King for the support and love that make writing and editing possible.

—Victor Wang

To adult learners around the world who inspire me daily and to Sharon, Jim, and Bill who support me with their perfect love.

—Kathleen King

CONTENTS

PREFACE

In most instances, vocational education is defined as organized instructional programs which are directly related to the preparation of individuals for paid or unpaid employment or for additional preparation for careers which do not require a baccalaureate or an advanced degree. In its contemporary context, vocational education is often referred to as career and technical education. Career and technical education encompasses different components such as agriculture education, business education, health occupations education, family and consumer science, vocational-industrial education, technology education, technical education, and vocational guidance. This book is designed primarily for potential and in-service vocational instructors who are pursuing a program of personal and professional development which will ensure competency in this specialty. In any state in the United States, there are a number of uncredentialed instructors who teach courses in vocational education. Although these individuals may be competent enough in their subject matter areas, there is an obvious deficiency in the foundations of vocational education. Foundations of vocational education help vocational educators lay a solid foundation from which they can better help students hold aloft the banner of the full range of education for work, which is career and technical education in its modern sense. From this standpoint, this book is an excellent textbook for undergraduate and graduate students at university settings. Appealing foundation books are normally concerned with historical, philosophical, and social considerations of vocational education. The basic principles of vocational education must be covered in these books. Such prominent elements can be found from Evans and Herr's (1978) *Foundations of Vocational Education* to Gray and Herr's (1998) *Workforce Education: The Basics*. This book is no exception. The first section of the book is devoted to historical, philosophical, and social concepts of career and technical education. Four chapters cover historical and current issues in vocational education. One of the features which makes this book unique is that it includes international perspectives. Without a doubt, these new perspectives will widen the horizon of our learners. Most foundation books in vocational education may be too Western as the views in these books reflect mainstream Western thinking only. This is not the case with this groundbreaking book. As globalization brings different cultures together, it is not only important but also necessary to compare American vocational education with that in other countries.

It is by examining the acts of others that we improve our own. With this purpose in mind, talented scholars who have many years of extensive academic research and field experience in vocational education contributed chapters to this book. These individuals provided first-hand perspectives on vocational education in their own countries and regions. In particular, they have compared vocational education in the United States with that in other countries. Together, the chapters they have devoted to this book make up the second section of the book.

As you delve into the field of vocational education and training and global issues, you probably will come across multiple journal articles and books written by the editors and the authors of this book. The expertise of this book's contributors is also evident in the field's literature.

Any book of this type is the result of collaboration by many people rather than solely the "editors." Particular acknowledgement is due to Professor Ernest W. Brewer, editor of *The International Journal of Vocational Education and Training*, who granted us permission to reprint three articles published by that journal. The journal's blind review process has supported our efforts in providing high quality chapters for the book. The three articles published by this journal are as follows: (1), "Perspectives of a Healthy Work Ethic in a 21st Century International Community" by Gregory C. Petty and Ernest W. Brewer; (2), "Comparing the Russian, the Sloyd, and the Arts and Crafts Movement Training Systems" by Victor C. X. Wang and Carol Koerner Redhead; and (3), "Training in China" by Victor C. X. Wang.

Last but not least, please watch for other volumes in this new book series from Dr. King and Information Age Publishing about special topics in adult learning as it will be including vocational education. The reason being is that research keeps generating new knowledge in this field.

Victor C. X. Wang, EdD
California State University, Long Beach
Long Beach, CA

INTRODUCTION

Kathleen P. King

In thinking about the role of career and technical education (CTE) or vocational education (Voc Ed) today, one has to be impressed with the critical place it has in the Digital Age. Having roots in agricultural field and championing of the apprenticeship system of education, CTE has a long history that continues to profoundly impact humanity's livelihood, education and *innovation*. In our rapidly changing global community, education that focuses on relevance to current commerce and technologies, and develops self-directed learners and lifelong learners is at the center of success.

When one considers the saying "Think Outside of the Box," perhaps CTE has led the way in formal and informal education circles more than any other educational movement. CTE has not held back from addressing such challenges as

- changing economic needs,
- supporting the integration of new technologies into traditional and new careers, and
- developing new instructional strategies.

With rapid technological, global change, the standard of our world, future educational efforts need the capability to embrace even more radical and frequent transformations. This book, *Innovations in Career and Technical Education: Strategic Approaches Toward Workforce Competencies around the Globe,* provides a powerful experience and resource for educators across many grade levels and content areas in exactly these areas.

AUDIENCE AND USES OF THE BOOK

Part I of this volume provides a compelling platform of the historical, theoretical and philosophical foundations of the book, while Part II covers a one-of-a-kind detailed global survey of history and practice of vocational education. *Innovations in Career and Technical Education* can be used in several ways and for several purposes. While it was primarily designed with CTE and vocational education instructors who are pursuing a program of personal and professional development in mind, it can also be used in many other settings and applications. Teachers of Voc Ed and CTE can use this book to ensure competency in the specialty of the foundations and global applications of the field for their formal and informal development. While some may be engaged in in-service, others may be seeking a resource for self-directed study or lifelong learning in the field. In addition the book provides a valuable balance of practical and academic perspectives and writing so that it can also be used as a text for foundation courses in vocational education. Finally, the comprehensive scope of the text serves the needs of both new and experienced professionals and academics in the field and will no doubt provide rich findings upon multiple readings.

OVERVIEW

Part I of this volume begins with an eye-opening and comprehensive discussion of *The History of Vocational Education Up to 1850 and a Rationale for Work* in chapter 1. Much more than a chronology of the history of the field, Dr. Victor Wang provides a thought provoking analysis of the development and evolution of the meaning of work for humankind and its interrelationship with vocational education. Across geographies, political, religious and cultural realms, the reader gains a multifaceted perspective of the breadth and depth of humankind's understanding and need for work and the related training and learning that developed to support those needs. Wang does us a great service by interweaving the story with the history of vocational education, teaching, learning and the greater questions of humanity. From Egypt to Europe, the Chaldeans to the Romans, he also includes vignettes of the contributions of individuals such as Luther, Comenius, Locke, Rousseau, Pestalozzi, and Della Vos, to name a few. In addition as the chapter traces the relationship of vocational education to academic education and practical arts, a thesis emerges which provides new direction for vocational education or CTE. Knowing the breadth of development of the field in thought and practice is vital in guiding practitioners, administrators, scholars, lawmakers and students in continuing to shape the future.

Chapter 2, is a vital contribution to the literature in providing a concise presentation of two critical themes in career and technical education—principles and funding—and how the historical pathways of vocational education informs it today and provides a solid basis for building its future. This chapter, *Principles and Philosophy of Career and Technical Education and Federal Funding for Vocational Education up to the Present*, by Drs. Victor Wang and Kathleen P. King concentrates on the nineteenth and twentieth century historical roots of the principles and philosophy of career and technical education. Starting with the principles advanced by Prosser in 1925, the work of Roberts in the 1970s and then Miller in the 1980s, one gets a close up look at the development of the field. In addition, this chapter provides a valuable examination of the critical federal funding acts and how they formatively shaped vocational education since the Morrill Act of 1862 through such familiar ones as the Manpower Act and the Perkins Act. Because of their impact on education and student lives, the coauthors effectively bring these vital legislations to life for the reader, surely this chapter is a must read.

Not shying away from the difficult questions, chapter 3, *Historical Perspectives of the Different Components of Vocational Education* by Drs. Victor Wang, Kathleen P. King, and Fredrick M. Nafukho takes on the task of tracing the historical roots of the varied components within the field of vocational education. From the more traditional manual training, manual arts, industrial arts or trade and industrial education, agriculture education, business education, health occupations education, family and consumer science (formerly known as home economics), vocational-industrial education, technology education, technical education, and vocational education, CTE has a much broader scope than that to which many people are accustomed. By providing an understanding of the historical development of the different components of CTE, educators who have come from different contexts and meet different needs can broaden their understanding of this vast field. This chapter is another one that proves the richness and depth of this field and can swiftly and significantly impact the understanding of current and prospective CTE teachers who read it. Be ready for an "Aha" experience when you read chapter 3.

With more than one fourth of high school students taking three or more CTE courses and 40 million adults participating in short-term postsecondary occupational training (U.S. Department of Education, 2006), chapter 4, *Current Instructional Programs in Career and Technical*

Education provides much needed information to understand the current state of the field. Drs. Kathleen P. King and Victor Wang cover not only the programs of study, related occupations, frequently included courses, instructional techniques, and more for each of contemporary business education, agricultural programs, health occupations education, high technology trends, current family and consumer sciences programs, and technology education. In addition, they provide an overview of related topics in vocational guidance. This quick paced chapter is a valuable source of current information for those planning CTE programs that can now be grounded in best practice.

In Part 2 of the book we begin a tour of CTE innovation, history, practice, and philosophy around the globe with chapter 5: *Comparing the Russian, the Sloyd, and the Arts and Crafts Movement Training Systems* by Drs. Victor C. X. Wang and Carol Koerner Redhead. Based on a research study conducted among vocational educators, this chapter provides unique and timely insight into teaching preferences relative to methods associated with each training system: Russian, Sloyd, and the Arts and Crafts Movement. In addition, the chapter provides an excellent historical background regarding each of the training systems. This background, combined with the findings, creates a chapter that is a powerful experience for considering teaching practice, teacher effectiveness and student preparedness for CTE teachers in their independent professional development, or as in-service or teacher education class assignments.

When one considers the learners/workers who are prepared through our vocational education programs today compared to those in the past, one cannot avoid the fact that there is a significant change in perspective about work and a shift in work ethic. Chapter 6 of this volume, *Perspectives of a Healthy Work Ethic in a 21st-Century International Community* provides a compelling and much needed discussion of this topic. Drs. Petty and Brewer couch their discussion in terms of the global community and instant communication of the twenty-first century and the impact these have on the perspectives and expectations of new generations of workers worldwide. The chapter's discussion fluidly spans diverse viewpoints of work, ancient historical perspectives, religious foundations, the effect of automation and globalization on work and work ethics. Be ready for a transformation of your own perspectives as you read this chapter and consider how the traditional views and ethics of work have been and are challenged around us moment by moment. If we are to be effective and relevant with our students and prepare them well for their lives ahead, we need current understandings about both them and our changing world. This chapter reveals these aspects of continuing change in our world for us.

Chapter 7's *Framing Strategic Partnerships Guided by Adult Learning* reveals how CTE is a valuable means to bridge the K-16 gap that is often experienced by learners in many educational systems. Dr. Kathleen P. King is an adult learning professor and former CTE instructor. The chapter is based on an extended research study of several successful CTE programs from across the United States in order to determine what characteristics of adult learning were evident among their best practices. The findings are unique in that they explicitly bridge the literature of adult learning with best practice of CTE. The K-16 gap depicts the chasm between compulsory and higher education. It is described as such because so many students never make it across to the ground of higher education. In this ground breaking chapter, we see many outstanding instructional strategies and program designs that help students succeed in continuing their learning, stay motivated and be best equipped for their future careers or additional academic study. Numerous practical examples are provided throughout the chapter in order to make it most valuable for practitioners of all levels of expertise.

Dr. Victor Wang's *Training in China* focuses the book's discussion in chapter 8 on training in the Asian context. Based on a survey research study among three training schools in China, this chapter explores how trainers in China respond to a Western trainer's view, teaching and the resulting perspectives and practices. The chapter freshly reveals characteristics of Chinese training. This chapter is another rare opportunity to explore and understand significantly different perspectives in the training field, to critically reflect on one's own work and to use the experience to improve teaching effectiveness and student preparation.

Dr. Fredrick Nafukho examines the development of vocational and technical education in Kenya in Chapter Nine, *Reforms in Education and Training Curriculum as a Strategic Approach to Workforce Development Competencies in Kenya*. By bringing our global discussion to Africa, this chapter provides a unique and valuable example of how the Kenyan government has sought to address the problems of low and middle income youth and other wage earners. The chapter describes not only the numerous legislations, but the story of a people, a nation, and CTE coping with sociocultural issues including racism, transitioning through governmental independence, and adopting a new educational system. This is another must read in order to appreciate the diversity of experience in our field around the globe and to grow in our understanding of the complexity of the choices involved in educational and governmental policy.

Moving on to the Caribbean, Dr. Henry O'Lawrence authored chapter 10, *Workforce Competencies: A Comparison of U.S. and Jamaican Experiences*, for this volume. Rather than solely a presentation of Jamaican workforce education, this chapter provides an important comparison of the U.S. and Jamaican experiences in workforce competencies. Fundamentally, Dr.

O'Lawrence presents his educational philosophy upfront and positions his discussion within the context of "the role of career and technical education in developing a nation's wealth." In doing so, he provides an historical overview of CTE around the globe and then focuses on the U.S. and in turn Jamaica. With the overview and analysis, the author is able to provide recommendations for workforce education from a global perspective as well as with specifics for Jamaica. The result is a very good chapter with dual purposes of an overview and comparative case study.

While the title of the eleventh chapter of the book might seem to solely compare China and U.S. CTE instructors, in reality, *Teaching Philosophies of Chinese Career and Technical Instructors and U.S. Career and Technical Instructors* by Dr. Victor Wang provides a comparison of dominant western perspectives with a sample of practitioners in China. Wang provides background that reveals how competency-based, or performance-based education has spread in CTE in various forms from Russia, across Canada, South America, the United States, Australia, and more. The research that is the foundation for this chapter compares the teaching philosophies of vocational education instructors' teaching in Chinese vocational agricultural universities and American land-grant universities. The results reveal similarities and differences among the groups in social settings, and philosophies of instruction. Readers will discover several significant implications from this chapter that may influence their understanding of varied cultures in an increasingly global world and their own educational goals, objectives and/or shape their philosophy of teaching.

Long known to be an innovator in distance learning and adult learning, Australia is the focus of chapter 12, Australia's vocational education and training. This chapter provides a seldom seen view of this specific topic. The scope and significance of this effort needs to be emphasized to those unfamiliar with the fact that the Commonwealth of Australia covers an entire continent and its outlying islands. It includes six states and two internal Territories: New South Wales, Queensland, South Australia, Tasmania, Victoria, Western Australia, the Australian Capital Territory, and the Northern Territory. In this chapter, Dr. Kitainge provides an interesting overview of the history and issues facing vocational education and training (VET). He clearly displays a case study that is instructive for CTE instructors and administrators worldwide to benefit from: VET educational system and practitioners have had to adapt to the needs of the industry and individual students. The implications of these findings are several; the story is persuasive. This chapter provides a unique basis for individual and group study of vocational education to see how the context, people and dynamics in which our field functions over time impacts the field. There is much room for provocative thought, reflective action, and effective practice to grow from reading and discussing this chapter.

SUMMARY

Whether you read *Innovations in Career and Technical Education* from cover to cover, or select individual chapters one by one, this book offers a vital foundation for vocational education practice, history, and development across the globe. With the initial chapters providing a conceptual framework and the latter chapters revealing our global tour of practice and research, readers will gain a profoundly greater appreciation and more comprehensive view of the field which has such a long and richly varied heritage.

Indeed, we as CTE teachers are lifelong learners ourselves. And this book can be an opportunity for us all to gain new teaching strategies, understand different perspectives, and grasp new opportunities to empower our students. While our world is rapidly changing and our adult learners, of all ages, are seeking careers, skills and knowledge that will enable them to cope and function in this environment, *Innovations in Career and Technical Education* provides a reinvigorating and insightful view of CTE as an innovative force for teachers and learners. We hope this volume will be a great aid to CTE and Voc Ed educators, educators-in-training and academics in their professional and personal lifelong learning. For as we continue to lead the way in "Thinking Outside of the Box," so will our learners and field.

REFERENCES

U.S. Department of Education. (2006). *Career and technical education*. Retrieved December 14, 2006, from http://www.ed.gov/about/offices/list/ovae/pi/cte/index.html

PART I

CHAPTER 1

THE HISTORY OF VOCATIONAL EDUCATION UP TO 1850 AND A RATIONALE FOR WORK

Victor C. X. Wang

The history of vocational education parallels the efforts of humanity from the Stone Age to modern civilization. Humans learned early in history that they could improve their lot by means of work (Roberts, 1965, p. 31). Some of the following information will give the reader some ideas of the growth of this system. Thus, knowing the history of vocational education gives the practitioner useful "feed-forward" signals about the present condition of the field (Gray & Herr, 1998, p. 5). David (1976) argued that the usefulness of history lies in its potential to explain why things are the way they are. Practitioners, scholars, and students cannot achieve an objective understanding of the current status of vocational education without first looking into its history.

Another discussion in this chapter focuses on the rationale for work. It is commonly understood that one's rationale for work stems from people's economic, psychological, creative, expressive, and social needs. This chapter also reveals an interesting discussion of how prominent

Innovations in Career and Technical Education: Strategic Approaches Towards Workforce Competencies Around the Globe, pp. 3–19
Copyright © 2008 by Information Age Publishing
3

leaders in the field view work and its relationship with career and technical education.

THE EARLY BEGINNING OF VOCATIONAL EDUCATION

Survival is the act to remain alive or continue in existence. This was the main concern during the Stone Age because most skills were learned as a result of the need for survival (Roberts, 1965). These skills were gained from watching one's elders at the campsite, and could consist of making an axe, building a fire, heating flint so it would chip in order to make a sharp instrument, and similar skills (Bennett, 1926). Learning is an act to gain knowledge or skill by observation. During the Stone Age period, there were no written documents and the way one could learn their survival skills was to observe someone performing them (Boyd, 1921).

A second type of learning is to gain knowledge or skill with language (Roberts, 1965). As humans progressed and language developed, instruction could be given and learning was accomplished by more than observation. The use of language allowed people to learn to improve one's ways to accomplish tasks. The ways that were productive and those that were unproductive could be documented and passed from generation to generation. Through this documentation, humans were destined to not continuously repeat earlier mistakes (Breasted, 1916).

Discoveries in Europe have indicated that humans used stone implements more than 50,000 years ago. This period lasted approximately 40,000 years. During this period, improved stone instruments were developed, wooden boats were constructed, animals were domesticated, pottery was made, and grain was grown (Erman & Blackman, 1927).

The following describes how ancient peoples in the Middle East region and in Europe contributed to vocational education during the early part of human history. Thus some international perspectives can be formed for our readers. As Gray and Herr (1998) describe it, the history of vocational education gives the practitioner useful "feed-forward" signals about the present condition of the field. Indeed, so many practitioners teach in the field of vocational education now without knowing where it comes from.

The recorded history of the Egyptians might mark the beginning of civilization, or people with a higher social order. Humans continued to make progress through learning and work. About 6,000 years ago the ancient Egyptians began to develop a civilization based on scientific knowledge, government, and religion in the valleys of the Nile, Tigris, and the Euphrates rivers (Good, 1962). The Egyptians developed a form of picture writing called hieroglyphics. They also developed a paper called papyrus and started schools to teach scribes how to write and make the papyrus paper. The schools were of two types: (1) schools to teach reading and writing and (2) apprenticeships where the students learned on-the-job with an experienced scribe. During this time scribes were trained through apprenticeships, however, being a scribe was considered a noble occupation (West, 1931).

When humans began to reduce copper ore to copper metal, the metal age began. Roads were built, buildings were constructed of bricks, and fields were irrigated. They began to grow modern day grains like barley and wheat and use domesticated animals for work. The Nile dwellers learned how to measure time and established a calendar (Roberts, 1965).

The Persian Gulf from the northern borders of Arabia to the Mediterranean Sea was the first home of the people of Western Asia. The people of this area had reclaimed the marshes and produced barley and wheat long before 3,000 B.C. During the Babylonian Age, which extended for 3,200 B.C. to 2,100 B.C., people constructed houses of brick and fashioned arts and crafts from stone and metal. Vocations became specialized and apprenticeship-training programs were organized and legalized (Roberts, 1965). The first historical reference to apprenticeship was in the Babylonian Code compiled about 2,100 B.C. The Assyrians conquered the Babylonians, brought cotton and iron to the fertile land, and organized a postal service. However, they in turn were conquered in 612 B.C. by the Chaldeans (Roberts, 1965, p. 35). The Chaldeans conquered the Assyrians in 612 B.C. Under their influence, commerce, and business flourished, religion and literature were cultured and notable progress was made in the science of astronomy (Erman & Blackman, 1927, p. 198). The Persians came into prominence in approximately 561 B.C. They maintained an organization of government controlled by one man. The farmland was divided into large tracts and held by powerful landowners. Silver and gold were coined into money and excellent roads were maintained. The Persian Empire, which lasted until about 330 B.C., has provided documents which have enabled present-day humans to read the cuneiform inscriptions of Western Asia (Breasted, 1916, p. 137).

Ancient Jews recognized the value of education. They felt that everyone should possess skill in a manual trade so that they could contribute to the society rather than become a parasite, which is dangerous to any community. Jewish law placed the duty of teaching a son a trade upon the parents (Breasted, 1916). The fundamental focus of ancient Jewish education was religion. Religious teaching was known as the Law. Next to instruction in the Law, instruction in vocations was of high esteem. Children were taught the Law and to follow it. The father taught each of his sons a trade, usually the trade he followed. Boys attended school in the morning, which were taught by rabbis and worked with their father in the afternoon. This was a similar format to our current cooperative program (Roberts, 1965).

Education in both Athens and Sparta was for the purpose of training both strong and courageous soldiers and citizens. The chief objective of education in Sparta was strength, courage, endurance, patriotism, and obedience (Roberts, 1965, p. 37). During the early Greek days, handicraft occupied a place of respect, but in later times, the work of handicraftsmen was designated as merely mechanical and was frowned upon. A person with callused hands was scorned (Roberts, 1965, p. 38). Apprenticeship instruction was approved for the lower class. Boys were taught drawing quite similar to the way orators, lawyers, physicians, and cooks were trained (Seybolt, 1917, pp. 91-92). The Romans were a practical and conservative people. They were especially noted for their codes of law and plans for public administration. Their civilization, much of which was borrowed from the Greeks, has had a strong influence on present day civilization (Roberts, 1965).

Early Roman education was carried on in the family. The father provided a practical education for his sons. The sons were taken to the fields and to the forums where they learned by observation and participation. In terms of schooling, three distinct levels were provided: elementary, secondary and higher. Elementary covered reading, writing, conduct, and memorization of laws. Secondary covered literature in Latin and Greek, and higher covered rhetoric, oratory, mathematics, music, history, and law. Public funds were used by the Romans to pay teachers of grammar and rhetoric from about A.D. 75 Most of the other funds for education were private funds.

With the fall of Rome in the fifth century, the influence of Roman culture declined, and the teaching in the schools became formal and superficial. This type of education began to have little appeal and by the sixth century most of the universities were closed. Western civilization at that time entered the Dark Ages of the medieval period. The Christian Monks devoted an excessive amount of care and attention to manual labor. Labor was required of everyone that was associated with the monasteries. St. Benedict (480-543) founded the order of the Benedictines at Monto Cassinor in Italy about 529. He made labor one of the cardinal principles of his rule. He felt that 7 hours a day should be expended in labor and 2 hours per day should be used for reading. This reading was done from manuscripts since books were not printed until about 1450. Scribe work was accepted as equivalent to out-of-doors work, so copying manuscripts become a favored occupation with the monks. Benedictines drained marshes, built roads and bridges and introduced new methods of farming. The Benedictines' enthusiasm carried them north of the Alps. Germany was filled with monasteries, which became centers of civilization. The Benedictines became the civilization of the region (Roberts, 1965). Monastic schools attracted men both young and old, who sought an opportunity for a life of reflection and study. Thus the monasteries came to be the schools for teaching, the place of professional training, the universities of research, the only publishers of books, and the only libraries for the preservation of learning; they produced the only scholars; they were the sole educational institution of this period.

The transition from medieval to modern times, which occurred in the fourteenth and fifteenth centuries, is known as the Italian Renaissance. One phase of the transition, the scholarly phase, is referred to as the "Revival of Learning." This revival was a return to the ancient literature of the Greeks and Romans that had been discarded at the beginning of the Dark Ages (Roberts, 1965). The invention and early development of the art of printing, and the Protestant Reformation with its center in Germany, beginning early in the sixteenth century, unfolded new educational possibilities and put new life into teaching methods. This new instruction was based upon two fundamental ideas: (1) sense impression is the basis for thought and consequently of knowledge and (2) the support of manual arts training with "learning by doing."

HISTORIC FIGURES WHO HELPED SHAPE VOCATIONAL EDUCATION

Many of the present-day views on vocational education still reflect the insights and philosophies of early historic leaders in the field. It is these historic leaders who helped shape vocational education. Their influences are still felt to this day. If you have never heard of these historic figures, this is a good opportunity to study their ideas and philosophies that offered the formative directions for vocational education throughout our history. Gordon (2003) argued that some of their philosophies of vocational education encompassed enduring ideas and concepts that have transcended the ravages of time (p. 34).

Martin Luther (1483-1546) objected to the system used by the Monastic school. He compared them to prisons. He indicated that the boy was like a "bird in a dark cage" or like "a young tree required to grow in a flower pot." Luther felt that schooling should be given to "all people, noble and common, rich and poor, and it should include both boys and girls." Schooling should be compulsory and it should be held 2 hours per day and arranged so those older children could carry on the ordinary economic duties of life uninterruptedly. Luther advocated that the curriculum should include Latin, Greek, Hebrew, logic, mathematics, music, history, and science (Monroe, 1905, pp. 410-412).

Rabelais (1494-1553) also disagreed with the way that the churches and schools were being conducted. Rabelais would approach knowledge through the use of objects and the observation of processes (Hodgson, 1908). His ideals were later brought out by Montaigne, Locke, and Rousseau.

Francis Bacon (1561-1626) felt that new learning could be obtained from nature and the arts of daily life. Bacon felt that to learn new things one must go straight to nature and learn through the senses. He held that all knowledge must be obtained by a careful and unprejudiced induction from facts, hence the importance of the experiment. Bacon's philosophy of realism gave support for applied science in our schools (Manzo, 2006).

John Amos Comenius (1592-1670) agreed with Rabelais in regard to the combination of words and things, which should be integrated in instruction. He would have children learn "as much as possible, not from books, but from the book of nature, from heaven and earth, from oaks and beeches." He also believed that learning should be pleasant for the learner. He felt that both sexes should be sent to school. He felt that the schools should be divided as follows: (1) infant school, (2) elementary, (3) secondary School, (4) university. Comenius has been called the "father of modern pedagogy" because he formulated principles and methods of instruction that were in harmony with the main current of pedagogical development (Comenius, n.d.).

John Locke (1632-1704) became a chief proponent of the idea that education should fit a boy for practical life, whether it be a trade or a profession (Fieser & Dowden, 2007). In 1697 when he was a commissioner of trade and plantations, he advocated that a system of "working schools" for all pauper children between 3 and 14 years of age should be available to teach spinning and knitting or some other part of the woolen manufacture. Locke advocated the learning of manual trades because (1) they afford good physical exercise, (2) the skill gained is worth having-it may be useful, and (3) they provide diversions or recreations.

Jean Jacques Rousseau (1712-1778) was the author of *The Social Contract* (Carrin, 2006), which has been blamed for the French Revolution (Mandler, 2007). He also wrote *Emile*, which is said to have been the cause for him to flee France to avoid arrest. This book is also said to have broken down the walls of educational formalism and initiated a new approach in education in which the student or child is the center of teaching. Rousseau believed profoundly that experience is the best teacher and he felt that everything possible should be taught by actions and that words should only be used for those things that cannot be taught by actions. Rousseau's statements concerning the value of the manual arts in education placed him ahead of his predecessors and many of those who came after him. His recognition of the fact that the manual arts may be a means of mental training marked the beginning of a new era in education. It prepared the way for the education methods of Pestalozzi and those who followed.

In the study of manual arts, **John Henry Pestalozzi** (1746-1827) is referred to as the "father of manual training." Pestalozzi was impressed by the writing of Rousseau. He originally studied the ministry, then began a study of law, but settled for the quiet life of a farm in Birr, Switzerland where he attempted to teach a group of poor children how to farm. The farming operation was not a financial success and he had to abandon it. On the other hand, the education of the children was successful. He went on to other areas of hands-on instruction. The instruction always seemed to be successful. Pestalozzi felt there were two ways to instruct: (1) from things to words and (2) from words to things. He used the first method. He was never in a hurry for the students to study books. He always wanted them to become actively involved in their learning by hands-on experiences so that the written material would have greater meaning. He also believed that children in school should learn to work not only because of the economic value of skill and the habit of labor, but because this experience gives sense-impressions which like the study of objects, becomes the basis of knowledge (Beyer, 2004, p. 3).

Just as Pestalozzi was the new and vital force in the realm of educational philosophy and methods during the early part of the 19th nineteenth, **Phillip Emanuel Von Fellenberg** (1771-1844) was the force in practical school organization and administration during the same period (Beyer, 2004). Von Fellenberg believed in the separation of people in different social levels and organized a series of schools and classes for these various social levels at Hofwyl, Switzerland beginning in 1800. The educational establishment at Hofwyl attracted more attention and exerted a wider influence than any one institution in Europe or America at that time. It was visited and studied by many educators and statesmen. It especially attracted an American, William C. Woodbridge; editor of the *American Annals of Education*, which featured many issues "Sketches of Hofwyl" which brought to American educators a wealth of information concerning this noble experiment in education. These ideas influenced the development in vocational education in the United States. Von Fellenberg demonstrated the importance of school organization and business management in the operation of a school system (Beyer, 2004). The chief characteristic of this system was manual labor. Von Fellenberg proved that manual activities, when properly organized and directed; could contribute both financially and educationally to the success of the student and the school system.

Victor Della Vos and his shop instructors developed a new system to teach manual trades in 1867. He developed a system where the students could learn entry-level skills for a craft or trade in a school setting (Anderson, 1926). The following were crucial for him to develop this system:

- Each art or distinct type of work was required to have its own separate instruction shop; for example, joinery, woodturning, blacksmithing, locksmithing, and so forth.
- Each shop was equipped with as many working places and sets of tools as there were pupils to receive the instruction at one time.
- The courses or models were arranged according to the increasing difficulty of the exercises involved, and were given to the pupils in strict succession as arranged.
- All models were made from drawings. Copies of each drawing were supplied in sufficient number to provide one for each member of a class.
- The drawings were made by the pupil in the class for elementary drawing, under the direction of the teacher of drawing with whom the manager of the shops came to an agreement concerning the various details.
- Pupils were not allowed to begin a new model until they had acceptably completed the previous model in the course.
- First exercises were accepted if dimensions were approximately correct; later exercises were required to be more exact according to the dimensions.
- Every teacher was required to possess more knowledge and skill of the specialty taught than were necessary to merely perform the exercises in the course of instruction. The instructor must also keep in practice so that demonstrations to students indicate a high level of skill.

Victor Della Vos exhibited his system of instruction at the Centennial Exposition in Philadelphia in 1876. As a result of this presentation, The School of Mechanic Arts was opened in connection with the Massachusetts Institute of Technology in Boston. Also, the St. Louis Manual Training School, in St. Louis, Missouri, adopted the principles of his system in 1880. These schools gave manual training in the high school, an impetus that spread over the United States in a short period of time (Schenck et al., 1984).

A RATIONALE FOR EDUCATION FOR WORK

Now that we have knowledge of how vocational education came into being and who helped shape it during the early part of human history, it is time to study the rationale for education and for work. Marx defined work as a process going on between humans and nature, a process in which humans, through their own activities, initiate, regulate, and control the material reactions between themselves and nature. (as cited in Wang, 2006, p. 39) According to Marx (1890/1929), work produces surplus value. Wang interprets this surplus value as "added value" in vocational education and training. As noted by Gordon (2003, p. 247), career and technical education generally has focused on helping people to understand the relationship between education and work and to acquire employment skills. People often ask the question, "Why education for work?" There are a number of reasons to educate for work in a modern society. In exploring why people work, Wenrich, Wenrich, and Galloway (1988) recognized that:

People Need to Work: There is ample evidence that people need to work and need assistance in learning to work and to appreciate work, and career and technical education is one phase of educating individuals for work.

Perceptions of Work: Each of us has a different perception of work depending upon our experiences. It may be a joy or a burden depending upon our idea about its place in our lives.

Work versus Leisure/Vocation versus Avocation: What is work for one person may be leisure or play for another or vice versa. For example, for a golfing professional, golf is work, but for an editor of a magazine, golf is play or leisure.

Work Through the Ages: Work has changed through the ages. For example, in early Christianity, work was viewed as punishment laid on man by God. The ancient Hebrews and Greeks thought of work as painful drudgery. During the Reformation Age work was thought of as the right and moral thing to do. Later, the Puritan Work Ethic promoted work as good and leisure or idleness as bad (as cited in Petty & Brewer, 2005, pp. 95-98).

People work because they need to work: For income, for activity, for self-respect and the respect of others, for social contacts and participation, and to express themselves creatively (Friedmann & Havighurst, 1954).

Work and Leisure: The shift from a labor intensive to a machine or robotic led society should provide more time for leisure. Society in

America has gone from a 60-hour workweek to a 32-40 hour workweek (Friedmann & Havighurst, 1954).

Developing Work Ethic: Experiences must be provided in elementary, secondary, and post secondary education to help individuals understand and appreciate the value of work and its functions in life and to help them develop their potential to become satisfied workers.

Individuals Want to Work: The old assumption that "people do not want to work," has not proved to be true. Individuals enjoy doing those things they are good at. This supports the idea that individuals need vocational education in order to become skilled in an area they would like to pursue, whether for work or for pleasure.

Equal Educational Opportunity: with public education in a democratic society, career and technical education should be available to all secondary and postsecondary students. This is an important part of the process of developing the individual's potential for work.

Relationship of Work and Education: As noted by Wenrich, Wenrich, and Galloway (1988, p. 16), primitive people did not need much formal education in order to work. Even in the early history of the nation (USA), most people learned to work by associating with experienced workers (apprenticeship). With the advent of the industrial revolution and the shift to an industrialized society, more formal education was necessary to work. The technological, or information society is requiring even more formal or technical education. Most individuals participate in formal education based on the expectation that it adds quality to their life. Fewer than 100 years ago in the United States, formal education for most individuals ended at the eighth grade. Economics was one of the main reasons why parents did not keep their children in school: it was not seen as increasing one's ability to earn money. Only when the promise of better-paying jobs was connected to more education did attending school longer become a motivating factor in education.

Gray and Herr (1998) defined workforce education (please note workforce education is the most current name for vocational education. Vocational education has had different names during different parts of human history) as follows:

> Workforce education is that form of pedagogy that is provided at the pre-baccalaureate level by education institutions, by private business and industry, or by government-sponsored, community-based organizations where the objective is to increase individual opportunity in the labor market or to solve human performance problems in the workforce. (p. 4)

They also suggested that workforce education has two functions: (1), Promote individual opportunity by making students more competitive in the labor force, and (2), Make a nation economically strong and firms internationally competitive by solving human performance problems of incumbent workers.

VOCATIONAL EDUCATION AND LIBERAL EDUCATION

Vocational ("Vocational Education," 2007) or career and technical education is education specifically designed to prepare one to enter into or advance in a specific vocation or career. Liberal education ("Liberal Arts," 2007) should assist persons to follow a number of vocations or careers. However, it does not provide them with specific skills for these vocations or careers. Instead, a liberal education prepares more for living or life in general rather than for work. Liberal education includes such disciplines as mathematics, physical sciences, natural sciences, biological sciences, and rhetoric, history, languages, and philosophy. Note that a person who works in practicing mathematics is making a vocational or career use of their education. The same can be true of virtually all subjects.

Evans and Herr (1978) wrote that some objectives of career and technical education that may be considered include:

- Meeting the manpower needs of society,
- Increasing the options available to individuals, and
- Providing a motivating force to enhance all types of learning.

All other objectives of career and technical education may revolve around the above three basic objectives.

Meeting the Manpower Needs of Society

Industry, government, the schools, and indeed all institutions of society require trained people if they are to survive. As Evans and Herr (1978) noted, while the needs of family are almost invariably ignored in statements of needs for workers, society is gradually recognizing that consumer education and homemaking education of high quality are essential to the survival of the family as well. As we live in this information age and knowledge society, the need for trained workers has become more pronounced.

Career and Technical Education Can Broaden the Options of an Individual

An individual can pursue a career and technical education, but will not necessarily be limited to that specific vocation or career. Many individuals who pursue a vocational curriculum take general education courses to broaden their horizons. They may also learn skills that can transfer to other work areas. For example, an individual may major in auto mechanics but obtain competencies and obtain employment as a mechanical maintenance person in an industrial plant (Evans & Herr, 1978).

Career and Technical Education Increases Options

For an individual who attends secondary and postsecondary schools, career and technical education provides skills which will give individuals more options than if they pursued a liberal education (Evans & Herr, 1978).

John Dewey and Occupational Education

John Dewey, America's first philosopher/educator, felt that occupations should be used as vehicles of instruction in elementary and secondary education. Dewey's philosophy was based upon the idea of a total organism interacting with its environment. He conceived of the mind as the process by which organisms and environment become integrated. He believed that occupations excite the interest of the student and cause them to be better students (Dewey, 1944, 1966). Dewey opposed vocational education which was limited only to the acquisition of job skills. He believed that the underlying principles of the work processes and social significance of work must be included. He further believed that through vocational studies, culture might be made truly vital for many students.

NEED FOR CAREER AND TECHNICAL EDUCATION

Wenrich, Wenrich, and Galloway (1988) make the point that career and technical Education as a responsibility of the public school system can be justified only if it is planned and organized so as to achieve its objectives to the maximum degree possible. The following will address the objectives as stated earlier.

Needs for Trained Personnel

Educators must be knowledgeable about the personnel needs within their service area in order to ascertain whether the programs they implement and conduct actually serve these needs. Continual research is needed in order to determine the needs and the fulfillment of those needs by the respective career and technical programs. Programs may need to be implemented, revised, or closed as needs change in the program service area.

Individual Options

The opportunity to choose from a number of alternatives is an important concept in a democratic society and in education. Education should provide for these alternatives. Options may include choices from among different occupations, kinds and levels of education, income, employment and many other areas (Evans & Herr, 1978).

Project Talent

A study of students in United States' high schools in 1966 by Flanagan and Cooley, found that the general curriculum enrolled 25% of the students, yet it produced 76% of the high school dropouts. The study also showed that graduates of the general curriculum ranked behind the college preparatory and the vocational graduates on nearly every measure of success including:

- Proportion who go on to college
- Annual earnings
- Job satisfaction
- Length and frequency of unemployment.

Individual options are increased when:

- A larger variety of specialized career and technical programs are available from which individuals may choose.

- Career and technical programs are offered by public schools, as opposed to the vocational training provided by employers.
- High school programs are broadened so that youth are prepared for clusters of occupations, thereby giving greater flexibility in the labor market.
- Adult programs are readily available for the upgrading and retraining of employed person.
- Job placement services are provided by the schools to assist youth in finding suitable employment.

Learning Enhancer

Career and technical education can serve as a motivating force to enhance all types of learning. Employment-bound youth in secondary and post secondary programs can be challenged by the occupation of their choice and the job-entry requirements. Subject areas take on new meaning when a student begins studying an occupation and discovers they are necessary for satisfactory completion of the program. Subject areas such as mathematics, science, reading, writing, and spelling suddenly take on new meaning since the student can now see relevance in pursuing them.

CAREER AND TECHNICAL EDUCATION VERSUS PRACTICAL ARTS EDUCATION

Perhaps it is safe to say that it is Wenrich, Wenrich, and Galloway (1988) who provided the similarities and differences of career and technical education and practical arts education. Their insights are still widely cited today. Wenrich, Wenrich, and Galloway (1988) recognize that:

> Career and technical education and practical arts education are special subject matter areas in which applied instruction is given. That is to say that a lot of hands-on or applied learning takes place where psychomotor skills are involved. Career and technical education is job specific in order to produce students with job entry skills. Much time is devoted to practice and application of job skills needed for the occupation. Practical arts is skill-oriented instruction, however, the purpose of this training is more for consumer knowledge than for job entry. It is more for a vocational use rather than for vocational use. For that reason, practical arts education is considered general education. That is, it is useful for anyone to take no matter what their career ambitions are. Practical arts could be considered pre-vocational since many students who enroll in practical arts decide to follow one of the career

and technical areas as a result of their hands-on experiences with the psychomotor skills. (pp. 5-6)

CAREER AND TECHNICAL EDUCATION AND DROPOUT PREVENTION

Educators and parents are always concerned with the large number of youth who leave school before completing the usual 12 grades of secondary education. Studies show that from 30 to 40% of the youth who enter the first grade drop out before the completion of high school. The junior high school, Grades 8, 9, and 10, show an unusually large number of dropouts. The larger schools with a greater variety of course offerings have a higher holding power than the smaller schools.

Some advocate that more students would complete the secondary school if they felt that the offerings were more interesting and relevant. Many suggest that practical arts and career and technical education could decrease the dropout rate. However, practical arts and career and technical education cannot effect much of a change unless the students enroll in the programs. Many students drop out of school before they ever enroll in practical arts and career and technical education courses. Since the "Nation At Risk" report (National Commission on Excellence in Education, 1983) was released in the early 1980s many school districts have raised graduation requirements for the nonpractical courses, math, science, reading, and English. This change in requirements is making it difficult for secondary students to enroll in practical arts or career and technical education courses. Since the 1976 Vocational Education Amendments were passed, the practical arts and career and technical education teacher has been involved with a number of "mainstreamed" disadvantaged and handicapped students some of whom may have difficulty in completing the work for the program. This could have an influence on the dropout rate of vocational students.

CONCLUSION

A closer examination of the history of vocational education and the rationale for work reveals that vocational education has been developed to meet the three objectives of vocational education in any form of society. The workforce needs of any society are even greater today than any previous part of human history as human beings have entered the so-called information age and globalization. No longer can we view vocational education just as education for work! It is also education for life, not just the preparation for life. During the primitive era, little formal education was needed for work; now for the full range of work much more formal education is needed in order to work. The relationship between vocational education and work is getting closer and closer given the nature of our technological society. The influences advanced by those early vocational educators in the field are still being felt today. In fact, their principles and philosophies will continue to guide the field of career and technical education into the future. Although federal legislation indicated that vocational instruction is designed to enable people to succeed in occupations requiring less than a baccalaureate degree, evidence shows many vocational education students are college bound students today. In other words, the distinction between vocational education and academic education is not that clear. At the same time to integrate vocational educa- tion in academic education does seem to be a viable option.

REFERENCES

Anderson, L. F. (1926). *History of manual and industrial school education*. New York: Appleton-Century-Crofts.

Bennett, C. A. (1926). *History of manual and industrial education up to 1870*. Peoria, AZ: Manual Arts.

Beyer, C. K. (2004). Manual and industrial education for Hawaiians during the 19th century. *Hawaiian Journal of History, 38*, 1-34.

Boyd, W. (1921). *The history of Western education*. London: Black.

Breasted, J. H. (1916). *Ancient times, A history of the early world*. New York: Ginn.

Carrin, G. J. (2006). Rousseau's "social contract": Contracting ahead of its time? [Review of the book The social contract]. *Bulletin of the World Health Organization, 84*(11), 917-918.

Comenius Foundation. (n.d.) *About John Amos Comenius*. Retrieved May 3, 2007, from http://www.comeniusfoundation.org/comenius.htm

David, H. (1976, October). *Education manpower policy*. Paper presented at the Bicentennial conference sponsored by the National Advisory Council on Vocational Education. Minneapolis, MN.

Dewey, J. (1944). Challenge to liberal thought. *Fortune, 30*(2), 155-190.

Dewey, J. (1966). *Democracy and education*. New York: The Free Press.

Erman, A., & Blackman, A. (1927). *The literature of the ancient Egyptians*. New York: Dutton.

Evans, R. N., & Herr, E. L. (1978). *Foundations of vocational education*. New York: Macmillan.

Fieser, J., & Dowden, B. (Eds.). (2007). *Educational writings*. Retrieved May 2, 2007, from http://www.utm.edu/research/iep/l/locke.htm #Educational%20Writings

Flanagan, J. C., & Cooley, W. W. (1966). *Project talent: One-year follow-up studies*. Pittsburgh, PA: University of Pittsburgh.

Friedmann, E. A., & Havighurst, R. J. (1954). *The meaning of work and retirement.* Chicago: University of Chicago Press.

Good, H. G. (1962). *A history of Western education.* New York: Macmillan.

Gordon, H. R. D. (2003). *The history and growth of vocational education in America.* Long Grove, IL: Waveland Press.

Gray, K. C., & Herr, E. L. (1998). *Workforce education.* Boston: Allyn & Bacon.

Hodgson, G. (1908). *Studies in French education from Rabelais to Rousseau.* London: Cambridge University Press.

Liberal arts. (2007). Encyclopedia Britannica [Electronic version]. Retrieved January 7, 2007, from http://www.britannica.com/eb/article -9048113/liberal-arts

Mandler, P. (2007). The idea of the self: Thought and experience in Western Europe since the seventeenth century. *American Historical Review, 112*(2), 575-576.

Manzo, S. (2006). Francis Bacon: Freedom, authority and science. *British Journal for the History of Philosophy, 14*(2), 245-273.

Marx, K. (1929). *Capital: A critique of political economy. The process of capitalist production* (E. Paul & C. Paul, Trans.). New York: International Publishers. (Original work published in 1890)

Monroe, P. (1905). *A textbook in the history of education.* New York: Macmillan.

National Commission on Excellence in Education. (1983). *A nation at risk: The imperative for reform.* Washington, DC: Author. (ERIC Document Reproduction Service No. ED 251 622)

Petty, G. C., & Brewer, E. W. (2005). Perspectives of a healthy work ethic in a 21st century international community. *International Journal of Vocational Education and Training, 13*(1), 93-104.

Roberts, R. W. (1965). *Vocational and practical arts education* (2nd ed.). New York: Harper and Row.

Schenck, J. P., & Others. (1984). *The life and times of Victor Karlovich Della-Vos.* Washington, DC: Education Resources Information Center. (ERIC Document Reproduction Service No. ED297 137) Retrieved May 3, 2007, from http:// eric.ed.gov/ERICWebPortal/custom/portlets/recordDetails/ detailini.jsp?_nfpb=true&_&ERICExtSearch_SearchValue_0=ED297137&E RICExtSearch_SearchType_0=eric_accno&accno=ED297137

Seybolt, R. F. (1917). *Apprenticeship and apprenticeship education in colonial New England and New York* (Contributions to education, No. 85, Bureau of Publications). New York: Columbia University.

Vocational education. (2007). Encyclopedia Britannica [Electronic version]. Retrieved January 8, 2007 from http://www.britannica.com/eb/ article-9075632/vocational-education

Wang, V. C. X. (2006). A Chinese work ethic in a global community. *International Journal of Vocational Education and Training, 14*(1), 39-52.

Wenrich, R. C., Wenrich, J. W., & Galloway, J. D. (1988). *Administration of vocational education.* Homewood, IL: American Technical.

West, W. M. (1931). *The story of man's early progress.* Boston: Allyn & Bacon.

CHAPTER 2

PRINCIPLES AND PHILOSOPHY OF CAREER AND TECHNICAL EDUCATION AND FEDERAL FUNDING FOR VOCATIONAL EDUCATION UP TO THE PRESENT

Victor C. X. Wang and Kathleen P. King

The principles of career and technical education emerged as vocational education was beginning in the late nineteenth and early twentieth centuries. The original principles were a reflection of circumstances, thinking and needs specific to a time in history (Snedden, 1920). The fundamental concepts behind these principles were influential in shaping the early development of career and technical education. In most instances, these concepts are still evident in contemporary restatements of principles of career and technical education. However, in some cases the concepts have been revised or dropped. The first person to have advanced the principles of career and technical education was Dr. Charles Prosser. Prosser, the first National Director of Vocational Education, developed and publicized

Innovations in Career and Technical Education: Strategic Approaches Towards Workforce Competencies Around the Globe, pp. 21–47
Copyright © 2008 by Information Age Publishing
21

16 theorems in the early days of vocational education in the United States. It is believed that Prosser also helped draft federal legislation to recognize and fund vocational education (Foster, 1997). Federal funding was available for vocational education as early as 1862 when the Morrill Act supported agriculture, engineering and military science in land-grant colleges (Allen, 1950, p. 72). Subsequently, federal legislation stimulated vocational education in many different ways. Vocational education was developed and shaped largely due to favorable guiding principles and philosophy and federal support.

PRINCIPLES AND PHILOSOPHY OF
CAREER AND TECHNICAL EDUCATION

Prosser advanced these theorems as a basis for sound and successful programs of vocational education, but he did not classify the theorems as he advanced them. The language in these theorems has been changed to reflect twenty-first century sensibilities, but the meaning has not been changed. Prosser's Theorems (Prosser & Allen, 1925) include:

1. Career and technical education will be efficient in proportion as the environment in which the learners are trained is a replica of the environment in which they must subsequently work.

2. Effective career and technical training can only be given where the training is carried on in the same way with the same operations, the same tools and the same equipment as in the occupation itself.

3. Career and technical education will be effective in proportion as it trains the individual directly and specifically in the thinking habits and the manipulative habits required in the occupation itself.

4. Career and technical education will be effective in proportion as it will enable individuals to capitalize their interest, aptitudes, and intrinsic intelligence to the highest possible degree.

5. Effective career and technical education for any profession, calling, trade, occupation or job can only be given to the selected group of individuals who need it, want it and are able to profit by it.

6. Career and technical training will be effective in proportion as the specific training experiences for forming right habits of doing and thinking are repeated to the point that the habits developed are those of the finished skills necessary for gainful employment.

7. Career and technical education will be effective in proportion as the instructors have had successful experience in the application of skills and knowledge to the operations and processes they undertake to teach.

8. For every occupation there is a minimum of productive ability, which an individual must possess in order to secure or retain employment in that occupation. If career and technical education is not carried to that point with an individual, it is neither personally nor socially effective.

9. Providers of career and technical education must recognize conditions as they are and must train individuals to meet the demands of the "market" even though it may be true that more efficient ways of conducting the occupation may be known and those better working conditions.

10. The effective establishment of process habits in any learner will be secured in proportion as the training is given on actual jobs and not on exercises or pseudo jobs.

11. The only reliable source of content for specific training in an occupation is in the experiences of masters of that occupation.

12. For every occupation there is a body of content, which is peculiar to that occupation and which has practically no functioning value in any other occupation.

13. Career and technical education will render efficient social service in proportion as it meets the specific training needs of any group at the time that they need it and in such a way that they can most effectively profit by the instruction.

14. Career and technical education will be socially efficient in its methods of instruction and in its personal relations with learners; it takes into consideration the particular characteristics of any particular group, which it serves.

15. The administration of career and technical education will be efficient in proportion as it is elastic and fluid rather than rigid and standardized.

16. While every reasonable effort should be made to reduce per capita costs, there is a minimum below which effective career and technical education cannot be given, and if this minimum of per capita cost is not available for a course or a program, the program should not be attempted.

Prosser believed that the more nearly a career and technical program can approach the full realization of these theorems in its operation, the higher the quality of the program. Any attempt to disregard any of these basic and fundamental concepts can only result in undermining and destroying career and technical education for the citizens of the community. Prosser's views were criticized for lacking the qualities of a formal philosophic system (Miller & Gregson, 1999). Rojewski (2002) indicated that Prosser's major goal of school was not individual fulfillment but meeting the manpower needs of society. Others such as Lewis (1998) criticized Prosser's views on vocational education as being class-based and tracking certain segments of society—based on race, class, and gender— into second-class occupations and second-class citizenship. Prosser's views are in striking contrast with Dewey's in that Dewey believed that the principal goal of public education was to meet individual needs for personal fulfillment and preparation for life. Rojewski (2002) cited Hyslop-Margison by noting:

> Dewey rejected the image of students as passive individuals controlled by market economy forces and existentially limited by inherently proscribed intellectual capacities. In his view, students were active pursuers and constructors of knowledge, living and working in a world of dynamic social being. (Hyslop-Margison, 2000, p. 25)

As time goes on, other leaders in the field of vocational education and training have created different principles of vocational education. For example, Roberts (1971) further developed and classified the principles into three broad categories: organization, administration, and instruction.

Organization

Principles of organization are concerned with definitions, functions, needs and procedures. They may be used to assist in arriving at decisions concerning the advisability of establishing programs of career and technical education.

- Federal aid for career and technical education is justified as a means of stimulating the further development of career and technical education and as a device for maintaining acceptable standards in it.
- The need for career and technical education in a specific area should be determined from the results of a community survey.

- Occupational information and guidance should be provided for career and technical students.

Administration

Career and technical and practical arts education present some problems of administration more complex than those of academic subjects. The use of federal funds causes some of the problems. Robert's principles for administration include:

- Representative laypersons should be appointed to boards of education concerned with the administration of career and technical education on federal, state, and local levels.
- Each state should maintain a complete program of career and technical and practical arts teacher education.
- Career and technical and practical arts educators should be technically competent and professionally qualified.
- Career and technical and practical arts education programs should be based on continuous research.

Instruction

Materials and methods of instruction in career and technical education and practical arts education differ from those of other educational areas, due to such factors as the interest and purpose of the learner, the demands of business and industry, the standards of achievement and performance, and the technological changes that are constantly occurring in a changing society.

- Career and technical instruction should be available for those who need, want, and can profit by it.
- The standards in career and technical education should be as high or higher than the accepted standards in the occupation concerned.
- Instructional programs in career and technical and practical arts education should be characterized by flexibility.
- Career and technical and practical arts instruction should include information and activities designed to protect and conserve human

life. Miller (1985) grouped the principles of career and technical education into three headings: People, Programs, and Processes as a matter of convenience. According to Miller, these headings are arbitrary, although well-reasoned.

People

Miller (1985) reasoned that the individual is the focal point for the activities for career and technical education.

- Guidance is an essential component of career and technical education.
- Lifelong learning is promoted through career and technical education.
- The needs of the community are reflected by programs of career and technical education.
- Career and technical education is open to all.
- Placement in the next step is a responsibility of career and technical education.
- Elimination of sex bias and sex-role stereotyping is promoted through career and technical education.
- Individuals with special needs are served through career and technical education.
- Student organizations are an integral feature of career and technical education.
- Teachers of career and technical education are both professionally qualified and occupationally competent.
- A positive work ethic is promoted through career and technical education.

Programs

The distinguishing characteristics for these principles are that they emphasize instructional activities in career and technical education.

- The career awareness and precareer and technical education components of career education complement career and technical education.

- Career and technical education is a part of the public system of comprehensive education.
- Curricula for career and technical education are derived from requirements in the world of work.
- Families of occupations are a basis for developing curricula for career and technical education at the secondary level.
- Innovation is stressed as a part of career and technical education.
- Persons are prepared for at least job entry level through career and technical education.
- Safety is paramount in career and technical education.
- Supervised occupational experience is provided through career and technical education.

Processes

Principles in the process group emphasize procedures that career and technical educators prefer in their efforts to effect change and improvement in career and technical education.

- Advice from the community is sought in providing programs of career and technical education.
- Articulation and coordination are central to the purposes of career and technical education.
- Evaluation is a continuous process in career and technical education.
- Follow-up is a vital extension of career and technical education.
- Federal legislation for career and technical education is a reflection of national priorities.
- Comprehensive planning is stressed in career and technical education.
- Research on a continuing basis is fundamental to the dynamics of career and technical education.

Many scholars and practitioners in the field have pointed out that the principles of career and technical education carry philosophical implications. The principles represent the preferred practices in career and technical education and may be characterized as representations of values held by career and technical educators. It is possible to translate the principles of career and technical education into a philosophy of career and technical education. The inductive process may be used to develop a philosophy from principles. Miller (1996) defined philosophy as making assumptions and speculations about the nature of human activity and the nature of the world ... ultimately, philosophy becomes a conceptual framework for synthesis and evaluation because it helps vocational educators decide what should be and what should be different (p. xiii). It is this philosophy that has prompted vocational educators to answer the following questions:

- What is the nature of the learner?
- What is the role of the teacher?
- How do we decide what should be taught?
- What is the role of schooling in America?
- Who should pay for the schooling?

These questions can be used to inductively arrive at a philosophy for career and technical education. The principles of career and technical education can be used to provide responses to these issues. Philosophy provides a framework for thinking about career and technical education. It helps the educator sort out competing alternatives and provides a basis for a final course of action. Philosophy also provides guidelines for practice, contributing to decisions about program development, selection of learning activities, curriculums, goals, resource utilization, and identification of other essential needs and functions in career and technical education. Action without philosophical reflection leads to a mindless activism (Elias & Merriam, 2005, p. 4). Philosophies of teaching lead to meaningful practice.

Good principles and philosophies do guide the field of vocational education. However, these are not enough. For career and technical education to thrive, federal funding has played a major role. Rojewski (2002) noted that since the beginning of federal support for public vocational education, the federal government has been a predominant influence in determining the scope and direction of secondary, and to a lesser extent postsecondary, vocational and technical training. Without federal funding, career and technical education would not have been developed to this day. A glimpse of federal funding and federal legislation can provide our readers and learners information regarding what contributions federal funding has made to vocational education. Readers and learners can also find out in what ways federal legislation can enhance the three objectives of vocational education, especially the very first objective, "meet the manpower needs of society."

1862—MORRILL ACT

Federal Support for the Agricultural and Mechanical Colleges (Land-Grant Colleges) (Allen, 1950) supported colleges that offered instruction for agriculture, engineering, and military science. Named for senator was Justin A. Morrill of Vermont who introduced the Morrill Act in 1857, but it failed to pass the Senate, reintroduced it in 1859, and it passed both houses of Congress. The bill was vetoed by President James Buchanan who said it was unconstitutional. The president feared the states would depend upon federal support for their own education systems (McClure, Chrisman, & Mock, 1985). The bill was reintroduced in 1862 and it was supported by Senator Benjamin Wade who took advantage of national wartime concerns, saying it would be ideal to train officers and engineers. The bill was passed and signed into law by President Lincoln and resulted in the rapid expansion of agriculture and engineering schools. The bill became a keystone of higher education in the mid and far west. The principle objective was to develop schools to teach agriculture and mechanical arts. The bill enabled higher education to open to a broader public and improve agriculture technology. The concept of integrated academics was first identified. Thirty thousand acres of land was granted to states for each senator and representative in congress for the purpose of endowing colleges for agriculture and mechanical arts. One hundred and six land grant colleges were established. As a result of the 1862 Morrill Act, Kansas State University was established in 1863. Kansas State Agricultural College developed a system of "industrials," in which shop work was more on the trade level in 1874. Victor Della Vos, from the Imperial Technical Institute in Moscow (Ham, 1990), exhibited at the Centennial Exposition in Philadelphia. The method of teaching mechanic arts was well received and it gave impetus to similar types of offerings in the United States in 1876 (Schenck et al., 1984). The first manual training school in the U.S. was established in St. Louis, Missouri. by Calvin Woodward 1880. Col. Richard Tylden Auchtmuty founded the New York Trade School in 1881.

Hebrew Technical Institute was founded in New York City in 1883. The first manual training school to be supported by public expense was located in Baltimore in 1884. Hatch Act provided Federal Funds for state agriculture experiment stations in 1887. The second Morrill Act provided $15,000.00 annually for each of the land-grant colleges in 1890. In 1905, the Douglas Commission, led by Governor William L. Douglas of Massachusetts, investigated the need for trade training in specific areas. In 1914, a presidential commission authorized by the Congress was appointed to study national aid for vocational education. The summary of the commission indicated that there was a need for federal funding for Vocational Education.

Table 2.1.   1917-Smith-Hughes Act Funding 1918-1926

Year	Agriculture	Trade & Industrial and Home Education	Teacher Education
1918	$500,000.00	$500,000.00	$500,000.00
1919	$750,000.00	$750,000.00	$700,000.00
1920	$1,000,000.00	$1,000,000.00	$900,000.00
1921	$1,250,000.00	$1,250,000.00	$1,000,000.00
1922	$1,500,000.00	$1,500,000.00	$1,000,000.00
1923	$1,750,000.00	$1,750,000.00	$1,000,000.00
1924	$2,000,000.00	$2,000,000.00	$1,000,000.00
1925	$2,500,000.00	$2,500,000.00	$1,000,000.00
1926	$3,000,000.00	$3,000,000.00	$1,000,000.00

In the 1917-Smith-Hughes Act was passed to provide federal support for vocational education. Funding began in 1918 with increments each year until 1926 (see Table 2.1).

The Smith Hughes Act of 1917 created a federal board for vocational education. It gave federal board control over state programs. The Act designated funds given to states annually to promote programs in agriculture, trade and industry, and home economics. The passage of this act was the fruition of a long legislative campaign to secure federal aid for vocational education (Douglas, 1921, p. 293). It provided annual appropriations for (1) salaries to teachers, supervisors, and directors of vocational education areas—50/50 with states; (2) teacher preparation in areas of agriculture, home economics, and trade and industry; (3) support for activities of the federal board for vocational education. According to the general standards of this act, teacher training should be given only to those who had had adequate vocational experience in line of work they were preparing to teach (Douglas, 1921). Further, to prevent the undue slighting of any subject, it was specified that not less than 20% nor more than 60% of the quota of any state for training teachers should be spent for agriculture, for the trades and industries, and for home economics (Douglas, 1921, p. 297). The Act mandated the creation of a state board and it required a development of a state plan. In addition, it required annual reports of state system to the federal board. The Act required states to designate 50/50 salaries for vocational education personnel and cooperate with local schools to provide funds to support high quality instruction in vocational programs—facilities, equipment and materials. Federal funds had to be under public supervision and control. It required vocational training to be provided to persons who: (1) have selected a vocational area and desire preparation in it; (2) have already been employed and seek greater efficiency in that employment; (3) have accepted employment and wish to advance to positions of responsibility; (4) vocational education was to be less than college grade for persons over 14 years of age in day time training and over 16 who seek evening class training. Many of the vocational education issues addressed in the Smith-Hughes Act endure to this day. The three salient parts of the Smith-Hughes Act of 1917 that are worthwhile to note may be summarized as follows:

- The Act provided an appropriation of $1.7 million for the year 1917-1918, with funding increasing at intervals to $7.2 million for 1925-1926.
- The Act also created a federal board for vocational education to administer the new law's provisions. The members included the secretaries of commerce, agriculture and labor, the Commissioner of education and three appointed citizens.
- States were required to create state boards for vocational education, which would prepare a plan, to be approved by the federal board, for operation of state vocational education programs. The state or local community was required to match each dollar of federal money appropriated to the state.

After the Smith-Hughes Act was successfully implemented, Congress recognized a need for additional funds for vocational home economics and vocational agriculture. In 1929, the George Reed Act was passed.

In 1934, the George Ellzey Act replaced the George Reed Act and more appropriations were provided for vocational education. In 1937, the George Deen Act increased the vocational funding for Agriculture home economics and trade and industry and included new funding for distributive education. In 1940, vocational training was provided for war production workers and trained workers were to assist with the war effort. Time did not permit the schools to produce finished craftsmen and training was limited to job units that could be learned quickly.

In 1946, the George Barden Act provided more funds for earlier areas of support and provided more flexibility in the use of these funds. The 1958 National Defense Education Act amended the George Barden Act of 1946. Funds were used to train highly skilled technicians or occupations necessary for national defense. The Act was passed in response to Russia launching Sputnik into space in 1957. The Act supported education by providing special institutes to train high school mathematics, science and foreign language teachers as well as high school guidance counselors (Anderson, Walker, & Beame, 1981). In 1961, Congress passed the Area Redevelopment Act and this act enabled the federal government together with the states to help areas of substantial and persistent unemployment and under employment to better plan and finance their redevelopment. The Act authorized occupational training in courses such as auto mechanics, carpentry, drafting, farm equipment, heavy equipment operation, sewing machine operation, needle trades, stenography, upholstering, and welding.

THE MANPOWER DEVELOPMENT AND TRAINING ACT (MDTA) (1962)

This act authorized the secretary of labor to appraise the manpower requirements and resources of the nation while working with the secretary of health, education, and welfare and with state agencies to provide training programs for the unemployed and underemployed (Manpower Development, 2006). These training programs were provided through the state vocational agencies. The original programs were 100% funded, however, after four years the funding level was reduced to 90%. The training was free to the participants and training allowances were available to eligible trainees to defray educational expenses. These allowances, which could be paid up to 104 weeks, could not exceed $1,000 more than the average weekly unemployment compensation payment with adjustments for other income received. Trainees under the MDTA were required to fit within in the following categories:

- Unemployed.
- Underemployed.
- Part-time workers.
- Workers with skills that are obsolete.
- Members of farm families with less than $1,200.00 annual net family income.
- Ages 16 through 22 and in need of occupational training.

The MDTA was amended in 1963, 1965, and 1968. The 1968 amendment consolidated the MDTA and the ARA. The MDTA enrolled more than a million trainees from its beginning in 1963 through 1968. About 70% of these were in institutional programs and most of the remaining were in on-the-job training. More than 600,000 trainees completed training during the period and 90% of these were employed at some time during the first year after they completed training.

THE 1963 VOCATIONAL EDUCATION ACT

In 1963, Congress enacted legislation designed to extend present programs and develop new programs for vocational education; encourage research and experimentation; provide work-study programs to enable youth to continue vocational education (Anderson, Walker, & Beame, 1981). The 1963 Act also amended the Smith-Hughes, George-Barden, and the National Defense Education Act. As seen in Table 2.2, the authorizations were made in the 1963 Act.

Funds from the 1963 VEA could be used to provide training for persons of all ages, levels of achievement, and all occupations except those requiring a baccalaureate degree. Funds could be expended for the following: (1) teacher training; (2) administration and supervision of programs; (3) instructional supplies and equipment; (4) development of instructional materials; (5) program evaluation; (6) construct area vocational school facilities.

State boards for vocational education administered the 1963 VEA program. A state plan was required in order to receive the federal funding. Table 2.3 illustrates the work-study authorizations.

THE 1968 VOCATIONAL EDUCATION AMENDMENTS

The Amendments of 1968 provided changes and additions to the 1963 VEA Act. The amendment amounted to changes in the amount of funds authorized and some new authorizations for new areas to be considered. New funding authorizations for the Act are listed in Table 2.4.

In addition, new funding for disadvantaged and handicapped were included:

| Fiscal Year 1969 | at $40,000,000.00 and |
| Fiscal Year 1970 | at $40,000,000.00 |

Table 2.2.   VEA Authorization

Fiscal Year 1964	$160,000,000.00
Fiscal Year 1965	$118,500,000.00
Fiscal Year 1966	$117,500,000.00
Fiscal Year 1967	$225,000,000.00
Fiscal Year 1968	$225,000,000.00

Table 2.3.   VEA Work-Study Authorizations

Fiscal Year 1965	$30,000,000.00
Fiscal Year 1966	$50,000,000.00
Fiscal Year 1967	$35,000,000.00
Fiscal Year 1968	$35,000,000.00

Table 2.4.   New Funding for 1968 VEA Amendment

Fiscal Year 1969	$355,000,000.00
Fiscal Year 1970	$565,000,000.00
Fiscal Year 1971	$675,000,600.00
Fiscal Year 1972	$675,000,000.00
Fiscal Year 1973	$565,000,000.00

This new funding was to pay the cost of the development and administration of state plans, advisory councils, evaluation, and dissemination. This new funding could be used for: (1) national and state advisory councils; (2) research and training; (3) exemplary programs and projects; (4) residential vocational education; (5) consumer and homemaking education; (6) cooperative vocational education programs; (7) Work-study programs; (8) curriculum development; and (9) training and development for vocational education personnel.

1972 VOCATIONAL EDUCATION AMENDMENTS

The 1972 Act was actually Title II of the Public Law 92-318 which amended the Higher Education Act of 1965, the Vocational Education Act of 1963, the General Provisions Act and the Elementary and Secondary Act of 1965 (Anderson, Walker, & Beame, 1981). Title II just amended the 1963 Act and the 1968 Amendments.

COMPREHENSIVE EMPLOYMENT TRAINING ACT (CETA) OF 1973

CETA was an extension of the 1962 MDTA. This Act superseded the 1962 ACT. Source of funding was from the Department of Labor (DOL).

Public Law 94-482

The 1976 Vocational Education Amendments (Anderson, Walker, & Beame, 1981) are contained in Title II of this Act. This title was an amendment and an extension of the 1972 amendments. Table 2.5 shows the authorizations that were supported by these amendments. In addition, $24,000,000.00 was authorized each year in fiscal year 1979-1982 for states to prepare 5-year plans; prepare annual plans and accountability reports; conduct evaluations as required; administer vocational education programs. New funds were authorized for the following: (1) sex equality programs; (2) program evaluation and accountability reports; (3) state advisory councils; (4) 5-year plans; (5) work-study programs; (6) cooperative vocational education programs; (7) energy education; (8) residential vocational Schoolsb(9) curriculum development; (10) vocational guidance and counseling; (11) program improvement; (12) bilingual vocational training. It was not until the Carl Perkins Vocational Education Act of 1984 that this Act and related funding was suspended.

Table 2.5. Public Law 94-482 Authorizations

Fiscal Year 1978	$80,000,000.00
Fiscal Year 1979	$1,030,000,000.00
Fiscal Year 1980	$1,180,000,000.00
Fiscal Year 1981	$1,325,000,000.00
Fiscal Year 1982	$1,485,000,000.00
Funds for Subpart Four for Disadvantaged	
Fiscal Year 1978	$35,000,000.00
Fiscal Year 1979	$35,000,000.00
Fiscal Year 1980	$45,000,000.00
Fiscal Year 1981	$50,000,000.00
Fiscal Year 1982	$50,000,000.00
Funds for Subpart Five for Consumer and Homemaking Education	
Fiscal Year 1978	$55,000,000.00
Fiscal Year 1979	$65,000,000.00
Fiscal Year 1980	$75,000,000.00
Fiscal Year 1981	$80,000,000.00
Fiscal Year 1982	$80,000,000.00

THE JOB TRAINING PARTNERSHIP ACT OF 1982 (JTPA)

This act replaced and superseded the 1973 CETA. Some new guidelines were developed to administer the funds differently (Workforce Investment, 2001). The source of funding for the JTPA was from the Department of Labor (DOL).

THE 1984 CARL PERKINS VOCATIONAL EDUCATION ACT

This was the first new Act passed since the 1963. The emphasis of this Act extended from of supporting existing programs to funding new, innovative and expanding vocational offerings (Weizenbaum, 1986). The major portion of the funds were directed to the unserved or the underserved populations. The following were listed as purposes of the Act:

- Assist the states to expand, improve, modernize, and develop quality vocational education programs in order to meet the needs of the nation's existing and future workforce for marketable skills and to improve productivity.
- Assure that individuals who are inadequately served under vocational education programs are assured access to quality vocational education programs, especially individuals who are disadvantaged, who are handicapped, men and women who are entering nontraditional occupations, adults who are in need of training and retraining, individuals who are single parents or homemakers, individuals with limited English proficiency, and individuals who are incarcerated in correctional institutions.
- Promote greater cooperation between public agencies and the private sector in preparing individuals for employment, in promoting the quality of vocational education in the states and in making the vocational system more responsive to the labor market in the states.
- Improve the academic foundation of vocational students and to aid in the application of newer technologies (including the use of computers) in terms of employment or occupational goals.
- Provide vocational education services to train, retrain, and upgrade employed and unemployed workers in new skills for which there is a demand in that state or employment market.
- Assist the most economically depressed areas of a state to raise employment and occupational competencies of its citizens.

Table 2.6.   Carl Perkins Vocational Education Title II Part A Funds

Handicapped	10.10%
Disadvantaged	22.0%
Adult training and retraining	12.0%
Single parents	8.50%
Sex bias	3.5%
Corrections	1.0%

- To assist the state to utilize a full range of supporting services, special programs, and guidance counseling and placement to achieve the basic purposes of this act.
- Improve the effectiveness of consumer and homemaking education and to reduce the limiting effects of sex-role stereotyping on occupations, job skills, levels of competency, and careers.
- Authorize national programs designed to meet designated vocational education needs and to strengthen the vocational education research process.

TITLE II: Part A Funds—Unserved and Underserved Populations

This comprised 57% of the basic grant to the state. Table 2.6 depicts the division of these funds:

TITLE II: Part B Funds—Vocational Education Program Improvement, Innovation and Expansion

This comprised 43% of the basic grant to the state. The following are purposes of this section:

- Improvement in quality of vocational programs.
- Expansion of vocational education activities.
- Introduction of new vocational programs.
- Training to revitalize business and industry in a state.
- Exemplary and innovative programs.
- Improvement and expansion of postsecondary and adult programs.
- Improvement and expansion of career counseling and guidance services.

- Curriculum development including basic skills training.
- Expansion and improvement of programs at area vocational schools.
- Acquisition of equipment and renovation of facilities.
- Conduct special courses and strategies to teach the fundamentals of mathematics and science through practical applications.
- Assignment of personnel to coordinate efforts to insure vocational programs are responsive to labor market needs and supportive of apprenticeship programs.
- Vocational Student Organization activities.
- Prevocational programs.
- Programs of modern industrial and agricultural arts.
- State Administration.
- Stipends for students in vocational education programs.
- Placement services.
- Day care services for children of vocational education students.
- Construction of Area Vocational School facilities.
- Acquisition of high technology equipment.
- Vocational education programs in private schools and institutions.
- Preservice and in-service teacher education.

TITLE III: Special Programs—The Following are Areas Which are Covered Under This Section

- Community Based Organizations.
- Consumer and Homemaking Programs.
- Adult training, retraining, and employment development.
- Career Guidance and Counseling Programs.
- Industry-education partnerships.
- For training in high technology occupations.

TITLE IV: National Programs—The Following are Covered Under This Section

- Research activities.
- Demonstration programs;

- Model Programs;
- State equipment pools;
- Demonstration centers for retraining dislocated workers;
- Model centers for vocational education for older individuals;
- Occupations information data systems;
- National Council for Vocational Education;
- Bilingual vocational training.

Guidelines for the State Board in the Administration of the Act

Guidelines for administration of the Carl Perkins Act of 1984 include coordination of the development, submission and implementation of the state plan and evaluation of the program services and activities; development of the state plan in consultation with the state council on vocational education, and submission of this document to the secretary; consultation with the state council and other appropriate groups and individuals involved in the planning, administration, evaluation, and coordination of programs funded under the Act; convening and meeting as a state board at such times as necessary to carry out its functions under the Act; adoption of procedures to implement state level coordination with the state job training coordinating council to encourage cooperation in the conduct of the respective programs.

THE CARL D. PERKINS VOCATIONAL AND APPLIED TECHNOLOGY ACT OF 1990

The Carl D. Perkins Vocational and Applied Technology Act of 1990 amended and extended for 5 years the original Carl D. Perkins Vocational Education Act of 1984. This Act authorized the United States government to spend up to $1.6 billion a year on state and local programs that teach the "skill competencies necessary to work in a technologically advanced society." The addition of "Applied Technology" to the name of this legislation suggests that Congress designed the new Carl Perkins legislation to improve America's high-tech competitiveness. Another focus of this new Carl Perkins Act is to provide greater vocational education opportunities to disadvantaged people. The following information gives a breakdown of areas covered under this legislation and the amount authorized under each section.

Basic State Grants

More than $940 million of the authorization: 75% of the $1.25 billion that has been authorized to go to states in the form of basic grants, is specifically earmarked for programs that address the vocational education needs of poor and handicapped, students and those of limited English-language proficiency (Office of Vocational and Adult Education, 2005). States are obligated to spend this money on schools, area vocational-technical centers and postsecondary institutions serving the greatest number of disadvantaged students. The Act requires that states be more accountable for the programs they are operating. States must be able to show that disadvantaged people have the chance for full and equitable participation in vocational education programs. States must set up extensive systems of evaluating programs and effects of Carl Perkins money on these programs. Each state must set up a core of standards and performance measures that will form the basis for Perkins-mandated evaluations. Each state must submit to the secretary of education a 3-year plan detailing how it will administer Perkins funds.

CARL PERKINS VOCATIONAL EDUCATION ACT OF 1998

This act replace the 1990 Carl Perkins Act and gives states and local districts greater flexibility to develop programs (U.S. Department of Education, 2003). It makes them more accountable for student performance and more money at the local level. The Act eliminates set-asides for gender equity and gives vocational education separate authorizing legislation. The Act ensures that education authorities, not governors or labor officials will oversee vocational education. It includes a separate authorization for tech prep and creates 10% reserve of local funding. Finally the Act strengthens academic and vocational technical instruction, places more emphasis on professional development and supports career guidance activities (Hayward & Benson, 1993, p. 3). According to Lynch (2000), the two most recent reauthorizations of the 1984 Perkins legislation are essentially grounded in school reform and the mandate to use federal funds to improve student performance and achievement (p. 10).

Other Programs

In addition to basic state grants, the reauthorized Perkins Act funding is divided into 11 other categories, which will be covered:

1. Tech Prep—The new Perkins Act authorizes $125 million to fund tech prep programs—cooperative arrangements that combine 2 years of technology-oriented preparatory education in high school with 2 years of advanced technology studies at a community college. These programs are to integrate academic and vocational education, which is a major emphasis of the new Act;

2. The national Tech Prep initiative establishes goals which may give all of education an opportunity to implement change. A major goal is to allow students to move from one level of learning to another without unnecessary repetition or duplication of coursework. Another major goal is to prepare students to assume the roles of a highly skilled workforce. The aim of the Tech Prep initiative is to help break down barriers between secondary and postsecondary institutions, resulting in a coordinated, integrated, focused and challenging education program. Tech Prep is a program consisting of 2 years at the secondary level and 2 years at the postsecondary level in higher education or apprenticeship training, which includes a common core of mathematics, science, communications, and technologies and leads to an associate degree or a certificate in a specific career. It is considered a dual-purpose program, which means that students are prepared to enter a vocational or technical program, a college prep program, or a combination of the two. Tech Prep does not undermine the academic system; in fact, research shows that the Tech Prep program of study can strengthen the academic achievement of all students;

3. Supplementary Grants for Facilities and Equipment—Up to $100 million has been authorized to improve vocational education facilities and equipment in economically depressed areas. These funds will flow to states and school districts with the highest concentrations of disadvantaged students;

4. Consumer and Homemaking Education—The Act authorizes $38.5 million for states to develop or improve instruction in nutrition, health, clothing, consumer education, family living and parenthood, child development, housing and homemaking;

5. Career Guidance and Counseling—The law authorizes $20 million for career development programs that assist people to

make the transition from school to work, maintain current job skills, develop skills needed to move into high-tech careers, develop job-search skills, and learn about other job training programs;

6. Community-based Organizations—Up to $15 million in Perkins funding may go to local non-profit and other community groups providing vocational education services to disadvantaged people;

7. Bilingual Vocational Education—The Act authorizes $10 million to fund programs specifically designed to provide bilingual vocational education and English-language instruction;

8. Business/labor/education Partnerships—$10 million has been authorized to help fund state grants to cooperative partnerships that team schools, local agencies, or state departments with business, industry or labor groups to provide vocational education;

9. Community Education/Lighthouse Schools—The Act authorizes $10 million to establish and evaluate model high school community education employment centers serving low-income urban and rural youth. So-called Lighthouse Schools—model vocational education institutions that provide information and assistance to other programs—are also eligible to receive the funding;

10. State Councils on Vocational Education—Up to $9 million may go to the state councils, established by the original Perkins Act. These groups advise and make recommendations to state agencies that set vocational education policy. Tribally Controlled Postsecondary Institutions—$4 million may go to postsecondary vocational institutions operated by Native American tribes;

11. National Council on Vocational Education—The law authorized $350,000 to fund the activities of the National Council through September 30, 1991. This advisory group created by the original Act was disbanded on October 1, 1991.

While it appears that the Perkins Act authorization was generous, it is important to remember that the law set maximum spending limits. Congress may and usually does, appropriate less than the amount set. For fiscal year 1991 Congress appropriated $1.003 billion, which is about 63% of what the Act allowed.

SCHOOL-TO-WORK (1994)

When the School-to-Work Opportunities Act (STWOA) was initiated in 1994, it was envisioned as a "systematic, comprehensive effort to help all young people (1) prepare for high-skill and high-wage careers, (2) receive top quality academic instruction, and (3) gain the foundation skills to pursue postsecondary education and lifelong learning" ("School to Work," 1994). Because school-to-work (STW) approaches to teaching and learning were seen as most appropriate for students not designed for college, however, it was considered by many to be just another vocational program. STWOA did call for the development of three main components in a STW system: School-based learning, work-based learning, and connecting activities. School-based learning consists of integrated academic and vocational courses that focused on a career area or industry with links to postsecondary education. Partnerships are created with business to develop opportunities for students to take part in worksite learning; these work-based activities coordinate with students' school-based learning. Connecting activities are developed to coordinate the school-based and work-based activities. STW is learner centered, provides authentic learning opportunities, and is based on principles that can benefit all students, including a focus on active learning, exploration of career possibilities and interests, and supervised experiences outside of the classroom. STW offers a seamless educational system that offers as many options as possible. STW begins at the elementary level with career awareness activities, progresses to career exploration in the middle grades and early high school and finally to career preparation during the later high school years. In summary, the following are key elements of STWOA:

- Collaborative partnerships.
- Integrated curriculum.
- Technological advances.
- Adaptable workers.
- Comprehensive career guidance.
- Work-based learning.
- Step by step approval.
- Grades K-6: develop Career Awareness.
- Grades 7-10: Career Exploration.
- Grades 11-12: Career Preparations

In addition, the respective work based, school based and connecting activities components of STW are:
Work based learning components of STW

- Job shadowing.
- Job training.

- Work experience (paid or nonpaid).
- Workplace mentoring.
- Instruction in workplace competencies.
- Instruction in all elements of industry.

School based learning components of STW:

- Career counseling.
- Career pathways.
- Rigorous program of study.
- Integration of academics and vocational education.
- Evaluation.
- Secondary/postsecondary articulation.

Connecting activities components of STW:

- Matching students with employers.
- Establishing liaisons between education and work.
- Technical assistance to schools, students and employers.
- Assistance to integrate school-based and work based learning.
- Encourage participation of employers.
- Job placement, continuing education or further training assistance.
- Collection and analysis of post-program outcomes of participants.
- Linkages with youth development activities and industry.

THE WORKFORCE INVESTMENT ACT OF 1998

This act provides the framework or a unique national workforce preparation and employment system designed to meet both the needs of the nation's businesses and the needs of job seekers and those who want to further their careers (U.S. Department of Labor, 2006). Title I of the legislation is based on the following elements: (1), Training and employment programs must be designed and managed at the local level—where the needs of businesses and individuals are best understood; (2), Customers, potential participants, must be able to conveniently access the employment, education, training, and information services they need at a single location in their neighborhoods; (3), Customers should have choices in deciding the training program that best fits their needs and the organizations that will provide that service. They should have control over their own career development; (4), Customers have a right to information about how well training provided succeed in preparing people for jobs. Training providers will provide information on their success rate; and (5), Business will provide information, leadership, and play an active role in ensuring that the system prepares people for current and future jobs.

The Act builds on the most successful elements of previous Federal legislation. Just as important, its key components are based on local and State input and extensive research and evaluation studies of successful training and employment innovations over the past decade. Federal funding has been available for all vocational-technical program areas since the 1963 VEA was passed. It has served well in stimulating vocational education in the United States for a number of years. Agriculture, home economics, and trade and industrial education have been stimulated ever since the 1917 Smith Hughes Act was passed.

CONCLUSION

Developed during the late nineteenth and twentieth centuries, principles of career and technical education were instrumental in shaping the early development of vocational education in our country. The concepts behind these principles are still evident in guiding today's career and technical education although in some cases, these principles need to be reinterpreted given the new contexts in our society. For the most part, federal funding has stimulated career and technical education in many ways. For example, the federal government has been obliged to use various types of agriculture programs to improve farm incomes during periods of declining prices and poor weather conditions. Although business education was not covered specifically in any federal legislation, the 1963 VEA, the Carl Perkins Act of 1984 and the 1990 Amendments provided monies for upgrading or expanding the business area.

As health occupations education was considered part of the trade and industrial (T&I) education, the Smith-Hughes Act of 1917 supported health occupations education. Later, a number of federal legislation supported Health Occupations Education. The same can be said about Family and Consumer Science. The Carl Perkins funding was used to purchase equipment as well as computers, which can be used to operate computer assisted design (CAD) and computer assisted manufacturing (CAM). This funding was also used to integrate math and science in the vocational curriculums and to support student organizational activities as an integral part of the instructional process. Federal funds have been used to support vocational guidance since 1938. The first funds used were not directly for vocational guidance but for supporting teacher training and indirectly assisting vocational guidance. In short, while principles and philosophy guide the development and direction of vocational education, federal legislation stimulated it in many different ways. Rather than defying one another, the two complement and supplement each other. Both were and continue to be necessary and important in shaping the further development of career and technical education.

REFERENCES

Allen, H. P. (1950). *The federal government and education: The original and complete study of education for the Hoover Commission Task Force on Public Welfare*. New York: McGraw-Hill.

Anderson, W. F., Walker, D. B., & Beame, A. D. (1981). *The federal role in the federal system: The dynamics of growth*. Washington, DC: Diane.

Douglas, P. H. (1921). *American apprenticeship and industrial education*. New York: Longmans, Green, & Co., Agents.

Elias, J. L., & Merriam, S. B. (2005). *Philosophical foundations of adult education* (3rd ed.). Malabar, FL: Krieger.

Foster, P. N. (1997). Lessons from history: Industrial arts/technology education as a case. *Journal of Vocational Technical Education, 13*(2), 1-14.

Ham, C. H. (1990). *Mind and hand: Manual training the chief factor in education*. New York: American Book Company.

Hayward, G. C., & Benson, C. S. (1993). *Vocational-technical education: Major reforms and debates 1917-present*. Washington, DC.: U.S. Department of Education, Office of Vocational and Adult Education. (ERIC Document Reproduction Service No. ED 369 959)

Hyslop-Margison, E. J. (2000). An assessment of the historical arguments in vocational education reform. *Journal of Career and Technical Education, 17*, 23-30.

Lewis, T. (1998). *Toward the 21st century: Retrospect, prospect for American vocationalism* (Information series No. 373). Columbus: The Ohio State University, ERIC Clearinghouse on Adult, Career, and Vocational Education.

Lynch, R. L. (2000). *New directions for high school career and technical education in the 21st century* (Information series No. 384). Columbus: The Ohio State University, ERIC Clearinghouse on Adult, Career, and Vocational Education.

Manpower Development. (2006). *Manpower Development and Training Act*. Retrieved December 29, 2006 from http://en.wikipedia.org/wiki/Manpower_Development_and_Training_Act

McClure, A. F., Chrisman, J. R., & Mock, P. (1985). *Education for work: The historical evolution of vocational and distributive education in America*. London: Farleigh Dickinson University Press.

Miller, M. D. (1985). *Principles and philosophy for vocational education*. Columbus: Ohio State University.

Miller, M. D. (1996). Philosophy: The conceptual framework for designing a system of teacher education. In N. K. Hartley & T. L. Wentling (Eds.), *Beyond tradition: Preparing the teachers of tomorrow's workforce* (pp. 53-72). Columbia, MO: University Council for Vocational Education.

Miller, M. D., & Gregson, J. A. (1999). A philosophic view for seeing the past of vocational education and envisioning the future of workforce education: Pragmatism revisited. In A. J. Paulter, Jr. (Ed.), *Workforce education: Issues for the new century* (pp. 21-34). Ann Arbor, MI: Prakken.

Office of Vocational and Adult Education. (2005). *State plan guide for the Carl D. Perkins Vocational and Technical Education Act.* Retrieved December 26, 2006, from http://www.ed.gov/about/offices/list/ovae/pi/cte/memo2004.html

Prosser, C. A., & Allen, C. R. (1925). *Vocational education in a democracy.* New York: Century.

Roberts, R. W. (1971). *Vocational and practical arts education: History, development and principles* (3rd ed.). New York: Harper & Row.

Rojewski, J. W. (2002). Preparing the workforce of tomorrow: A conceptual framework for career and technical education. *Journal of Vocational Education Research, 27*(1), 1-27.

Schenck, J. P., & Others. (1984). *The life and times of Victor Karlovich Della-Vos.* Washington, DC: Education Resources Information Center. (ERIC Document Reproduction Service No. ED297 137) Retrieved May 3, 2007, from http://eric.ed.gov/ERICWebPortal/custom/portlets/recordDetails/detailini.jsp?_nfpb=true&_&ERICExtSearch_SearchValue_0=ED297137&ERICExtSearch_SearchType_0=eric_accno&accno=ED297137

School to work opportunities act of 1994. (1994). School to Work. Retrieved December 22, 2006 from http://www.ncrel.org/sdrs/areas/issues/envrnmnt/stw/sw3swopp.htm

Snedden, D. (1920). *Vocational education.* New York: Macmillan.

U.S. Department of Education. (2003). *Carl D. Perkins Vocational and Technical Education Act of 1998.* Retrieved December 24, 2006 from http://www.ed.gov/offices/OVAE/CTE/legis.html

U.S. Department of Labor. (2006). *Workforce Investment Act of 1998: Its application to people with disabilities.* Retrieved December 22, 2006, from http://www.dol.gov/odep/pubs/ek01/act.htm

Weizenbaum, J. (1986). *Technology and structural unemployment: Reemploying displaced adults.* Washington, DC: Diane.

Workforce Investment. (2001). *History: Job Training Partnership Act, 1982-2000.* Retrieved December 28, 2006 from http://www.picsf.org/about/jtpa.htm

CHAPTER 3

HISTORICAL PERSPECTIVES OF THE DIFFERENT COMPONENTS OF VOCATIONAL EDUCATION

**Victor C. X. Wang, Kathleen P. King,
and Fredrick Muyia Nafukho**

INTRODUCTION

This chapter contains a description and discussion of the historical perspectives of the different components within career and technical education (CTE). When one considers career and technical education, readers may just think of manual training, manual arts, industrial arts, or just trade and industrial education. In fact, career and technical education encompasses agriculture education, business education, health occupations education, family and consumer science (formerly known as home economics), vocational-industrial education, technology education, technical education, and vocational guidance. Each component of career and technical education was developed in response to the needs of people in a given society.

It is well known that the last quarter of the nineteenth century saw the development of manual training. It quickly spread into the secondary

Innovations in Career and Technical Education: Strategic Approaches Towards Workforce Competencies Around the Globe, pp. 49–67
Copyright © 2008 by Information Age Publishing

49

schools of the United States. Proponents of the manual training movement wanted to use manual training as a vehicle of achieving educational and intellectual values in vocational education and training. Since its early inception, manual training has fostered much debate concerning its value in the field. Some educators promoted the value of manual training while others opposed it bitterly. Manual training did not gain strength and acceptability until the waning years of the 1880s. Bitter opposition of manual training resulted from the lack of understanding of the history of manual training movement. Over the years, manual training has evolved. In the early 1900s, it was once called manual arts and later called industrial arts. Then in 1905, it was formally called vocational education. While vocational educators, students, and many in business and industry know the value of vocational education, it did not seem to have achieved the same status with liberal arts education. Therefore, leaders in the field suggested that career and technical education be used to replace the name vocational education.

Regardless of the name change and bitter opposition, career and technical education has been and will continue to be a vehicle by which millions of students will obtain and upgrade occupational competencies. Working around the world is not a dream but a reality as globalization brings different cultures together. As America changed from a mixture of peoples from many countries often described as a melting pot to a tossed salad, it is imperative that vocational educators help students develop workforce competencies by using strategic approaches so that our students can remain competitive in the global economy. Nowadays, competition comes not only from within the United States but also from other industrialized and developing nations. Indeed, career and technical education has come a long way. The study of historical perspectives of different components of career and technical education perhaps can help us understand the plight of vocational education and defend its value in the field. What is more, the study of historical perspectives of different components of CTE can help us look to the future when intense competition is sure to arise given the nature of our global economy.

Why the Historical Perspective?

Understanding the context and history of the different components of vocational education and how the field has developed over time is important to scholars, practitioners, and students. By learning the historical perspective of the field, we are in a position to know the changes that have taken place, what led to the changes and how the professionals in the field responded to these changes. This vantage point provides an opportunity to improve on current practices and to develop the relevant material such as this book required to advance the field.

Scholars and practitioners with limited history of how their disciplines have developed over time are at a disadvantage since they do not know where they are coming from, nor can they adequately anticipate trends for the future (Nafukho, Amutabi, & Otunga, 2005). The history of vocational educational education and training in the United States of America is important since the U.S. model has been adapted in many regions of the world. Knowledge of history also helps in the development of the principles that extend beyond mere impressions of current facts. This knowledge also improves practice by suggesting what has worked or not worked in practice before, why it did or did not work, and options or alternatives for consideration (Long, 1990; Nafukho, 2007).

The importance of the historical perspective of any discipline is noted as follows, "history is to a people what memory is to the individual. People with no knowledge of their past would suffer from collective amnesia, groping blindly into the future without guide-posts of precedence to shape their course" (Fafunwa, 1974, p. 13). Since the vocational education field has changed from various names such as manual training, manual arts, industrial arts, vocational education, and now career and technical education, we feel that this chapter fills an important gap by providing the historical perspective of the field that we now refer to as career and technical education.

DEVELOPMENTS IN AGRICULTURE EDUCATION

In 1887, Congress passed an act providing for financial support for agricultural experiment stations. The provisions for the scientific study of agriculture were carried out in the land grant colleges having departments organized as experiment stations and in separate institutions organized for that purpose (Barlow, 1967). The 1862 Morrill Act provided for additional federal aid to the land grant colleges. In the next 18 years, agreement was difficult to reach regarding how much federal support would be provided. Finally in 1890, the second Morrill Bill provided further support for the land grant colleges. Evidenced in just these few examples is how federal funding has played a major role in the development of agriculture education.

Agriculture is not only one of the oldest vocations but one of the most significant in the development of civilized life. As primitive people began to settle and rise from the level of wandering hunters to that of home builders, agriculture became an important aspect of self-preservation. As agriculture developed in effectiveness as a means of food supply our society progressed (Bellwood, 2004). Hence, from an early period in man's history, agriculture has been of very great importance in the climb toward civilization; and it is today as basic as ever to the maintenance and progress of human life. Farmers, from the beginning of time, have encountered many troublesome problems. In early times, farmers worked long hours with inadequate equipment. They endured physical discomforts and frequently were subject to attack from unfriendly people.

Farm life has undergone many changes over a period of time. New farming equipment has made the work less of a drudgery. However, the following are problems, which are currently encountered in farming careers:

1. Weather and climate—floods, hail storms, windstorms, temperature, and adequate rainfall;
2. Erosion and urban expansion—Floods and winds remove good soil and highway and airports, housing developments, and sports complexes displace good farmland;
3. Insects and wild animals—insects eat crops, deer, rabbits, raccoons, squirrels, damage crops, and coyotes eat animals;
4. People—in early days rustlers were a problem. The farmer still has to contend with rustlers, hunters and drug dealers. Many farmers lose cattle and other farm animals to careless hunters. Hunters also drive over land where crops have not been harvested and destroy the crops. Many also drive over fields when they are wet and produce ruts from four-wheel drive vehicles;
5. Increased mechanization—this is both an advantage and a disadvantage. The disadvantage being that the farmer must be able to maintain the farm equipment. The farm equipment is becoming more and more technical; therefore it is necessary to try to purchase farm equipment on which service can be obtained (see for example Cochrane (1993) and University of California (2003)).

An agriculture revolution has been taking place as a result of the changes in mechanization. Farming dramatically changed from animal power to tractor power in the 1930s. The increase in use of hydraulics and combines occurred in the 1950s and 1960s and still greater use of minimum till machinery and herbicides occurred in the 1970s (Cochrane, 1993). New farm combines are utilizing many high tech options to control the harvesting units. These changes have resulted in fewer farmers, larger farms, higher farm incomes and greater capital investments. Success in farming currently requires knowledge and skill far beyond the requirement of those needed in the 1950s or earlier.

BUSINESS EDUCATION

Vocational business education had its origin in apprenticeship programs (Barlow, 1967). The early scribes, for example, were trained under an apprenticeship program. When the apprenticeship agencies failed to meet the need for bookkeepers and clerical workers, training programs were organized in academies and proprietary schools. However, commercial subjects reappeared in high schools at the turn of the twentieth century. The courses become more vocational as a result of the stimulation of federal funds under federal legislation, especially the 1963 Vocational Education Act (VEA). The English grammar schools and academies of the United States offered courses in arithmetic, handwriting, and bookkeeping in the eighteenth and nineteenth centuries. These courses were said to prepare students for "life" as well as college entrance. Bookkeeping was included in the curriculum of the English high school of Boston in 1823 (Graham, 1933) Massachusetts enacted a law in 1827 in which instruction in bookkeeping among other subjects was specified for certain high schools.

Business education received less emphasis in public schools during the latter part of the nineteenth century because of the rise of private business colleges. These private commercial schools or colleges flourished in the United States between the years 1852-1893. Commercial courses were introduced into public high schools about 1890 through popular demand. The curriculums were borrowed from the private business colleges and the principle courses were bookkeeping, shorthand, and typewriting.

> The public schools were slow to accept these subjects and frequently the commercial courses were used for the placement of slow learners. Because of this fact, the public schools were unable to compete with the private business colleges, especially in the quality of output. However, the popular demand for this type of program increased and by 1893 it was estimated that 15,000 students were enrolled in commercial education courses in the public high schools in the nation. (Roberts, 1965, p. 111)

Renewed interest in business education in the public schools occurred in the twentieth century. Committees of the National Education Association in 1903 and again in 1919 pointed to the need for business education not only for vocational usage but also for mental discipline and general education. Business education was introduced into the junior high school curriculum at this time for general knowledge, exploratory values, and as means of reducing school dropouts. Specialized courses were used at first but later unified courses in business education were introduced (Roberts, 1965).

HEALTH OCCUPATIONS EDUCATION

Humans have required health care since the beginning of time. The early Egyptians accumulated some knowledge of healing from witchcraft and magic. In time, they learned to recognize and treat many diseases. Hippocrates of ancient Greece, usually referred to as the "Father of Medicine," changed the magic of medicine into the science of medicine and wrote many treatises on medicine. During the Dark Ages and early Middle Ages, the Catholics founded some hospitals in the Western World, and the Moslems, utilizing the knowledge of the early Greeks, erected many hospitals for the care of the sick. During the Middle Ages, medicine in Europe was influenced by the Roman traditions remaining after the Dark Ages and the ecclesiastical medicine that existed in the monasteries. The Moslem ideas about hospital construction were accepted throughout Europe. The renaissance in medicine came during the sixteenth century when William Harvey treated medicine as a science rather than a tradition. Practical nursing became regarded as a profession rather than a charitable act or an unskilled service occupation (see Ackerknecht, 1982; and Clendening, 1960 as general examples of the history of medicine).

Florence Nightingale became the dominant figure in nursing and nursing education was a result of her work in health care during the Crimean War (1854-1856). She established a school of nursing at St. Thomas Hospital in London about 1860. This school became the worldwide pattern for schools of nursing. Ms. Nightingale believed that nurses should live in homes or dormitories where moral responsibility and discipline could be developed (Clendening, 1960).

Early schools of nursing in the United States included one at Bellevue Hospital in 1873, and the University of Minnesota in 1909 as part of the university. Table 3.1 shows a detailed chronology of early hospitals. However, many of the hospitals of the nineteenth century were simply a place of sojourn for the sick and incidentally a convenient place for practical training of physicians (Williams, 2000).

Hospital improvement began in the United States in 1910 as a result of a study of the nation's medical schools by Dr. Abraham Flexner, which was funded by the Carnegie Foundation (Williams, 2000). The shortcoming of the medical profession, as revealed by this study led to state laws requiring high standards in the care of the sick. Many substandard hospitals were closed while others were improved. Patient care shifted from the home to the doctor's office and thence to the hospital. In 1935 1 in every 15 citizens was admitted to a hospital. By 1966 this became 1 in every 7 persons; see Table 3.2 for a comparison of the number of hospital beds across these years. The increased use of hospitals was due to many factors

Table 3.1.   History of Hospitals

The Greeks first used hospitals to isolate the sick	
Moslems during the eighth and ninth century built well-planned hospitals	
Royal London Ophthalmic Hospital in	1804
Charity Hospital-New Orleans	1737
Massachusetts's General Hospital	1821
St. Louis Hospital	1830
Johns Hopkins Hospital	1889

including the introduction of new medicines and new techniques for the care of individuals and the prevention of disease.

FAMILY AND CONSUMER SCIENCE

Human survival throughout the ages has depended upon choice of food. During this time humans have selected the kind and quantity of food that has provided the proper nutrients for growth and development. Some people through the years have been less fortunate than others and have chosen or been forced to accept food that was lacking in some of the essential elements. These people have contracted dietary-deficiency diseases.

Some well-known examples of dietary-deficiency diseases are scurvy and beriberi, which have been cured by the use of proper diet. Human beings do not instinctively choose their food in accordance with the principles of good nutrition, but they must learn the kinds of foods that are needed, the methods of producing food, and the techniques of preparing the food for consumption.

Much progress has been made since the beginning of the twentieth century in understanding the relationship between food and health. Scientists have discovered that more than 50 known nutrients found in food are necessary for the normal operation of the body. When any of these are lacking, some health problems may arise.

Table 3.2.   Increase in Hospitals and Hospital Beds

Date	Hospitals	Beds
1910	4,385	42,500
1935	6,000	1,000,000+
1966	7,127	1,700,000

Early vocational home economics programs required that home experience become a part of the home economics program. This home experience is actually a home project where the student planned and carried out a project in relation to the home. Many of these were projects sanctioned by the parents and supervised by the home economics teacher and could be carried out during the summer months. Early in the 1880s, a plan for teaching the household arts to children in the form of play was originated and became known as the Kitchen Garden Movement (Barlow, 1967). According to Barlow (1967), the Industrial Education Association of New York in 1884 developed from the Kitchen Garden Association. This association endeavored to teach the poor of the city how to sew. Finally, this association established the New York College for training teachers in 1888. This college has become what is known as Teachers College of Columbia University. The Lake Placid, New York conferences contributed much to the development of home economics. During the summer of 1898, Ellen Richards was a visitor at the summer home of Mr. and Mrs. Melvin Dewey at Lake Placid. Dewey was the secretary of the New York State Board of Regents. Based on Barlow's 1976 accounts, Mrs. Richards spoke to the members of the Lake Placid Club on domestic problems, and through a suggestion that arose at that meeting, invitations were sent to a selected group of individuals to attend a conference of the Dewey home during the summer of 1899. The purpose of this kind of organization was to discuss the economic and social problems of the home. Courses of study for all areas of education were considered in relation to the growing home economics movement.

Many changes have occurred in family and consumer sciences programs as a result of new legislation and studies that have been made by various groups. Since the passage of the 1963 VEA the classes have been titled secondary, postsecondary, and adult. With the passage of the 1984 and 1990 Carl Perkins Vocational Education Acts, there has been an emphasis on programs that assist the displaced homemaker and the single parent. As a result of the back-to-the-basics movement from the "Nation at Risk Report" in the early 1980s, family and consumer sciences programs have had to compete for students as well as work with less funding. All of these changes have made an impact on what is being offered in the various programs. The Consumer and Homemaking Programs must now serve the following students:

1. Male and females
2. Disadvantaged
3. Handicapped
4. Single parents
5. Economically depressed

VOCATIONAL-INDUSTRIAL EDUCATION

Apprenticeship is an old form of education, used generously by the ancient nations, the Greeks and Romans, and throughout the Middle Ages, and the Renaissance (Barlow, 1976a). According to Barlow (1976b), apprenticeship in Colonial America was one of the fundamental educational institutions of the time. It represented a pathway to literacy for the boy or girl who could not pay for an education. It is also worth pointing out that in the Colonial period, there were the abundance of land, the mobility and freedom of the people, the willingness of the frontiersman to "make do" with makeshift implements and furnishings, and the immigration of mechanics and craftsmen who had been trained in Europe, all working against the apprenticeship system. The factory in the nineteenth century delivered the heaviest blow to the system. Rapid development of labor-saving machinery contributed much to the decline of apprenticeship (Barlow, 1976c).

The early settlers came to colonial America for many reasons, but few came for educational purposes. With few exceptions these settlers were satisfied with the educational programs of the mother country, and as a consequence the first schools of the New World were similar to those of the country from which the settlers came. Four main types of educational activity were conducted in the colonies during the seventeenth century. These were apprenticeship, religious schools for instruction in reading and writing, Latin grammar schools, and practical schooling in mathematics.

The early training of craftsman and industrial workers was conducted through on-the-job training and/or apprenticeship training. Apprenticeship came to the New World in the early Colonial period. This type of training in the colonies resembled that of the mother countries, except that it developed directly under the laws of the towns and counties. The English apprenticeship system was modified to suit conditions and became the most important educational agency during the period of colonization and settlement.

In 1803 there were four cotton mills in operation in the United States. By 1812 manufacturing had a good beginning. The expansion of trade brought about the invention of new machines and the improvement of others in the agricultural and manufacturing industries. The development of the power loom in 1814, the locomotive in 1829, the mechanical reaper and the telegraph in 1835, the sewing machine in 1846, together with the development of coal and iron mines and the growth of the railroads, brought about rapid changes in the nations economy. All of these changes put a strain on the apprenticeship programs.

The Mechanics' Institute originated in England during the early years of the nineteenth century (Barlow, 1967). It attempted to regain the educational values lost with the coming of the factory system. These same institutes soon spread to the United States.

Mechanical Institutes were first organized in New York City in 1820 by the General Society of Mechanics and Tradesmen. The society established a library for apprentices and a school for children of mechanics. The school was organized to meet the need for elementary education for the children of indigent members. The New York public school system assumed responsibility for the society's day school instruction in 1858. The second and most noted of the mechanics schools was the Franklin Institute of Philadelphia, which was established in 1824 for the purpose of extending the knowledge of mechanical science to its members (Barlow, 1967). Two other representative institutes are the Maryland Institute for the Promotion of the Mechanics Art, founded in Baltimore in 1826, and the Ohio Mechanics' Institute of the Cincinnati, founded in 1828. In keeping with the westward movement, the San Francisco Mechanics Institute was founded in 1854 (Barlow, 1976a).

About the time mechanical institutes were being organized in cities to provide adult education for city workers, the American Lyceum was organized for adult education in small towns and in the country. Josiah Holbrook, a teacher and founder of an agricultural and manual labor school, published a handbook in 1826 providing for a comprehensive plan for popular education. The plan consisted of the organization of local lyceums, to be affiliated with state lyceums and these in turn with a national lyceum (Holbrook, 1826). This movement began in about 1830 and by 1833 there were about 1,000 lyceums in the United States. The lyceum movement which lasted until near the middle of the nineteenth century, served as a means of building up useful knowledge in the natural sciences among people of the smaller towns of the United States.

Technical schools came into prominence during the first quarter of the nineteenth century. These schools had objectives somewhat similar to those of the mechanics institutes and lyceums. They were designed to provide education in the practical applications of science and mathematics. The first of these was the Gardiner Lyceum established in Gardiner, Maine in 1821. The second and most important of the technical institutes was the Rensselaer School established in Troy, New York in 1824. Many more of these institutes were established through 1895. These schools played an important part in the development of vocational education in the United States. While the mechanics' institute was interested primarily interested in the vocational needs of the population, the lyceum planned for the educational and cultural needs as well. The artist, the farmer, and the mechanic were supposed to find in the lyceum areas of interest and value (Barlow, 1967).

Many trade schools for employed and prospective workers in industrial vocations were organized during the last quarter of the nineteenth century. Beatty (1918) chronicles the history of these schools as they included corporation, proprietary, and endowed schools. Among the first corporation school in the United States was the one developed in 1875 by the R. Hoe Printing Press Company of New York City. Other corporation schools that were organized were: Baltimore and Ohio Railroad in 1855, Westinghouse Machine Company in 1888, and General Electric Company in 1901 (Beatty, 1918). These schools also provided a much-needed service for developing industrial workers in the United States. A number of states were interested in developing vocational schools at the beginning of the twentieth century. Massachusetts, Wisconsin, New York, Connecticut, New Jersey, Indiana, Pennsylvania, and Rhode Island all had some vocational schools in operation before 1915.

TECHNOLOGY EDUCATION

Apprenticeships were conducted by the people of ancient times; however, like other forms of education, apprenticeships reached a low ebb over time. During the Middle Ages, a formalized apprenticeship system became the mode of instruction for the working class. This revival of interest was due in part to the programs of apprenticeship training organized by the guilds of this age. The guilds recognized early the importance of taking apprentices and requiring then to go through a course of training before being admitted to the trade as a journeyman or master craftsman. Records indicate that apprenticeships were practiced in England as early as the thirteenth century.

Apprenticeships established in the early colonial period resembled those that were practiced in England. However, since there were no guilds or similar craft organizations, the apprenticeship system was set up under the laws of the towns and counties. Hands-on training was learned while studying under a Master Craftsman of the trade. After a required period of training the individual became a journeyman. Then after a required length of time as a journeyman, an individual could become a master craftsman.

Significant American beginnings in industrial training took place at the Philadelphia Centennial Exposition in 1876, at which Victor Della Vos of Moscow's Russian Imperial Technical School displayed a series of student exercises in wood and metal (Barlow, 1976b; Bawden, 1950). This exhibit introduced to American educators an organized, systematic method of teaching hand skills. One of the visitors at the Centennial, who familiarized himself with the Russian exhibit, was John D. Runkle, president of the Massachusetts Institute of Technology. Realizing the value of tool instruction in general education, Runkle recommended that instruction shops be introduced at MIT. His recommendations were accepted and became a reality the following year (Barlow, 1967). John Runkle adapted the system to create the School of Mechanical Arts at the Massachusetts Institute of Technology in 1877, and Calvin Woodward opened a Manual Training High School at St. Louis' Washington University in 1879 (Coates, 1923; Miller & Smalley, 1963). Both promoted training as necessary to the education of all youth. According to Gerbracht and Babcock (1969, p. 8), manual training's threefold purpose in the late nineteenth century was to keep boys in school, provide vocational skills and develop leisure-time interests which did not deviate too far from Locke's philosophy in vocational education covered in chapter one of the book.

As a result of this movement, a widespread establishment of secondary-level courses in mechanical drawing, woodworking, pattern making, foundry, forging and machine shop soon followed. Publicly funded manual-training schools and high schools bearing the labels "technical," "polytechnic," and "mechanic arts" opened in the mid 1880s. "Shop" became an accepted subject in general high schools shortly after the turn of the century.

In 1888 Gustaf Larsson, a leader in the Scandinavian Sloyd Movement, came to Boston to educate teachers. His work at Boston's Sloyd Training School, which educated teachers from across the nation, did much to spread manual training, especially at the elementary level. The Sloyd approach for the first time had students construct well-designed and useful projects as a part of skill training. At this time, a secondary-level trade and industrial vocational education movement was also emerging. Trade and industrial (T&I) education schools tended to follow the Russian approach to skills training, while the manual arts movement grew from the Sloyd system and England's arts and crafts movement.

John Dewey's publication of *The School and Society* (1907) placed industrial occupations at the very center of the elementary school curriculum. In "The Place of Manual Training in the Elementary Course of Study" Dewey (1901) again expressed the use of the occupations as a vehicle of instruction. Professor Charles R. Richards (Bawden, 1950) in an editorial in the *Manual Training Magazine* (1904) suggested that the term "Industrial Arts" be used in place of "Manual Training." This gave rise to the industrial arts (IA) movement. Trade and industrial (T&I) vocational education emerged as a major education program with the passage of the Smith-Hughes Act of 1917.

Since both T&I and IA were implemented about the same time, there was competition between the two in regard to the consistency of each. Some in IA wanted to make it prevocational while others wanted to keep its conception broad and make it an essential part of general education.

The period after World War II was a time of much curriculum study and recommendation. William Warner and his graduate students at Ohio State University published the first IA curriculum proposal in 1946-47 (Herschbach, 1997). It established the use of personnel management structures in the laboratory and concentrated on five areas of study: communications, construction, power, transportation, and manufacturing.

Curricular refinements that followed promoted content based on the technology of industry, inclusion of mass-production procedures, and further use of business structures. Donald Maley of the University of Maryland proposed student activities organized around investigation, exploration, analysis, testing, and the use of tools and materials to solve problems. Many states, including California, developed their own plans for industrial arts education. These plans may be found at the Web sites of the several state departments of education (ERIC Education Resources Information Center, n.d.).

TECHNICAL EDUCATION

For many years higher education institutions have educated engineers, doctors lawyers, veterinarians, home economists, and other professional workers. The public vocational schools have provided workers for industry, farming, wholesale, and retail selling, homemaking, and other occupations since about 1920. During the 1960s a need surfaced for workers that required both technical knowledge and skills of a different nature than those needed by tradesman, engineers, scientists, and other professional workers. This area of training was that known as technical education, which is a level of education that trains technicians and technologists.

Many factors have been responsible for the development of technical education. Among these are technological developments in industry, impacts of war, increases in the initial employment age, the mushrooming of technical information, larger high school enrollment, and an increased interest in adult education.

With the Information and Digital Ages, technological development has increased even more rapidly since the 1990s. Scientist, engineers, technicians, and skilled workers have been developing new materials, processes, and products during the years. These discoveries and inventions have improved levels of living and reduced, by mechanization, much of the drudgery of handwork. The roboticization of industry has replaced the worker in hot, heavy and hazardous occupations. The manufacture and use of many new processes and products have demanded workers and operators with new knowledge and skills different from those obtained heretofore in either trade or professional courses. These new knowledge and skills have been in the area of technical education.

More and more adults are becoming interested in educational programs. This increased interest is partly due to changes in the requirements of occupations in which adults are employed. New technological developments require new skills. Ordinarily these must be acquired by employed workers, especially if the new content is not so extensive as to make training on the job impractical. The rising trend in the educational level of all citizens, especially noticeable in recent years, has made adults more conscious of the need for both general and career and technical courses. In addition, continued developments and changes in technology underscores the need for continuing education across the lifespan.

The need for technicians, laboratory assistants, testers, supervisors, inspectors, and other technical workers is evident in many occupational fields. The more important areas of need at this time appear to be in agriculture, business, health, family and consumer sciences, industry, and public service (U.S. Department of Labor, 2005).

VOCATIONAL GUIDANCE

The vocational guidance movement developed almost simultaneously with the vocational education movement (Barlow, 1967, p. 52). John M. Brewer, a Harvard University Professor, considered vocational guidance as both the vestibule and the back porch for vocational education.

Vocational guidance is concerned with the problems and techniques involved in choosing an occupation and in becoming adjusted in it. Vocational guidance, like vocational education, had its origins in the changing nature of work and has developed concurrently with, but independently of, vocational education. The development of vocational guidance has been due to the efforts of individuals and organizations interested in the problems of workers and prospective workers who were struggling with occupational choices or were dissatisfied with choices previously made (Technical & Vocational Education & Training (TVET), n.d.). Vocational educators learned early in the history of vocational education that the choice of an occupation and the adjustment thereto were important factors in the efficient production of the worker.

The relationship of vocational guidance to the efficiency of work stimulated vocational educators to acquire some proficiency in vocational

Table 3.3.   Early Philosopher's Views on Occupations

- Plato (427 B.C.-347 B.C.) suggested that each worker should be assigned to the one occupation for which he was naturally fitted.
- Cicero (106 B.C.-43 B.C.) stated, "We must decide what manner of men we wish to be and what calling in life we would follow; and this is the most difficult problem in the world."
- Pascal (1623-1662) discussed the importance of a wise choice of an occupation in his writings.
- John Locke (1695) suggested that children's natures and aptitudes should be studied as a means of determining their capabilities for earning and the extent to which improvement might be secured.
- Charles Dickens (1853) published the *Bleak House*, which depicted a youth who was in need of vocational guidance to find out what his natural bent was.
- Samuel Smiles (1859) published a volume entitled *Self Help*, which was designed to assist an individual in developing habits of industry.

guidance to enable them to counsel more intelligently with vocational students. The need for more extensive knowledge and skill in vocational guidance led vocational educators to seek an expansion of guidance services and, as a result, federal funds were made available as a reimbursement for certain vocational guidance services. The use of federal funds and the parallel development of vocational education and vocational guidance have led to some difference in points of view in the relationship between the two. Some changes have occurred in the administration of the public school guidance program as result of the National Defense Education Act of 1958, which authorized federal funds for guidance services. This lesson is concerned with various aspects of vocational guidance programs.

Human's choice of an occupation prior to the industrial revolution was influenced by such factors as heredity, tradition, and superstition. The usual procedure during this time was for the son to learn the trade or profession of his father. Little consideration was given to such factors as aptitude, interest, and personal preference.

Early beginning: as illustrated in Table 3.3, the writing of the philosophers of ancient times indicates that some of them were concerned about occupational choices.

WORK OF FRANK PARSONS

Present-day programs in vocational guidance developed as a result of the work of Dr. Frank Parsons. Parsons was instrumental in founding the Vocational Bureau of Boston, which was organized to deal with occupational adjustment problems of both youth and adults (Barlow, 1967,

Table 3.4. Dr. Parson and Vocational Choice Milestones

- He developed the Vocation Bureau, which formally opened in January 1908, in the Boston Civic Service House.
- The Vocational Bureau served individuals for ages 15-72.
- The Bureau furnished information so that individuals could choose an occupation or career.
- Dr. Parsons established a vocation department at the Boston YMCA in 1908. A school for training counselors was initiated in the department.
- Dr. Parsons' book *Choosing a Vocation* was published in May 1909. He had died in September 1908.

p. 53). He found that people were greatly interested in seeking advice about occupations. In time, individual counseling gave way to vocational guidance. Parson's work in this area is represented in a timeline in Table 3.4.

In his book Dr. Parsons suggested the method of the vocational counselor involved the following consideration:

a. Personal data; b. Self-analysis; c. The person's own choice and decision; d. Counselors analysis; e. Outlook in the vocational field; f. Induction and advice; g. General helpfulness in fitting into the chosen work.

The counselee was expected to record on paper his personal data and self-analysis. The counselor was instructed to test the counselee's choice of an occupation and to provide him with occupational information. Parsons is said to have been the first person to use the term vocational guidance in his first report on the work of the Vocational Bureau (Barlow, 1967, p. 53), and he paved the way for organizing vocational guidance programs in public schools by suggesting the educational institution should undertake this responsibility. However, according to Hershenson (2006), Pauline Agassiz Shaw, Meyer Bloomfield, and Ralph Albertson should be credited with initiating vocational guidance in the field. Parsons organized the work of the Vocation Bureau for the collection and study of information about occupations and workers. He recognized the importance of publicity and enlisted the assistance of friends and co-workers to carry on the work.

CONCLUSION

The origins of the different components of career and technical education and historical considerations reveal clear pathways regarding when and where vocational education came into being. Knowledge of the history of career and technical education will assist readers and learners in better understanding the current concept of vocational education. Without this knowledge of the history of career and technical education, readers or learners may find it hard to relate to current issues of career and technical education. As Kincheloe (1999) noted:

> Without historical insight, vocational educational policy makers fail to gain insights into the relationship between schooling and work that the past may provide. As a result, vocational educational leaders may devote great energy to reinventing a pedagogy incapable of addressing the demands of democracy and the needs of an evolving economy...Historical consciousness can help vocational educators recognize the inherent problems in particular assumptions or particular ways of operating and facilitate the development of pragmatic alternatives. (p. 93)

Rather than trying to convince anyone, vocational education reflects the concept that education is life, not just the preparation for life. It is built upon the ideal of individual differences among people; individual differences created and emphasized through the interaction of biological inheritance, the specific environment which surrounds the individual and the unique characteristics of each person. As you read this chapter, you have probably developed some common themes such as "survival," "progress" and "civilization." Indeed, such connections are quite accurate as vocational education has its roots in pragmatism (Evans & Herr, 1978).

REFERENCES

Ackerknecht, E. H. (1982). *A short history of medicine.* Baltimore: John Hopkins University.

Bawden, W. (1950). *Leaders in industrial education.* Milwaukee, WI: Bruce.

Barlow, M. L. (1967). *History of industrial education in the United States.* Peoria, AZ: Charles A. Bennett.

Barlow, M. L. (1976a). 200 years of vocational education, 1776-1976: The awakening, 1776-1826. *American Vocational Journal, 51*(5), 23-28.

Barlow, M. L. (1976b). 200 years of vocational education, 1776-1976: Independent action, 1826-1876. *American Vocational Journal, 51*(5), 31-40.

Barlow, M. L. (1976c). 200 years of vocational education, 1776-1976: The vocational education age emerges, 1876-1926. *American Vocational Journal, 51*(5), 45-58.

Beatty, A. J. (1918). *Corporation schools.* Bloomington, IL: Public School Publishing Company. Retrieved April 25, 2007, from http://books.google.com/books/pdf/Corporation_Schools.pdf

Bellwood, P. (2004). *First farmers: The origins of agricultural societies.* Ames, IA: Blackwell.

Clendening, L. (1960). *Sourcebook of medical history.* Mineola, NY: Courier Dover.

Coates, C. P. (1923). *History of the manual training school of Washington University.* (Dept. of the Interior, Bureau of Education Bulletin, 1923, No. 3). Washington, DC: U.S. Government Printing Office.

Cochrane, W. W. (1993). *The development of American agriculture: An historical analysis* (2nd ed.). Minneapolis: University of Minnesota Press.

Dewey, J. (1901, February). The place of manual training in the elementary course of study. *Manual Training Magazine,* 193-199.

Dewey, J. (1907). *The school and society: Being three lectures by John Dewey supplemented by a statement of the University Elementary School.* Chicago: University of Chicago Press.

ERIC Education Resources Information Center. (n.d.). *Suggested master plan for industrial arts programs in North Dakota schools final report research series number 22.* Washington, DC: Education Resources Information Center. (ERIC Document Reproduction Service No. ED 115 979).
  Retrieved April 26, 2007, from http://eric.ed.gov/ERICWebPortal/ Home.portal?_nfpb=true&_pageLabel=RecordDetails&ERICExtSearch_Sea rchValue_0=ED115979&ERICExtSearch_SearchType_0=eric_accno&objectI d=0900000b800ec8bf

Evans, R. N., & Herr, E. L. (1978). *Foundations of vocational education.* New York: Macmillan.

Fafunwa, A. B. (1974). *History of education in Nigeria.* Ibadan: NPS Educational Publishers.

Gerbracht, C., & Babcock, R. (1969). *Elementary school industrial arts.* New York: Bruce.

Graham, J. (1933). *The evolution of business education in the United States and its implications for business.* Berkeley: University of Southern California Press.

Herschbach, D. R. (1997). From industrial arts to technology education: The search for direction. *Journal of Technology Studies 23*(1), 24-32 Retrieved April 25, 2007, from http://140.126.32.4/NTNU/read-TEES02/JTS-IATE-Haerschbach.pdf

Hershenson, D. B. (2006). Frank Parsons's enablers: Pauline Agassiz Shaw, Meyer Bloomfield, and Ralph Albertson. *Career Development Quarterly, 55*(1), 77-84.

Holbrook, J. (1826). *American Lyceum, or Society for the Improvement of Schools, and Diffusion of Useful Knowledge.* Boston: Perkins & Martin.
  Retrieved April 25, 2007, from http://books.google.com/books/pdf/ American_Lyceum__Or_Society_for_the_Impr.pdf

Kincheloe, J. L. (1999). *How do we tell the workers?* Boulder, CO: Westview Press.

Long, H. B. (1990). Psychological control in self-controlled learning. *International Journal of Lifelong Education, 9*(4), 331-338.

Miller, R., & Smalley, L. (1963). *Selected readings in industrial arts.* Bloomington: McKnight & McKnight.

Nafukho, F. M. (2007). Ubuntuism: An African social philosophy relevant to adult and workplace learning. In K. P. King, & V. C. X. Wang (Eds.), *Comparative adult education around the globe* (pp. 59- 67). Hangzhou: Zhejiang University Press.

Nafukho, F. M., Amutabi, M. N., & Otunga, R. N. (2005). *Foundations of adult education in Africa.* Cape Town, South Africa: Pearson/UNESCO.

Roberts, R. W. (1965). *Vocational and practical arts education: History, development, and principles.* New York: Harper and Row.

University of California, Santa Cruz. (2003). *Teaching organic framing and gardening: Resources for instructors.* Santa Cruz: UC Santa Cruz Center for Agroecology and Sustainable Food Systems.

Technical & Vocational Education & Training (TVET). (n.d.). *Introduction.* Retrieved December 25, 2006, from http://www.tvet-pal.org/counseling/intro.html

U.S. Department of Labor. (2005). *Tomorrow's jobs.* Retrieved April 26, 2007, from http://www.bls.gov/oco/oco2003.htm

Williams, S. J. (2000). *Essentials of health services.* Florence, KY: Thomas Delmar Learning.

CHAPTER 4

CURRENT INSTRUCTIONAL PROGRAMS IN CAREER AND TECHNICAL EDUCATION

Kathleen P. King and Victor C. X. Wang

Career and technical education (CTE) is a massive enterprise in the United States. Thousands of comprehensive high schools, vocational and technical high schools, area vocational centers, and community colleges offer career and technical education programs (U.S. Department of Education, 2006). On the importance of career and technical education, it is noted, "CTE is about providing knowledge and skills to individuals of all ages, allowing them to have choices in their future and to reach full earning potential. It is about learning for life, citizenship and career success" (Bray, 2007, p. 6). Virtually every high school student takes at least one career and technical education course, and one in four students takes three or more courses in a single program area. One-third of college students are involved in career and technical programs, and as many as 40 million adults engage in short-term postsecondary occupational training (U.S. Department of Education, 2006). This figure provides a compelling demonstration of the importance of career and technical education in the nation.

Innovations in Career and Technical Education: Strategic Approaches Towards Workforce Competencies Around the Globe, pp. 69–97
Copyright © 2008 by Information Age Publishing
All rights of reproduction in any form reserved.

Instructional programs vary from current business education to vocational guidance within career and technical education. They have been offered largely in response to the *Nation At Risk* report (National Commission on Excellence in Education, 1983), which was released in the early 1980s. According to this report, many of our high school students were dropping out of schools and they did not compete with students from other industrialized nations. It may be true that U.S. students do not even compete with students from developing countries such as India and China. Educators in the field of career and technical education felt a strong need to offer interesting and relevant courses to high school students in order for them to complete high school. However, since many school districts have raised graduation requirements for the non-practical courses, math, science, reading, and English and many schools have added exit exams in recent years, it has become more difficult for secondary school students to enroll in vocational education courses (Rothrock & Walker, 2007; Stone, Kowske, & Alfeld, 2004).

In fact the No Child Left Behind (NCLB) initiatives have placed such a great emphasis on outcomes rather than curricula that at this time educators and public constituencies see that the legislation may be leaving many students of different socioeconomic and/or racial strata (Lee & Wong, 2004) and different learning or vocational interests behind. The most recent approach to counteract these trends in decreasing emphasis and/or interest in CTE is to integrate technology and general education content into vocational education courses (John Hopkins University, 2004; King, 2007). In this chapter, readers have the opportunity to compare and contrast all of the courses offered in the different components of career and technical education program and help determine whether they are adequate enough given the nature of the information age within which we live.

CONTEMPORARY BUSINESS EDUCATION

Business Education has come a long way since 1980. It has taken most of that time to fully accept the idea that keyboarding should be taught on a computer keyboard or electronic typewriter. Some typewriting teachers resisted this inexorable change, clinging instead to teaching obsolete skills like mechanical centering and other formatting details. Some of the newer areas that are covered in business programs besides keyboarding skills include:

- Word processing
- Desktop publishing

- Electronic mail
- Development of human capital

For example, the development of human capital in a technological environment is important if a business is going to be competitive in the local and global market and survive. Some of the topics that should be covered are:

Globalization: Students should be aware of the social values and mores, cultures, politics, business protocols, religions, and general working habits of other countries in order to be better prepared to communicate with people worldwide.

Technological Integration: People must be educated to accept the fact that products, services, equipment, and working environment capitalize on integration and connectivity. In many cases people must decide on what combination of components to use to get a job completed efficiently. Beyond mastering the basics in technology, employees must understand how an information system relies on the interrelationship among many components. They must develop alternative ways of approaching a task, because the familiar way of doing something might not mesh with the work of other employees who are contributing to the product.

Knowledge Specialists: The demand for information specialists and knowledge engineers will increase as knowledge continues to grow at exponential rates. Workers need not memorize vast amounts of information. Instead they must find efficient ways to retrieve information from databases. Skills for searching and sorting information are extremely valuable. These skills will become even more vital as information database services proliferate.

Business Competitiveness: The importance of understanding business ethics and politics cannot be over emphasized. As greater amounts of information become available to consumers, business will be forced to become more accountable for their products and services. Future workers must learn that competitiveness does not mean unwillingness to share, especially as more and more large businesses enter into joint ventures.

The Work Ethic: It appears that our nation has come full circle in our personal values and ideals of work. Most people no longer work because of job satisfaction, but because monetary gains can upgrade their standards of living. It is important to develop attitude and skills that stress dependability, punctuality, loyalty, and the willingness to give an honest day's work.

Change: Change is a constant in our world today. It must not only be accepted but also sought. With the computerization of nearly every facet of life, individuals can become comfortable with technology; however, the technology is constantly changing so the business educator must continually pursue cutting-edge techniques and procedures lest their skills and knowledge become obsolete. In addition they need to pass along the vital perspectives of changing knowledge and lifelong learning to their students.

Diversity: It is a reality that we live, learn and work in a diverse world. Diversity refers to "any dimension that can be used to differentiate groups and people from one another" (Giovannini, 2004, p. 22). Within business education, diversity of learners and educators can be categorized into three dimensions, internal (age, gender, ethnicity, race, physical traits), external (geographic location, social economic status, personal habits, appearance), and organizational (work experiences, work location, work and learning content, and environment). For business education programs to develop workforce competencies among learners, there is an urgent and compelling need to teach diversity (Adams, Sewell, & Hall, 2003).

These issues directly influence the development of human capital and affect society's ability to meet future challenges. Career and technical educators and especially business educators have a vast array of resources with which to address these issues (Darling, Greenwood, & Hansen-Gandy, 1998; Foxman & Easterling, 1995; Gay & Howard, 2000; Sabo, 2000). Addressing these issues is part of educating for life as well as training a better work force (Hill, 2006; King & Biro, 2006).

COURSES USUALLY COVERED IN BUSINESS EDUCATION

As mentioned earlier, the business education curriculum has more or less evolved as the public and industry made demands for more and more commercial or business education (Schmidt, 1990). For a number of years the secondary and post secondary offerings remained somewhat static. The following are generally accepted as indicative of the various offerings at secondary and post secondary levels:

Secondary offerings:

- Bookkeeping
- Shorthand
- Keyboarding
- Penmanship
- Economics
- Merchandising
- Salesmanship
- Entrepreneurship
- Marketing

Postsecondary offerings: In the case of graduate level programs which are mainly offered in business colleges or in colleges of education, Gaytan (2006) identified the following courses as forming the core curriculum of business education programs:

- Accounting
- Secretarial Science
- Computer Programming
- Web Page Design
- Legal Environment of Business
- Fundamentals of Computer Application
- Methods of Teaching Business Education
- Professional Writing in Business
- Instructional Strategies for Technology
- Managerial Communications
- Advanced Keyboarding
- Technology Support Systems
- Document Processing
- Managerial Reporting

Postsecondary programs are usually integrated or combined so that some of the course work covered in high school evolves as a combination course. Postsecondary programs are also more fortunate to have more sophisticated machines, so higher technological instruction can be provided at this level.

INSTRUCTIONAL PROGRAMS IN AGRICULTURE

Agriculture education is defined as resources for agriculture education programs, including classroom instruction, leadership, and supervised agricultural experience programs that prepare students for college or entrance into agricultural careers (California Department of Education, 2006). Since 1917, with the passage of the Smith-Hughes Act, federal and state legislation has provided leadership for the implementation and improvement of agricultural education programs. A successful agriculture education program must be based on three components: classroom instruction, Future Farmers of America (FFA) leadership activities, and Supervised Occupational Experience Projects. Two major federal and state programs provide support for agricultural education programs: the Carl D. Perkins Vocational and Technical Education Act of 1998 (20

U.S.C. 2301 *et seq.*, as amended by Public Law 105-332), and the Agricultural Education Vocational Incentive Grant Program. The programs seek to accomplish four major purposes (California Department of Education, 2006) which stated:

- Enable local education agencies to improve the curriculum for students enrolled in agricultural education programs through the development and implementation of (a) an integrated academic and vocational curriculum, (b) curriculum that reflects workplace needs and instruction, and (c) support services for special populations.

- Increase the competence of future and current high school, middle grades, and regional occupational centers and programs agricultural education instructors in developing and implementing a new integrated curriculum, student and program certification systems, technical preparation strategies, and effective instructional methodologies.

- Promote the development and use of curriculum, instructional materials, and instructional strategies that prepare students in all aspects of the agricultural industry and foster critical thinking, problem solving, leadership, and academic and technical skill attainment.

- Increase linkages between secondary and postsecondary institutions offering agricultural education programs; between academic and agricultural educators; and among agricultural educators, the agricultural industry, professional associations, and local communities.

According to the literature, many benefits of agricultural education programs have been identified. Such benefits include:

- Collaboration, articulation, and networking with all levels of delivery systems (elementary through postsecondary) for instructors.
- Supervised entrepreneurial and workplace learning experiences for students.
- Linkages and partnerships with business and industry for instructors and students.
- Professional development opportunities for teachers, administrators, and counselors.
- Curriculum development based on performance and content standards for instructors on-site technical assistance in programs for instructors and students.

- A foundation for students in the academic and technical skills necessary for career and personal success.
- Student leadership and interpersonal skills.
- An authentic assessment of knowledge, skills, and abilities through on-demand demonstrations and portfolios (California Department of Education, 2006).

Agriculture education programs consist of classroom work, shop work, organized youth activities, and in some cases supervised agricultural experiences. This kind of instruction requires that the instructors have college instruction and work experience to be able to manage agricultural educational program.

- Responsibilities of the teachers include: Classroom teaching, supervising the farming, and other experiences of students; engaging in community service; developing satisfactory public relations; maintaining adequate teaching facilities, materials, and equipment; organizing, supervising and conducting student club work; and making records and reports.
- Qualifications of the teacher: Professional qualification dictates that the teacher graduates from an approved 4-year agriculture education program from a land grant college. The teacher should have a minimum of 2 years of farm experience after the age of 14, preference is usually given to those that are farm reared. The teacher should have experiences with agriculture student organization and should have experience as a student in high school vocational agriculture. The teacher must have knowledge in teaching methods for both classroom and shop activities. The teacher must possess leadership abilities, resourcefulness, industriousness, open-mindedness, and dependability.
- Teaching methods: The agriculture teacher must use a number of teaching techniques including: lecture, demonstration, group discussion, field trips, contests, group projects, and student club activities.
- Teaching materials: Such materials depend upon what course is being taught. However, textbooks, extension bulletins, shop manuals, handout materials, homework, slides, videos, and computers can be used to teach the classes.
- Related class instruction: In some cases an agriculture instructor may utilize other high school classes to supplement agriculture classes. These may be salesmanship from the distributive education program, or typing from the business program.

- Building utilized: An agriculture program should have a classroom, shop or laboratory tool room, washroom and an office/conference room.
- Equipment: These should include all kinds of farm mechanics, metalworking, woodworking, sheet metal and welding equipment. A good set of hand tools are also needed to be able to show the students how to use them in maintaining farm equipment and facilities.

Courses Taught in Agriculture Programs

For most agriculture programs, courses in animal care and production, plant care and production, farm mechanics, building construction, hydraulics, electricity, welding, lathe work, sheet metal work, masonry work, fence building, and business management are included (see for example, Arizona Department of Education, 2006; and Georgia Agricultural Education, 2006). Certainly local geography, climate and industry indicators may have originally influenced local agricultural programs. However contemporary agricultural education programs cast a wider net of knowledge and skills for learners in order for them to realize the broad expanse of this innovative and essential field of study.

HEALTH OCCUPATIONS EDUCATION

Health science occupations education (HSOE) prepares students for careers related to medicine, nursing, dentistry, and allied health programs. Students preparing for health careers or for teaching careers in health occupations can gain valuable career information and network with other professionals by participating in the HSOE program. This program provides students technical skills, health care competencies, and opportunities to obtain the knowledge necessary to satisfy the requirements for entry-level health care jobs. HSOE is dedicated to educating today's students for tomorrow's health-care community (Wisconsin Department of Public Instruction, 2006).

These programs are planned to prepare individuals below the professional level to provide patient care in health related settings. These settings may be long-term facilities (rest homes), clinics, hospitals, doctor's offices, hospitals, and so forth. This means that training is below the registered nurse as well as the medical doctor. The following areas could be included in this continuum at a vocational school (ROP in California) or a community college:

Regional Occupational Program

Practical Nurse
Dental Assistant
Medical Laboratory Assistant
Occupational Therapist Assistant
Medical Office Assistant
Medication Aide
Geriatric Aide
Home Health Care Worker

Community College

Dental Laboratory Technician
Radiological Technologist
Medical Records Technician
Respiratory Therapist

For further examples of occupations and related resources, HSOE programs may include the following helpful resources: North Carolina Public Schools (2006), Illinois State Board of Education (n.d.), and Health Occupations Students of America (HSOA) (2007).

These programs all use classroom instruction along with clinical instruction in a health care facility so that students spend 50 percent or more of their instructional time on-the-job under the supervision of a clinical instructor. The programs are under strict guidelines furnished by the appropriate State Boards in regard to:

- What is taught?
- When it is taught?
- Where it is taught?
- The maximum size of class for classroom instruction
- The maximum size of class for clinical instruction

All graduates of these programs must pass state board examinations after completing the program and before they are certified.

HEALTH OCCUPATIONS INSTRUCTION

A number of states have promoted the use of competency profiles as a system of planning the content of the various health occupations programs

(Illinois State Board of Education, n.d.; North Carolina Public Schools; 2006). The use of these competency profiles assists the instructor and the student in evaluating whether or not the instructor or student has covered the items, which are listed on the profile.

Another use of the competency profiles is that of assisting the instructor in using competency-based education as a technique for guiding instruction. This competency based instruction can be modularized and it can also be individualized so that the students can progress at their own pace and in many cases be able to understand the material better (Illinois State Board of Education, n.d.; North Carolina Public Schools; 2006). If the health occupations curriculum is modularized, a number of the modules may be used in various health areas so that a sharing of materials such as multimedia can be used by the institution.

A good example of a module that could be produced that all health care programs could use would be one on how one should handle a patient with acquired immune deficiency syndrome (AIDS). This is one of the major problem areas that health care workers must face. Other areas that may be modularized so that all health care students may cover would be one on dealing with an aging population, and one on some new technological developments that all may need instruction on in relation to their program. Competency profiles could be used to determine some common core curriculum materials that could be modularized and individualized. Some areas that may be examined are:

Medical Terminology
Anatomy
Physiology
Microbiology
First Aid
Taking Vital Signs
Observation Skills
Microscope use
Nutrition
Aseptic Techniques
Computer skills
The Metric System
Cardiopulmonary Resuscitation (CPR)
Moving and transferring patients
Simple Lab Tests
Blood Pressure Measurement

With the use of video enhanced instruction, students can view the videos over and over to be able to master any of the procedures, terms, and so forth, that need to be covered in a course. Only when the course is individualized and mediated, can the course be set up for the individual learner and individual differences.

Health occupations educators should take advantage of all the new technologies that are available to assist the instructor in providing good instructional material for their students. Carl Perkins vocational education funds are available to upgrade instruction through the use of video, computer assisted learning, and so forth. Increasingly more institutions will be able to use more DVDs, CDs, online video, streaming video, and laser disks for instructional material since more of those are available.

Some writers are indicating that Health Occupations Educators should be considering offering a program, which would allow a student to become a multiskilled practitioner (Hoberty, 1996). This would indicate that individuals should cross train in order to practice in more than one health related job. The student would obtain the required competencies to qualify for more than one job title. For example, a student may be qualified as a medical laboratory technician, radiographer, and respiratory therapist.

This movement has emerged as an effort to relieve workforce shortages in rural hospitals. Alabama and Illinois pioneered the development of programs to cross-train health care workers in the early 1970s and were widely adopted in the late 1980s (Bamberg & Blayney, 1989). Some hospitals and systems in California have also tried cross-training with limited successes.

If Health occupation educators utilize competency profiles as mentioned earlier, it should be fairly easy to decide on the core competencies and then have options that the student would follow for specific areas. If the student then decides to follow three or more options, cross training would be quite simple. Perhaps the greatest challenges are in obtaining agreement from the various governing boards as new health occupations continue to emerge.

CLINICAL INSTRUCTION

The clinical instruction for health occupations varies from program to program. For a number of the programs, such as licensed vocational nursing (LVN), an instructor from the school also instructs at the clinical site. However, in some instances with other kinds of health programs the on-site instructor may be an employee of the facility in which the clinical is held (North Carolina Public Schools, 2006). In the case of LVN programs, the instructor who teaches the classes in the institution also teaches on the clinical site. However, in some cases the institution employs persons who are strictly clinical instructors. This occurs because most instructors at a clinical site are limited to a maximum of 15 students when they may have 30 enrolled in the program. This would either require the instructor to have 2 clinical assignments with 15 students each or an extra clinical instructor is employed to assist in the clinical setting. These numbers vary by type of program.

Students in the clinical setting are required to perform the various tasks required of the health worker in the particular occupation for which they are training. Since this is a requirement for the training, no reimbursement is required from the participating clinical institution. However, in some cases a small stipend may be given by the clinic institution while the student is training in the clinical setting.

HIGH TECHNOLOGY TRENDS IN
VOCATIONAL-INDUSTRIAL EDUCATION

The fundamental problem that has faced vocational industrial education in recent years has been the rapid change from person-to-machines (Freeman, 1996; National Clearinghouse for Educational Facilities (NCEF), 2006). Economic and technological advancement have lead leading manufacturers to use more robots and computer controlled manufacturing centers and to employ fewer people in the skill area (El Camino College, 2006). The thought of robots and the computer-controlled machines doing work for us is fascinating, but it raises several important questions for career and technical education and society in general.

The fundamental problems facing industry in the United States are the cost of productivity and the maintenance of quality products. Economic planners promote reindustrialization with the use of robots and computer controlled manufacturing wherever possible in order to decrease costs of production and to increase the quality of the product being produced.

The manufacturing sector is feeling the influence of technology far more than most persons realize. The work force employed at the turn of the twenty-first century was drastically different than that employed only 15 years earlier. The widespread use of computer-aided design (CAD) and computer-aided manufacturing (CAM) has, for example, brought machine shops and engineering departments closer together (Connecticut State Department of Education, 2006). This affects the jobs of assembly-line workers dramatically. Workers will not assemble the products but rather direct the robots to do the work. Some of the contemporary terms being utilized in manufacturing are flexible manufacturing and just-in-time delivery. Flexible manufacturing simply means that a computer controlled manufacturing system is used. Just-in-time delivery means that parts and subassemblies are made just in time to be shipped and/or assembled. This dynamic decreases the stocking and warehousing of parts. These two concepts have greatly affected how manufacturing industries conduct their business.

Workers in factories will need to be better educated, especially in the field of computers. As technology advances, workers will need retraining on a continual basis in order to keep abreast of changes in the technology being used. Vocational industrial education programs need to keep up as well if competent, up-to-date workers are to be effectively prepared or retrained (Connecticut State Department of Education, 2006; El Camino College, 2006; National Clearinghouse for Educational Facilities (NCEF), 2006; Smith, 2000). Craft areas are also experiencing some new methods of conducting their tasks. For example, computers are used for material purchases and to track costs for projects. Designing and estimating of costs are also conducted with computers and software designed for those purposes. Building trades programs will need to incorporate computer instruction into their classrooms. If the vocational industrial education programs do not include instruction in these areas for future carpenters, contractors, and builders they will not be prepared to enter the labor market.

Service areas such as auto mechanics are also experiencing drastic changes as the automobile is being controlled more and more by computers. Automotive students will need to be trained on the newest computer based diagnostic equipment if they are to enter the automotive technology area and be able to service the modern automobile or truck (Connecticut State Department of Education, 2006).

The image of the skilled trades person does not appeal to a number of high school students. The number of persons who are counseled into these programs seems to be diminishing. Also the increased need for persons who have a good grasp of mathematics and science will limit the number of persons who can profit from some of the "High Tech" training needed for the manufacturing, craft and service sectors. Unless these deficiencies are corrected, the United States could face a serious shortage of properly trained persons for a technological society (Flanagan, 2006; Friedman, 2005; King, 2007). There is a definite need to develop programs with government, industry, and education all working together in an effort to establish, once again, a high level of quality productivity in the United States.

Perhaps one of the ways that vocational industrial education can produce quality persons will be to work cooperatively with industry, the crafts and the service sector. Basic competencies in cognate, psychomotor and the affective domain can be addressed in the classroom at schools but the more in-depth cognate and psychomotor competencies can best be accomplished through cooperative programs or apprenticeships where the student works on-the-job with up-to-date equipment to be current with the industry, craft or service area. This would alleviate the cost to schools in obtaining the expensive machines being used in the crafts, industry or service areas.

CURRENT FAMILY AND CONSUMER SCIENCES PROGRAMS

Originating from the domain of "home economics" and expanding to a more comprehensive and problem-solving orientation, family and consumer sciences, human sciences, human ecology or home economics, is an academic discipline which combines aspects of consumer science, nutrition, cooking, parenting and human development, interior decoration, textiles, family economics, housing, apparel design and resource management as well as other related subjects. Today, family and consumer sciences combine social science, including its emphasis on the well-being of families, individuals, and communities, and natural science with its emphasis on nutrition and textile science. The discipline as it originated from home economics in the United States was first established at Iowa State University in 1875 and spread to other land grant universities (Schneider, 2000; Stage & Vincenti, 1997) The field appealed to women to have their own niche while men studied subjects such as agriculture or shop courses of study. For many years it was traditional for junior high and high school girls to study "Home Economics" (primarily cooking and sewing) while boys of the same studied "Shop" (carpentry, drafting, auto repair, etc.). Students of either gender were excluded, strongly discouraged or outright banned from taking the other subjects (Stage & Vincenti, 1997). Courses that are related to the traditional home economics and shop designations now are recognized subject areas in secondary education and have become universal subjects, in that students of both genders may participate in them.

Home economics developed in the last 100 years to a broader cluster of studies which is termed family and consumer sciences. Family and consumer sciences has gained great prominence in high schools and CTE schools across the United States and evolved as a field itself overtime. Originally family and consumer sciences placed major emphasis upon the following due to societal needs:

1. Consumer Educations and Management
2. Nutrition and Food Management
3. Human Developments and Family Living

4.   Housing and Living Environment

5.   Clothing/Apparel and Textile Products

However, in the 1990s and 2000s, we experienced further development in the understanding of this field, especially through the continuing efforts of the national association, American Association of Family and Consumer Sciences as it continued to labor to keep the field relevant to societal needs.

> The Body of Knowledge for the discipline and profession was identified more than twenty years ago to facilitate several evolving developments. Evolutions within the profession continue and include renewal of the certification examination and the standards for Accreditation of FCS programs. During this past year, several members of the Association have provided leadership in the revision of the CIP codes. Finally, dialogue during the FCS Higher Education Summit, held in February 1999 and a session at the 1999 Annual Meeting addressing a comprehensive vision for the future contributed to the decision to invite the elected leaders of professional organizations and societies of the family and consumer sciences profession to discuss the Body of Knowledge for the future.

> A continuing trend in the field is the need for Family and Consumer Sciences professionals to function as specialists, requiring both considerable depth in one subject area specialization and the ability to integrate concepts from other areas of the family and consumer sciences knowledge base. The proposed conceptual framework addresses this need.

> Basic Human Needs is one of the key elements. Basic Human Needs may be operationalized to include subject area specializations. Basic Human Needs may be conceptualized broadly to allow flexibility for programs and professionals to articulate in unique and varied ways the role of the specialist in Family and Consumer Sciences. New specializations and programs may emerge to focus on the interaction between the common body of knowledge, cross-cutting themes, and basic human needs. Basic Human Needs, as an organizing principle, include traditional specializations and make possible the emergence of new specializations. The dynamic nature of the framework provides a mechanism for continual reflection, enhancement, and development of programs and specializations in the field. (Baugher et al., 2003, p. 4)

Indeed, the reader may also see how family and consumer science understanding of critical thinking skills and interaction among the specializations of the field one with the other is seen in the following quote,

> During the past two decades, the curriculum in family and consumer sciences (FACS) education has undergone many changes. These changes are partly due to such events as the series of publications by Marjorie Brown

and those she coauthored with Beatrice Paolucci (1978, 1979, and 1980) and The Carl D. Perkins Vocational and Applied Technology Education Act Amendments (1990 and 1998). The effects of these two phenomena are recognizable in the FACS education curriculum through both program and course offerings. In fact, secondary FACS education programs are moving toward career preparation and an interdisciplinary curriculum, and many programs deliver the content using a critical science perspective. (Smith & Hall, 1999)

This development is a significant leap forward from the original domain of Home Economics of the nineteenth century. It also critically demonstrates the continued insight and innovation of CTE educators and the capability of CTE careers to keep pace with hi-tech innovations, societal, and economic developments.

Current Occupational Programs

Programs which are offered to assist individuals in developing competencies to become employable in occupations related to family and consumer sciences are offered at high schools, regional occupational programs, area vocational technical schools, and community colleges. Since all of these programs have an on-the-job or work-experience component, the instructors are required to become certified as instructor/coordinators so that they will have the competencies needed to coordinate the on-the-job experiences.

U.S. State Departments of Education (SDE)—have specific guidelines under which these family and consumer science programs are to be operated. These are usually published on the SDE Web site. Two of these are described here.

Occupational Home Economics (OHE)—this is an institution based program that prepares students with attitudes and entry level skills for employment in home economics and related occupations through a combination of classroom instruction, simulation, and supervised work experience.

Home Economics Cooperative Education (HECE)—this is a cooperative instructional program where the student obtains skills through classroom and on-the-job training. Students receive direct related and indirect related instruction in the institution through regular classroom instruction. The psychomotor skills are obtained on-the-job through a training agreement with the training station in regard to what the student is going to be taught at the work place.

In addition to state standards, national standards have been developed for the field of Family and Consumer Sciences (Indiana Department of

Education, 2006). These include comprehensive standards and content standards with the following major headings that are further subdivided and delineated in detail:

1. Career, Community, and Family Connections
   1.0 Integrate multiple life roles and responsibilities in family, career, and community roles and responsibilities.

2. Consumer and Family Resources
   2.0 Evaluate management practices related to the human, economic, and environmental recourses.

3. Consumer Services
   3.0 Integrate knowledge, skills, and practices required for careers in consumer services.

4. Early Childhood, Education, and Services
   4.0 Integrate knowledge, skills, and practices required for careers in early childhood, education, and services.

5. Facilities Management and Maintenance
   5.0 Integrate knowledge, skills, and practices required for careers in facilities management and maintenance.

6. Family
   6.0 Evaluate the significance of family and its impact on the well-being of individuals and society.

7. Family and Community Services
   7.0 Integrate knowledge, skills, and practices required for careers in family and community services.

8. Food Production and Services
   8.0 Integrate knowledge, skills, and practices required for careers in food production and services.

9. Food Science, Dietetics, and Nutrition
   9.0 Integrate knowledge, skills, and practices required for careers in food science, dietetics, and nutrition.

10. Hospitality, Tourism, and Recreation
    10.0 ntegrate knowledge, skills, and practices required for careers in hospitality, tourism, and recreation.

11. Housing, Interiors, and Furnishings
    11.0 Integrate knowledge, skills, and practices required for careers in housing, interiors, and furnishings.

12. Human Development
    12.0 Analyze factors that impact human growth and development.

13. Interpersonal Relationships
    13.0 Demonstrate respectful and caring relationships in the family, workplace, and community.
14. Nutrition and Wellness
    14.0 Demonstrate nutrition and wellness practices that enhance individual and family well-being.
15. Parenting
    15.0 Evaluate the impact of parenting roles and responsibilities on strengthening the well-being of individuals and families.
16. Textiles and Apparel
    16.0 Integrate knowledge, skills, and practices required for careers in textiles and apparel (Indiana Department of Education, 2006).

TECHNOLOGY EDUCATION—NEW PURPOSES—NEW STUDENTS

The nation has been besieged with reports on how U.S. students do not compare with students from other industrialized nations in terms of scores on mathematics and science (Baker, 2006; Friedman, 2005; Nussbaum, 2006). The solution most school districts have taken has been to add more mathematics and science courses for high school graduation. Many times students will only obtain more of the same instruction. If this did not work the first time, why should *more of the same* indicate better results? Education should mirror life. Given the complexities of life in our society, it would seem unwise to suggest that learning can effectively take place in isolated disciplines with the expectation that the students can effectively acquire and synthesize knowledge from the different areas.

Perhaps the leaders in our school systems should consider fundamental changes in regard to how these competencies are being taught. If the students are going to apply or use mathematics and science in business and industry, it would seem that it would be best to study these concepts in an integrated system as in technology education. With technology education at the core of schools offerings, they would be preparing students for our technological world. This preparation would be helpful to those that are going to follow the professions such as engineering or medicine as well as those that plan on pursuing technology as a career. Technology education is returning to the system that John Dewey supported years ago when he stated that we should use the occupations as the vehicle of instruction. At this time technology education can be the vehicle for all instruction especially for mathematics and science, which is crucial.

Some universities are requiring that Liberal Arts majors study technology education as a requirement for graduation. The University of Illinois at Champaign-Urbana, for example, suggests that study in "technologies" is equivalent to study in the sciences, as they propose major reforms of undergraduate education. The University of Illinois considers technological literacy a requisite for any person considered "liberally educated" at the bachelor's degree level.

Technology education instructors will have a full agenda if they are to serve higher-ability, college-bound students. The future is very positive but also very demanding. The study of technology forces thinking and interaction across disciplines. The integration of math and science with technology education as the core will facilitate student understanding of mathematical, scientific and technological principles. A multidisciplinary approach toward technology education is desirable and inevitable if higher-ability college-bound students are going to be taught. (John Hopkins University, 2004; King, 2007). Instructors also need to satisfy a number of learning styles and recognize that students can be different. Lessons will need to be directed toward capitalizing on individual differences. Meaningful learning activities that integrate math, science and technology will need to include more problem solving and analytical skills. With technology rapidly changing, technology instructors will be required to remain flexible, adaptable, and open-minded in order to stay current. (Bray, 2007; Connecticut State Department of Education, 2006).

With technology education as a core subject, college-bound students can apply mathematical and scientific concepts in an experiential, hands-on environment. Current literature suggests that hands-on experiences increase knowledge by as much as a factor of two or more. Beyond increased knowledge, retention is increased with the application of newly acquired knowledge (Connecticut State Department of Education, 2006; King, 2007). Technology education is about applying knowledge and we have learned that active learning is critical for preparing students for college. Technology education must go beyond only hands-on experiences—it must become hands-on/minds-on education if it is to be effective.

In addition, the school is a melting pot of diverse backgrounds. And in the midst of this diversity, the educational system must retain and provide students with worthwhile, relevant experiences. Technology education as a core subject can provide these worthwhile experiences with a hands-on application approach.

As a core subject in the college preparatory program, technology education can educate high-ability students in schools (Nussbaum, 2006) as well as those that originally were scheduled in industrial arts. This "new" student population will require new approaches to instruction, approaches that are rigorous and that are based on design, critical thinking, problem solving, and application (Friedman, 2005; Gura & King, 2007).

CHARACTERISTICS OF TECHNICAL EDUCATION

A technical education program is a terminal program not preparatory to a college degree but geared to meet the needs of agriculture, business health occupations, family and consumer sciences, and industry types of careers. Technical education programs vary in length from a single unit course of a few weeks to an integrated program operating on a part-time basis for several years.

Preemployment programs in technical education are usually 1 to 3 years in length. These programs are available at community colleges, or at the 13th and 14th grade levels.

Technical education programs are especially effective for young adults, and most other technical education students who have a mature attitude. Most preemployment programs require high school graduation or a GED as a prerequisite for entrance. However, they may have an open-enrollment policy which has no academic requirements beyond these.

TEACHING METHODS AND MATERIALS

Teaching methods for technical education emphasize shop and laboratory skill, fieldwork, and actual performance on the job as well as curriculum materials. Individualized instruction, home study, and small classes with extended opportunities for individual progress are important characteristics of the program (Bray, 2007). Modern curriculum materials are used with the computer, online learning, and continued workplace partnerships/internships facilitated through technology being core elements of instruction.

TECHNICAL PROGRAM INSTITUTIONS

A variety of institutions provide education for technical occupations, but the range of courses and the number of students enrolled frequently fall short of the demand for these trained persons. Technical courses are offered in community colleges, technical institutes, engineering schools, area vocational-technical schools (AVTS), technical high schools, and regional occupational programs (ROP). Some of these institutions, together with other special schools, offer correspondence courses in technical education. Technical education courses are also offered through trade associations and in industry. These courses are offered in both public and private institutions.

Area Vocational-Technical School Offerings: Many Area vocational-techni-cal schools and ROPs are offering a great number of technical courses as a result of the new "High-Tech" industry explosion. Career and technical schools may serve both secondary and postsecondary students in areas throughout most states. Many of the former vocational areas have become so specialized that a technical approach is required so that graduates are able to enter the technical field areas. For example, auto mechanics and auto body repair were formerly considered vocational areas of instruction, however, with the new emphasis on computers in auto mechanics and the uses of new construction and materials in auto body repair, persons enter-ing the labor market in these two areas are required to have a more "in-depth" technical training.

Career and technical schools usually offer certificates of attendance, and many of the community colleges accept the training from the AVTS as a portion of an associate degree. There has been a movement to 2 + 2 agreements where AVTS program hours can be converted to credit hours and used toward an associate degree at a community college and in some cases toward a BS degree in 4-year institutions.

Community College Offerings: Many types of curriculums are usually pro-vided in community colleges, including:

- Curriculums that will coordinate with continuing study at a four-year liberal arts college or university program (transfer courses).
- General education curriculum of a terminal nature.
- Career and technical education of a terminal nature.
- Technical education of a terminal nature.
- Career and technical education that may be transferred.
- Community Service courses that could be career and technical in nature. This could be college credit, continuing education units (CEUs), or noncredit.

Community colleges issue associate in arts (AA) degrees, associate in science (AS), certificates of attendance, continuing education units (CEUs) and a variety of other 2-year degrees. Some community colleges are part of state systems, some may be branches of state colleges or uni-versities, and many of them are single institutions with their own boards or are part of a larger community college district. Community colleges may be both public and private.

Technical High School Offerings: High schools seldom offer more than one or two programs that may be considered technical education. Some of the high schools are highly selective in who may be enrolled in these programs, and are usually called "magnet schools." Selection may be based upon scholastic records, examinations, and recommendations from school officials. With the current emphasis on obtaining the basics, usually English, foreign language, mathematics, and science, for graduation requirements, competition exists for the student's time while attending high school. Normally high school students would not have the time to devote to courses which are technical in nature.

Technical Institute Offerings: Technical institutes are usually directed to offering technical education curricula. While technical institutes are often operated as a separate school, sometimes they are administered through a board of control of a public school system. This may also include the board of regents for higher education systems. The technical institute is usually a postsecondary institution. The principal objective of a technical institute is to educate men and women for occupations that require specialized knowledge supplemented by a broad range of operational procedures. Technical institutes may operate both day and evening programs.

Technical institutes offer programs different from those of the community college. Many times they are more intensive and do not include the general education component required of community college programs. The admission practices are different from community colleges and the students who attend may be older. Instruction in a technical institute follows more closely that which may occur in industry rather than that which occurs in community colleges.

Extension and Correspondence Study: These offerings are organized to assist persons to prepare for or progress in technical occupations. They are offered by both public and private schools and colleges. Most universities have extension divisions that provide class instruction in various extension centers and public schools throughout a state. The extension centers are usually located in towns and cities some distance from the parent institution where the need for these courses is evident. The extension center facilities may include laboratories, a library, a dormitory, and conference and assembly rooms.

Technical education appears to be especially suited to home study because much of the technical content involves basic sciences and applied technology which may be acquired from home study courses. Many persons are unable because of economic and personal reasons to attend day school and extension classes. They are willing to engage in home study, and the wide variety of home study courses enables these persons to select a course or series of courses in which they are interested. Correspondence courses of a technical nature are available for agriculturists, businessmen, health workers, homemakers, industrial workers, and social workers. Course offering include a wide range of subject matter similar to the course offerings of day schools. The maintenance of high standards of achievement is an especially important consideration in home study programs. The National Home Study Council, which was organized to promote high standards and ethical practices in this field, has been instrumental in improving home study programs.

TECHNICAL PROGRAM CURRICULA

The curriculum in technical education includes both technical and general activities, and these activities are arranged or grouped into subjects or other categories for instructional purposes. The general education content, such as English, psychology, social science, and speech, is usually included in preemployment technical education curriculums and frequently omitted in in-service programs. The technical content of the curriculum is designed to provide occupational competency. This content is usually determined by means of an occupational analysis. For example, see Connecticut State Department of Education (2006).

As a general rule a technical curriculum will consist of:

1. 1.50% specific technical studies (information necessary for the technical area)
2. 2.25% direct related studies (math and sciences)
3. 3.25% indirect related studies (English, speech, psychology)

CURRENT CONCEPTS OF VOCATIONAL GUIDANCE

Vocational guidance is the process of helping a person to develop and accept an integrated and adequate picture of himself and of his role in the world of work. It has a specific goal; it assists individuals to find satisfying, interesting and realistic roles in the environment. Vocational guidance is the process of helping individuals know themselves, their interests and abilities and the world of work and its needs to be able to reach a mature career decision (Technical & Vocational Education & Training (TVET), n.d.). Vocational guidance refers to the services that may assist individuals of any age and at any point throughout their lives, to make educational, training, and occupational choices and to manage their careers. It includes services provided to those who have not entered the labor forces services to job seekers and services to those who are employed (Organisation for Economic Co-operation and Development, n.d.).

Concept and Content

The concept of counseling and vocational guidance refers to expert (science based) assistance and support with the aim to help individuals (EKEP-National Resource Centre for Vocational Guidance (EKEP-NRCVG), 2003):

- explore, analyze and develop the factors constituting their self-concept (interests, personal qualities and characteristics, values, skills, etc.),
- explore, evaluate, process and classify information and alternative education and vocation pathways with respect both to their needs and choices and to labor market requirements,
- integrate information about education and vocation/career with information derived from self-observation so that they develop to decision-making capabilities both with respect to their orientation in education and choices in occupation(s) befitting their particular psychosocial make up,
- create and implement their own education and vocation plans.

Ultimately, the individuals will be able to make the correct choices with respect to their future occupation/vocation and thus be (re)included into active life.

Counseling and Vocational Guidance activities target individuals who are:

- about to make a choice with respect to their education and vocation,
- in search of new fields of study/training,
- already employed but dissatisfied with their current occupation, hence in search of new areas of training and professional development,
- unemployed or have lost their jobs for whatever reason and wish to resume employment, and
- threatened with social exclusion owing to personal circumstances or misfortune (EKEP- NRCVG, 2003).

Vocational guidance is not a device for finding the one job an individual can do best. Experience has shown that almost every person can achieve success in a number of occupations. These concepts recognize the fact that individuals may have occasion to make a number of occupational choices and adjustments throughout their life-span, and therefore vocational guidance becomes a continuous process of assisting individuals understand themselves better as a basis for making decisions concerning their careers. Perhaps the 1966 definition developed by the American Vocational Association (AVA) states this fairly clearly:

> Vocational Guidance is the process of assisting individuals to understand their capabilities and interests, to choose a suitable vocation, and to prepare for, enter, and make successful progress in it.

CONCLUSION

Eighty-five years after the passage of the first piece of federal vocational education legislation, career and technical education is evolving from its original and sole focus on preparing students for work immediately following high school (U.S. Department of Education, 2006). Today's career and technical education programs increasingly incorporate rigorous and challenging academic content standards and provide a nonduplicative sequence of courses leading to an industry-recognized credential or certificate, or an associate or baccalaureate degree (U.S. Department of Education, 2006).

For the most part, content of the curricula within career and technical education is designed to provide occupational competency and it is quite scientific according to principles of learning and principles of teaching. Educators in the field take great care to group together both technical content and general education content. The most recent move is to integrate technology into vocational education curricula. All of these efforts are geared toward raising the competitiveness of our students in this so termed globalization. As Rojewski (2002) noted:

> Overall, a number of consistent themes emerge from the myriad educational reform reports and initiatives advanced over the past several decades. Prominent themes include the integration of academic and vocational education: emphasis on developing general (transferable) work skills rather than focusing on narrow, job-specific work skills; articulation between secondary and post secondary vocational programs; adjustments in programs to accommodate changing workforce demographics; preparation for a changing workplace that requires fairly high-level academic skills; familiarity and use of high technology; higher order thinking skills including decision making and problem solving; and interpersonal skills that facilitate working in teams. (p. 7)

However, whether instructional objectives can be reached largely depends on qualifications and certification of instructors in the field. In many states in the United States, a number of uncredentialed instructors teach various subjects in the field of career and technical education. Some of them have no knowledge of instructional theories. If this practice continues, the quality of instruction will be negatively affected in the long run. Unless this problem is fixed, regardless of how scientific the content of the curricula is, our students will not achieve the required learning objectives in career and technical education.

In addition, career and technical education programs should seek to offer innovative programs that aim at developing workforce competencies. Such programs should include in their content important topics such collaboration, adaptability, lifelong learning, cultural sensitivity, inclusion and globalization, reflective thinking, entrepreneurial and entrepreneurial thinking, critical thinking skills, problem solving skills, proactive teaching and learning, decision making, management skills, and leadership.

REFERENCES

Adams, A., Sewell, D., & Hall, H. C. (2004, Spring). Cultural pluralism and diversity: Issues important to family and consumer sciences education, *Journal of Family and Consumer Sciences Education, 22*(1), 17-28. Retrieved April 17, 2007, from http://www.natefacs.org/JFCSE/v22no1/v22no1Adams.pdf

Arizona Department of Education. (2006). *Current CTE program and curriculum frameworks.* Retrieved April 17, 2007, from http://www.ade.az.gov/cte/CurriculmFramework/

Baker, S. (2006, January 23). Math will rock your world. *Business Week.* Retrieved February 1, 2006, from http://www.businessweek.com/magazine/content/06_04/b3968001.htm

Bamberg, R. R., & Blayney, K. D. (1989). The education of multiskilled health practitioners: Results of a national survey. *Journal of Health Occupations Education, 4*(2), 72-93.

Baugher, S. L., Anderson, C. L., Green, K. B., Shane, J., Jolly, L., Miles, J., et al. (2003). *"Body of Knowledge" for family and consumer sciences.* Retrieved April 17, 2007, from http://www.aafcs.org/about/knowledge.html

Bray, A. (2007). Leading edge: The beginning of 2007 is an exciting time for career and technical education. *Techniques: Connecting education and careers, 82*(1), 6.

California Department of Education. (2006). *Agriculture Education.* Retrieved December 21, 2006, from http://www.cde.ca.gov/ci/ct/ae/

Connecticut State Department of Education. (2006). *Connecticut Technical High School System curricula.* Retrieved April 21, 2007, from http://www.cttech.org/central/curriculum/main-menu.htm

Darling, C. A., Greenwood, B. B., & Hansen-Gandy, S. (1998). Multicultural education in collegiate family and consumer sciences programs: Developing cultural competence. *Journal of Family and Consumer Sciences, 90*(1), 42-48.

EKEP-National Resource Centre for Vocational Guidance. (2003). *Concept & content.* Retrieved December 22, 2006, from, http://www.ekep.gr/english/Guidance/main.asp

El Camino College. (2006). *Robotics academy.* Retrieved April 17, 2007, from http://www.elcamino.edu/academics/cte/robotics.asp

Flanagan, D. L. (2006, Fall). U.S. competitiveness and the profession of Engineering, *The BENT of the Tau Pi*, 16-22.

Freeman, L. (1996). Vo-Tech goes hi-tech. *School Planning and Management 35*(3), 3-8.

Friedman, T. (2005). *The world is flat: A brief history of the Twenty-First Century.* New York: Farrar, Straus and Giroux.

Foxman, E., & Easterling, D. (1995). Diversity issues and business education. *Journal of Education for Business, 71*(1), 22-29.

Gay, G., & Howard, T. C. (2000). Multicultural teacher education for the 21st century. *The Teacher Educator, 36*(1), 1-16.

Gaytan, J. (2006). Focusing on accountability in business teacher education. In S. D. Lewis, M. Balachandran, & R. B. Blair (Eds.), *Meeting the challenges of business education through innovative programs* (pp. 87-98). Reston, VA: NBEA.

Georgia Agricultural Education (2006). *Georgia agricultural curriculum resource and reference.* Retrieved April 17, 2007, from http://aged.ces.uga.edu/Browseable_Folders/Curriculum/curriculum.htm

Giovannini, M. (2004, Winter). What gets measured gets done: Achieving results through diversity and inclusion. *The Journal for Quality and Participation*, 21-27.

Gura, M., & King, K. P. (2007). *Classroom robotics: Case studies of 21st century instruction for the millennial student.* Charlotte, NC: Information Age Publishing.

Health Occupations Students of America (HSOA) (2007). *HSOA homepage.* Retrieved April 17, 2007, from http://www.hosa.org

Hill, R. (Ed.). (2006, Winter). Challenging homophobia and heterosexism: Lesbian, gay, bisexual, transgender and queer issues in organizational settings. *New Directions in Adult and Continuing Education*, Issue 112. San Francisco: Jossey-Bass.

Hoberty, P. (1996). *The extent of multi-skilling education in respiratory care educational programs* (Respiratory Abstracts No. OF-96-122). Retrieved April 17, 2007, from http://www.cardinal.com/mps/focus/respiratory/abstracts/abstracts/ab1996/A00001282.asp

Illinois State Board of Education. (n.d.). *Health occupations (CTE occupational programs area).* Retrieved April 17, 2007, from http://206.166.105.35/career/html/cte_health.htm

Indiana Department of Education. (2006). *National standards for family and consumer education.* Retrieved April 17, 2007, from http://www.doe.state.in.us/octe/facs/natlstandards.htm#order

John Hopkins University (2004). *Why technology? A brief history of CTE history.* Retrieved April 17, 2007, from http://cte.jhu.edu/aboutus_history.html

King, K. P. (2007). Robotics: Prime opportunities for careers and student learning. In M. Gura, & K. P. King. *Classroom robotics: Case studies of 21st century instruction for the millennial student* (pp. 133-144). Charlotte, NC: Information Age Publishing.

King, K. P. (2007). Bridging the gap in K-12 education with career and technical education: The view from adult learning. In V. Wang & K. P. King (Eds.), *Innovations in career and technical education: Strategic approaches towards workforce competencies around the globe* (pp. 131-163) Charlotte, NC: Information Age Publishing.

King, K. P. & Biro, S. (2006, Winter). A transformative learning perspective of continuing sexual identity development in the workplace. In R. Hill (Ed.), *New Directions in Adult and Continuing Education, Issue 112* (pp. 17-27). San Francisco: Jossey-Bass.

Lee, J., & Wong, K. K. (2004). The impact of accountability on racial and socioeconomic equity. *American Educational Research Journal, 41*(4), 797-832.

National Clearinghouse for Educational Facilities (NCEF). (2006). *Career and technical education classrooms and facilities.* Retrieved April 17, 2007, from http://www.edfacilities.org/rl/tech_ed.cfm

National Commission on Excellence in Education. (1983). *A nation at risk: The imperative for reform.* Washington, DC: Author. (ERIC Document Reproduction Service No. ED 251 622)

North Carolina Public Schools (2006). *CTE-Health Occupations Education.* Retrieved April 17, 2007, from http://www.ncpublicschools.org/workforce_development/health_occupations/index.html

Nussbaum, B. (2006, January 23). Davos will be different. *Business Week*, p. 96.

Organisation for Economic Co-operation and Development. (n.d.). *Annex 6 glossary.* Retrieved April 20, 2007, from http://www.oecd.org/dataoecd/27/53/27573989.pdf

Rojewski, J. W. (2002). Preparing the workforce of tomorrow: A conceptual framework for career and technical education. *Journal of Vocational Education Research, 27*(1), 1-27.

Rothrock, D., & Walker, C. J. (2007). *Get R.E.A.L.: Aligning California's public education system with the 21st century economy.* Retrieved April 17, 2007, from http://www.lhc.ca.gov/lhcdir/CTE/RothrockWalkerMar07.pdf

Sabo, S. R. (2000). Diversity at work. *Techniques, 75*(2), 26-28.

Schmidt, J. (1990). *A chronology of business education in the United States.* Reston, VA: National Business Education Association.

Schneider, A. (2000, Oct. 13). It's not your mother's home economics. *The Chronicle of Higher Education 47* (7), p. A18. Retrieved April 21, 2007, from http://chronicle.com/weekly/v47/i07/07a01801.htm

Smith, J. (2000). Rethinking school design. *Buildings, 94*(8), 50, 56, 59.

Stage, S., & Vincenti, V. B., (Eds.). (1997). *Rethinking home economics: Women and the history of a profession.* Ithaca, NY: Cornell University Press.

Stone, J. R., Kowske, B. J., & Alfeld, C. (2004). Career and technical education in the late 1990s: A descriptive study. *Journal of Vocational Education Research 29*(1) Retrieved April 21, 2007, from http://scholar.lib.vt.edu/ejournals/JVER/v29n3/stone.html

Technical & Vocational Education & Training. (n.d.). *Introduction*. Retrieved December 25, 2006, from, http://www.tvet-pal.org/counseling/intro.html

U.S. Department of Education. (2006). *Career and technical education*. Retrieved December 14, 2006, from http://www.ed.gov/about/offices/list/ovae/pi/cte/index.html

Wisconsin Department of Public Instruction. (2006). *Health science occupations education*. Retrieved December 21, 2006, from http://dpi.state.wi.us/cte/hoe-home.htm

PART II

CHAPTER 5

COMPARING THE RUSSIAN, THE SLOYD, AND THE ARTS AND CRAFTS MOVEMENT TRAINING SYSTEM

Victor C. X. Wang and Carol Koerner Redhead

This chapter investigates vocational educators' preferences among three foreign systems that have been used frequently in vocational education in the United States: the Russian system, the Sloyd system, and the Arts and Crafts Movement. Thirty-two (64% of 50) in-service vocational educators enrolled in teacher credentialing programs in the Department of Occupational Studies at California State University, Long Beach during the fall of 2003 completed a 6-point Likert-type scale designed to measure teaching preferences relative to methods associated with each training system. Data were analyzed using descriptive statistics and analysis of variance. Results indicated a slight preference for the Sloyd system and the Arts and Crafts Movement over the Russian system, although differences were not significant ($p > .05$).

Innovations in Career and Technical Education: Strategic Approaches Towards Workforce Competencies Around the Globe, pp. 101–118
Copyright © 2008 by Information Age Publishing
All rights of reproduction in any form reserved.   101

INTRODUCTION

At the beginning of the twentieth century, the educational system of the United States had adopted methods from three foreign training systems: the Russian system, the Sloyd system, and the Arts and Crafts Movement (Bott, Slapar, & Wang, 2003; Brehony, 1999; Grubb, 1998; Roberts, 1965; Roche, 1995). These approaches were adopted primarily in response to the sharply increased need for skilled workers during the period of the industrial revolution. At the time of the Industrial Revolution, the expansion of capitalism, an increase in world trade, and a rapid shift from farm work and small business to large business enterprises, with a concurrent emphasis on increased manufacturing production, placed a burden on schools, including colleges and universities, to supply needed skilled manpower (Grubb, 1998; Roberts, 1965). Education was perceived as the solution to the related problems of increased job dissatisfaction associated with industrial labor, including factory sweatshops, unsafe working conditions, pollution, and a general decline in work satisfaction (Chen, 1999; Oklahoma State University, n.d.a.). Other problems in the late 1880's that eventually led to changes in U.S. education included a growing dissatisfaction with dull and impractical academic curricula, the lack of practical training available for architects and engineers, and the unavailability of alternative academic options for students who performed poorly in traditional academic subjects (Oklahoma State University, n.d.a.). At the same time, a movement to revamp the public education system according to a variety of philosophies began in the Scandinavian countries, England, France, Germany, and the United States, and other countries. These philosophies were influenced by religious beliefs, politics, and economics in a general social upheaval that eventually became global in scope (Brehony, 1999; Cumming, 2001; Roberts, 1965; Roche, 1995). The Russian System, the Sloyd System, and the Arts and Crafts Movement all contributed to the remodeling of the U.S. educational system, and the influence of these approaches can still be felt to this day (Grubb, 1998; Roberts, 1965).

We were interested in identifying vocational educators' teaching preferences relative to the Russian system, the Sloyd system, and the Arts and Crafts Movement, especially in light of the advantages and disadvantages of each system. We sought to determine if vocational educators preferred one of the foreign training methods over the remaining two methods. Specifically, we wanted to know what were the preferences of vocational educators relative to

1.   Emphasizing a logical procedure where students advance based on results from a series of graded exercises (Russian system).

2. Encouraging student self-direction and initiative (Sloyd system).

3. Emphasizing aesthetic and creative side of work (Arts and Crafts Movement).

4. Reaching large groups of students in the least possible time (Russian system).

5. Focusing on neatness and accuracy (Sloyd system).

6. Utilizing rotation of work (Arts and Crafts Movement).

According to Bott et al. (2003), an experiment conducted in Boston in the 1890s explored whether the Sloyd system or the Russian system better met the needs of American students. As a result of this experiment, the Boston schools began to use the Sloyd system almost exclusively.

Today's teachers face problems that are similar to those faced by teachers in the late 1880s. The present technological revolution can be compared to the Industrial Revolution because it has created the same needs for changes in curricula, teaching methods, and skills and knowledge of students (Oklahoma State University, n.d.a.). With technology advances increasing exponentially, employers need highly skilled workers as well as workers who are flexible, able to solve problems, self-initiating, and foresighted about their possible advancement in the workplace (Grubb, 1998). Instructional methods employed by instructors can have drastic effects on how well students learn. By examining foreign historical systems of education, answers to the problems of the present may be revealed.

HISTORICAL BACKGROUND

Since the inception of the Russian manual training method advanced by Victor Della Vos in 1876, vocational education instructors of the United States have adopted and adapted a series of foreign training methods. After the Russian training method was successfully introduced into America, the Sloyd system (which originated in Scandinavia) and the Arts and Crafts Movement (which originated in England as a protest against poor craftsmanship) were brought to the United States for the purpose of improving American vocational education instructors' training methods (Bott et al., 2003). Each of these teaching designs is different and distinct from one another, and all were explored by American educators. Victor Della Vos brought his ideas of rigidly formal instruction from Russia to an exhibit at the 1876 Centennial Exposition in Philadelphia. Swedish educators Lars Erickson and Gustaf Larson started classes in the Sloyd system in Anoka, Minnesota in 1884 and in Boston in 1888. The Arts and Crafts

Movement exerted its influence in the United States during the latter part of the nineteenth century. Whereas The Russian and Sloyd systems focused upon the skill of the student and worker, the Arts and Crafts Movement emphasized the creative and aesthetic side (Brehony, 1999; Crawford, 1997; Cumming, 2001; Fish, 1997; Roche, 1995). A description of each training system follows.

The Russian System

Victor Della Vos, who in 1868 became the director of the Moscow Imperial Technical School, developed the Russian System of competency-based instruction, which was partly influenced by Pavlov's research on conditioning (Grubb, 1998). His task analysis approach, developed in Moscow in the 1860s and brought to America at the 1876 Centennial Exposition in Philadelphia, was wholeheartedly accepted by John D. Runkle, who was the president of the Massachusetts Institute of Technology (MIT) where he introduced laboratories in his institution. The Russian system was also adopted by Professor Clavin M. Woodward, Dean of the Polytechnic faculty of Washington University in St. Louis, Missouri (Oklahoma State University, n.d.a.). Both of these men, for the first time, developed and introduced shop courses for their engineering students (Oklahoma State University, n.d.a.). At that time, engineers and architects did not receive a good educational foundation in theory and practice of construction techniques (Oklahoma State University, n.d.a.). Partly for this reason, the Russian System of industrial education, including the theory and principles behind it, was adopted throughout the United States and also in many parts of the world. The object of the Russian system during this global industrial revolution was to instruct as many students in as little time as possible in order to supply skilled manpower for the country's needs (Bott et al., 2003; Roberts, 1965).

Teachers of the Russian system of manual training utilized a systems approach in which a specific curriculum was devised by breaking training into its components, and each of those were taught as a separate entity. The system consisted of three stages: the first being the study of the materials and tools, the second was acquisition of the skills to use the materials and tools, and the third was actual construction of a part of a whole item (Bott, et al., 2003; Roberts, 1965). For instance, students studied woodworking, then rotated to another discreet lesson such as blacksmithing, then joinery and so on; each module contained its own shop, tools, and curriculum (Roberts, 1965). Lessons began with drawings, and each student had his or her own tools and a place to work. After drawings were mastered, students progressed to an increasingly difficulty, but students did not graduate to another activity without complete mastery of the first (Grubb, 1998; Roberts, 1965). Teachers of the Russian system were expected to be expert models of knowledge and skill and to upgrade their skills continually.

Advantages of the Russian System

The logical, sequential aspects of the Russian system create a structured atmosphere of concentrated effort and focus where knowledge is built upon knowledge in a logical fashion. This system benefits students in that they are taught in a manner that allows for no confusion in the acquisition and application of knowledge and skills (Grubb, 1998). Students of this method graduate with a known body of knowledge, learned in the materials and tools as well as the uses of both. This method is especially beneficial to both the student and the employer because the students gain skills and the employers can trust that the graduates will be assets to the companies. This consistency of results translates into increased earnings for both the new employee and the company (Grubb, 1998). Another benefit of the method is that it produces a large number of skilled workers in a relatively short time, as was needed during the Industrial Revolution (Bott et al., 2003; Roberts, 1956).

Disadvantages of the Russian System

Although the Russian system produces students who are learned, they often do not have the ability to create something on their own or to even to finish a project (Bott et al., 2003; Roberts, 1965). Their learning is relegated to only small exercises, and when on the job after graduation, students may lack skills to be self-initiating or to solve problems, such as in engineering and other higher-order work, a limitation which fails students and employers (Grubb, 1998). Furthermore, although students graduate in the Russian System with a certain amount of skill, they may lose individual creativity in the training process. A secondary criticism of the Russian, skills-oriented method of teaching is that because teachers focus exclusively on skills, they may not keep abreast of new forms of problem solving, which limits their ability to teach needed knowledge to their students, leads to an incomplete curriculum, thereby cheating the students of valuable information (Grubb, 1998).

The Sloyd System

The Sloyd System was adopted in schools in Boston and Albany, New York in the late 1880s and in Chicago in 1894 (Bott et al., 2003). This system emphasized individualized instruction instead of the assembly-line teaching of the Russian method. Sloyd, which means "handcrafts" in Scandinavia, began in Scandinavia in response to the increasing demand for new types of workers, such as clerks, technicians, and engineers. After much travel and study in Alaska, Uno Cygnaeus, a Finnish preacher and teacher, developed a system of folk education for the Finnish school system. He observed the differences between civilized and uncivilized peoples of the region. Melding the ideas of Johann Heinrich Pestalozzi, the father of manual training who espoused the use of objects and manual labor to teach and to help poor children improve their social conditions, and Friedrich Froebel, a student and coworker of Pestalozzi, Cygnaeus devised his own system to teach manual studies based on hand-eye coordination (Brehony, 1999). These educators believed that children learn best by doing handwork because, among other reasons, they are naturally creative. Cygnaeus believed that handcrafts should be taught by the traditional teacher and not in a technical school, and that handcrafts should be a part of the regular curriculum. In 1866, his system was adopted in all Finnish schools.

During the 1880s, educator Otto Salomon of Sweden, through the influence of Cygnaeus, developed the Sloyd system, which is still used throughout the world today. Salomon took a more structured approach that comprised three key elements: (a) making useful objects; (b) analysis of processes, and (c) educational method. The Sloyd system, especially as espoused by Froebel, was based on a religious belief that children should be prepared for work at an early stage because of God's own model of hard work (Brehony, 1999). Some followers of the European Froebel Movement believed in race capitulation, the concept that former stages of evolution are evident, physically as well a culturally, as people pass from embryo to adulthood and that childhood is but one stage of an evolving series of hierarchical ordered stages with the inherently hierarchical notion of race (Brehony, 1999). They believed that manual dexterity was a stage of development that preceded the development of the brain; subsequently, they believed that use of the hands could train the mind (Brehony, 1999).

The Sloyd system became a fashion, a popular movement that expanded into England and the United States at about the same time as did the Russian system. This new idea spread in response to government demands for workers who were knowledgeable in areas of trade and finance, which quickly became highly competitive on a global scale

(Brehony, 1999). Children in grammar schools were given cards on which to sew, do cardboard work, and woodwork because it was believed that the mind could be trained by the use of hands (Brehony, 1999). The movement evolved in the United States to encompass morality and respect for workmanship. Moreover, unlike book learning, the Sloyd system led to the creation of self-motivation among students and to students taking an interest in their studies; thus, it encouraged children to transfer learned skills to other activities. Children learned by doing, displayed initiative, and exhibited an understanding of the importance and the value of those who worked with their hands (Brehony, 1999).

Individualized instruction and the use of a good model were the key points of Sloyd system (Roberts, 1965). Classes began in a small way by Erickson and Larsson, and when an experiment was conducted in Boston in the 1890s to see whether the Russian or Sloyd system was the preferred method of teaching grammar grades, the Sloyd system won (Roberts, 1965). Consequently, the Sloyd system spread to other schools, and by 1893-1894, the Report of the U.S. Commissioner of Education stated that "25% of all schools offering manual training in Grades 7 through 12" incorporated the Sloyd method, or 18 schools altogether (as cited in Bott et al., 2003, p. 38). The Sloyd method, unlike the Russian system, encouraged the use of measuring tapes and other devices, freehand work and individualized expression, neatness and accuracy, pride in workmanship, and regular teachers were to be used rather than artisans (Bott et al., 2003). Another distinction between the two teaching systems was that Sloyd students could make a whole item, while the students of the Russian System were limited to an exercise that produced nothing of value. By 1904, however, Sloyd, as a specialized approach, began to disappear, as the philosophy of John Dewey took precedence (Brehony, 1999). Dewey presented the case for combining academic instruction with manual training, and Sloyd ideas, with their emphasis on learning skills for work for work's sake, were set aside (Brehony, 1999). Dewey believed that children should be taught through a trade rather than be taught a trade for work's sake (Oklahoma State University, n.d.b.)

Advantages of the Sloyd System

Benefits to students of the Sloyd method of instruction include more freedom of artistic expression and the advantages of teaching from whole-to-part, which allows students to learn the concept of the whole project, thus enabling them to finish a product that can be later used or sold (Bott et al., 2003; Roberts, 1965). Students make a completed model rather than participate in a limited exercise, as in the Russian style. Because a variety of tools and materials and self-expression are involved, students are more motivated to learn with this method than with the others (Roberts, 1965). The Sloyd method brings out the whole individual more than the Russian because students can better relate work to the world and to themselves (Bott et al., 2003: Roberts, 1965).

Disadvantages of the Sloyd System

Educators have criticized the Sloyd method as being too formal and inflexible, a criticism also levied against the Russian System (Bott et al., 2003). Also, because of the increased flexibility and the decreased formality and rigidity associated with learning in the Sloyd system in comparison to the Russian system, there may be a loss in expertise compared to the Russian method. Educators employing the Sloyd system also have more responsibility for keeping up-to-date on technological developments in order to be effective teachers (Grubb, 1998). Faced with a difficult and time-consuming task instead of a purely structured approach, a teacher employing the Sloyd system must integrate skills as well as theory to teach students how to make a whole item and then be able to use it.

The Arts and Crafts Movement

The Industrial Revolution brought many changes to the world, including advances in machinery, medicines, a global economy, and large factories. Thousands of workers spent their days in mindless and often dangerous work on assembly lines. Reacting to the loss of fine craftsmanship, pride in workmanship, and freehand labor, the Arts and Crafts Movement began in England and spread to the United States (Bott et al., 2003; Cumming, 2001). The movement claimed many followers. The famous architect Frank Lloyd Wright and the prominent educator and philosopher John Dewey were influenced by this movement, with Dewey becoming its spokesperson. Other supporters of the movement emerged from discontent with conditions wrought by the Industrial Revolution. Social philosopher Thomas Carlyle expressed concern about the loss of personal freedom and expression, and John Ruskin vehemently attacked the value of objects created by an impersonal system rather than through a labor of love (Cumming, 2001). Another main leader of the movement in England was architect and writer William Morris. Morris spoke for the movement and built a showplace for art and design where ordinary men and women could peruse for ideas to use in their own homes and churches (Cumming, 2001; Roche, 1995).

This outpouring of protest gained strength and support as artisans and craftsmen of all types organized a movement against the poor craftsmanship promulgated by factory methods of mass production (Cumming, 2001; Roberts, 1965; Roche, 1995). The Arts and Crafts Movement was characterized by Roche as an ideology that could be interpreted as a sort of renaissance of the spirit of man, as a struggle against oppression of machines upon man, and as an overcoming and taking control of one's own life and destiny. The Arts and Crafts Movement stressed the importance of good craftsmanship and aesthetic quality. When incorporated into elementary schools, the movement utilized a method that rotated students among classes in drawing, designing, clay modeling, and wood-carving (Bott et al., 2003).

Three principles guided the Arts and Crafts Movement in England: (a) unity of art, which defined all forms of art as equal rather than in a hierarchy where one type of art was worth more than other types of arts and which opposed the superiority of professionalism; (b) joy in labor, which was the idea that people could use their imaginations to derive pleasure from the experience of work as opposed to working in stultifying factories; and (c) design reform, whereby the designs of objects used by ordinary people were changed to look as if they belonged in the place where they were used (e.g., a kettle looked like it belonged in a kitchen), but objects also were stylized, representing taste as opposed to wealth and refinement and craftsmanship as opposed to ostentation (Crawford, 1997). Factory-made items and late-Victorian ostentatiously styled pieces of jewelry were no longer valued, whereas finely crafted, artistic items were valued.

Advantages of the Arts and Crafts Movement

When the Arts and Crafts Movement was introduced, many educators turned to its ideas to counteract criticisms of the rigidity and inflexibility of the Russian and Sloyd systems. The movement invited students to create using good craftsman skills and brought new value to honest work. Students took pride in workmanship, and they experienced pleasure in work, which had been largely missing to that point (Brehony, 1999; Roberts, 1965). They were allowed to use improved models for their work, take field trips, use other types of materials, and enjoy the benefits of a large, less constrictive curriculum (Roberts, 1965). Drawing skills were related to other schoolwork, and students were allowed to make their own designs (Roberts, 1965). Students of the Arts and Crafts Movement, because of their lack of constriction, were better equipped than students of the Russian and Sloyd systems to solve problems and express initiative and creativity. Consequently, they were well suited for high-paying jobs that required cognitive thinking skills (Grub, 1998). Innovative study motivated students, creating an interesting learning environment (Roberts, 1965).

Disadvantages of the Arts and Crafts Movement

The Arts and Crafts Movement encouraged teachers and students to be creative and innovative, but this freedom may have cost students the in-depth skills and knowledge afforded by the more rigid curricula of the Russian or Sloyd systems. Although Arts and Crafts students were creative and self-initiating, they had less self-discipline in their learning habits than their counterparts in the Russian and Sloyd systems. The Arts and Crafts Movement was wrapped in social, religious, and political overtones, and some students may have lost sight of educational objectives in favor of the glamorous prospects of joining a movement for the movement's sake (Crawford, 1997). During the early days of the movement, philosophical discussions were an essential part of the process. Because it was difficult to separate the making of an object from the reason behind it, these discussions addressed questions of whether the item derived from practical necessity or political purposes. In this milieu, students may have become more interested in extra-curricular activities than in academic duties.

Summary

Vocational educators in the United States have adopted numerous training methods associated with the Russian system, the Sloyd system, and the Arts and Crafts Movement. Each of these training systems has its own set of advantages and disadvantages. Table 5.1 provides a summary of the advantages and disadvantages of the training methods associated with the Russian system, the Sloyd system, and the Arts and Crafts Movement.

INSTRUCTIONAL PREFERENCES OF VOCATIONAL EDUCATION INSTRUCTORS OF THE UNITED STATES

Although there are disadvantages associated with training methods from the Russian system, the Sloyd system, and the Arts and Crafts Movement, each training system's influence can still be felt to this day (Grubb, 1998; Roberts, 1965). The laboratory experiences that John Runkle started at MIT are in use in almost every vocational education classroom, whether it be welding, horticulture, cosmetology, or family and consumer sciences. In fact, it is probable that most or all vocational education teachers find a

Table 5.1.   Advantages and Disadvantages of the Russian System, Sloyd System, and Arts & Crafts Movement

Training Systems	Advantages	Disadvantages
Russian system	Emphasizes a logical procedure where students advance based on results from a series of graded exercises. Reaches large groups of students in the least possible time.	Loses individual creativity in the training process. Limits ability to teach needed knowledge.
Sloyd system	Encourages student self-direction and initiative. Focuses on neatness and accuracy.	Loses expertise in comparison with the Russian method. Lacks unity of theory and practice.
Arts & Crafts Movement	Emphasizes aesthetic and creative side of work. Utilizes rotation of work.	Costs students the in-depth knowledge. Become less self-disciplined in students' learning habits.

lab of some sort indispensable because students cannot learn enough to apply their trade of study successfully without hands-on experience. Competency-based education, which the Russian and Sloyd systems advocated, has been the basis of many curricula, including the modules of employable skills developed by the International Labor Office, the Developing a Curriculum (DACUM) process initiated in Canada, and the *serie metodica ocupacionis* (i.e., shopwork methodological series) that developed in Brazil and then spread throughout South America (Grubb, 1998). Many secondary schools in the United States have included competency-based curricula since the 1960s, as have schools in Australia and England (Grubb, 1998).

Teachers and curriculum designers of today can avail themselves of texts and other information developed over the years by the research and development of individuals and companies. Those who design a curriculum can use catalogs that list competencies for a particular curriculum. For instance, The Vocational and Technical Education Consortium of States (V-TECS) has produced extensive catalogs for many professions that delineate duties, tasks, and performance objectives in an employment-referenced data base that is used for curriculum development (Finch & Crunkilton, 1999). Other similar catalogues are used for exploratory programs and information for competency-based education is offered by texts such as, *Curriculum Development in Vocational and Technical Education: Planning, Content, and Implementation* by Finch and Crunkilton. Incorporating Russian and Sloyd ideals in content and purpose, this textbook is an example of the comprehensive nature of curriculum planning used in the United States today. Also, the Sloyd pedagogical library at Naas, Sweden contains thousands of books, periodicals, and other references in a large data base on Sloyd and is open to students and educators interested in the system.

Woodwork and shop have been included in many grammar schools and high schools as well as in tech-prep schools and other types of schools across the United States. Tasks taught in these classes use the methods delineated by Finch and Crunkilton (1999), such as the V-TECS task analysis approach in which all the tools used in various trades are listed and taught, as well as the tasks associated with them. This approach is in line with the Russian system. The DACUM approach also uses this method, listing all the tools needed and the curriculum for that class (Finch & Crunkilton, 1999). Each task relates to the next task, as in the Russian system, and then the whole is completed, as in the Sloyd system. This is an example of combining two systems so that students learn each individual tool and task and then complete a whole product in a logical and systematic manner. However, Grubb (1998) pointed out that most vocational instructors in Secondary schools in the United States use the skills-only method in which students work on needed skills with little attention to the overall picture (i.e., the Russian system). In community colleges observed by Grubb, students used the Russian approach in which they devoted a specified unit of time to learning a particular skill, or they learned on a whole-top art basis, as advocated by the Sloyd system, when a problem solving approach was necessary, such as in such trades as computers and automobile systems. Although type of class can dictate the type of teaching used, most teachers in secondary schools and community colleges, as observed by Grubb, used the skills-oriented Russian system, with a few teachers incorporating the systems-oriented Sloyd system. The practice of working at one's own pace while crafting an item of one's own design disintegrated during World War I when objects were mass-produced, and slowly crafted items became a luxury (Cumming, 2001). However, as Cumming reported, teachers maintained that students did not want to work in factory assembly lines producing cheaply designed objects; rather, they valued craftsmanship and the beauty of natural materials.

METHODS

Sample

The Occupational Studies Department, California State University, Long Beach enrolled approximately 90 in-service instructors who were employed in the secondary, postsecondary schools, and regional occupational programs in the state of California. In the fall semester of 2003, 50 in-service instructors were enrolled in teacher credentialing programs in the department. Of the 50 in-service instructors, 32 (64%) participated in the study. These 32 instructors represented almost all of the secondary and postsecondary schools and regional occupational programs in California that were actively involved in vocational teacher credentialing programs. Participation in the study was voluntary, and responses were kept confidential.

Instrumentation

We designed the instrument used to collect data, modeling it after existing surveys used at two universities. We distributed a survey to each instructor. The survey included two sections: a demographics section and a 6-point Likert-type scale designed to measure the instructors' preferences of the three foreign training systems. The demographics section asked for area of instruction and number of years in the occupation. On the second section, participants responded to six items, rating their teaching preferences relative to training methods associated with the Russian system, the Sloyd system, and the Arts and Crafts Movement. Designed to reflect the advantages of the training systems, the items were as follows:

1. I use a training method that emphasizes a logical procedure where students advance based on results from a series of graded exercises. (Russian system)
2. I use a training method that encourages student self-direction and initiative. (Sloyd system)
3. I use a training method that emphasizes the aesthetic and creative sides of work. (Arts and Crafts Movement)
4. I use a training method that reaches large groups of students in the least possible time. (Russian system)
5. I use a training method that focuses on neatness and accuracy. (Sloyd system)
6. I use a training method that utilizes rotation of work. (Arts and Crafts Movement)

Participants rated their teaching preferences relative to each item on a 6-point Likert-type scale: 1 (always), 2 (almost always), 3 (often), 4 (seldom), 5 (almost never), and 6 (never). Three vocational educators in the Department of Occupational Studies at California State University, Long

Beach, who were not included in the study sample, comprised the sample for a pilot study conducted to validate the instrument. Data gathered from the pilot study were used to determine where there was a need to revise the instrument. The pilot study also was used to test for understanding of items on the instrument. Results indicated that there was no need to revise the instrument. Thus, the questions were considered content valid. The alpha reliability coefficient for the instrument was .78.

Data Analysis

We calculated means and standard deviations for each of the six items on the instrument. Mean scores were used to determine instructors' teaching preferences. An analysis of variance was used to determine if there were significant differences among instructors' preferences for methods associated with the Russian system, the Sloyd system, and the Arts and Crafts Movement.

FINDINGS

Responses on the demographics section of the instrument indicated that among the 32 respondents, 3 (9.4%) were trade instructors (e.g., welding, electronics, mechanics, automotive service, air conditioning and refrigeration, industrial maintenance, tool and die technology, industrial processing); 10 (31.3%) were literacy instructors; 5 (15.6%) were academic instructors; and 1 (3.1%) was a business instructor; 1(3.1%) was a health instructor; and 12 (37.5%) were instructors who taught other occupational skills (e.g., cosmetology, food science, woodworking, hotel management). Years of experience as an instructor ranged from 1 to 27 years, the average being 6 years.

Table 5.2 presents the means and standard deviations for the six items regarding respondents' preferences for each training method. The item numbers correspond with the numbers of the items as noted in the Instrumentation section; the training system measured by the item is indicated in parenthesis. Overall, the results demonstrated that the instructors preferred methods from the Sloyd system and the Arts and Crafts Movement to methods from the Russian system, although they also preferred some aspects of the Russian system, as indicated by the mean of the responses to item 1 ($M = 3.00$), which indicated that instructors almost always or often used methods associated with the Russian system in teaching. The mean for item 4 indicated that instructors in the sample seldom used methods associated with the Russian system in teaching. The means for

Table 5.2. Means and Standard Deviations

Item	M	SD
Item 1 (Russian system)	3.00	1.24
Item 2 (Sloyd system)	2.41	1.16
Item 3 (Arts and Crafts Movement)	2.66	1.31
Item 4 (Russian system)	3.13	1.24
Item 5 (Sloyd system)	2.72	1.20
Item 6 (Arts and Crafts Movement)	2.41	1.32

items 2 and 5 showed that instructors almost always used methods associated with the Sloyd system in their teaching. The means for items 3 and 6 indicated that instructors often or almost always used methods from the Arts and Crafts Movement in their teaching.

Although there were differences in the mean scores for the items related to each system, results from the ANOVAs indicated that the differences were not significant ($p > .05$). Results from the ANOVAs are summarized in Table 5.3 and Table 5.4.

DISCUSSION AND RECOMMENDATIONS

The Russian system, the Sloyd system, and the Arts and Crafts Movement have long influenced the curricula that vocational educators use. Results from this study indicate that vocational educators prefer training methods associated with the Sloyd system and the Arts and Crafts Movement over methods associated with the Russian system, although differences are not statistically significant. These findings support results from the 1890s historical experiment conducted in Boston that indicated that the Sloyd system met students' needs better than the Russian system (Bott et al., 2003)

American society currently is characterized by rapid technological changes, innovation, and creativity. To meet these demands, vocational educators must emphasize student self-direction and the aesthetic and creative sides of work, which are the heart and soul of the Sloyd and Arts

Table 5.3. Comparing Means for Training Methods: Items 2, 3, and 4 (One-Way ANOVA)

Item	F	p
Item 2 (Sloyd System)	1.30	0.31
Item 3 (Arts and Crafts Movement)	0.86	0.62
Item 4 (Russian System)	0.90	0.58

**Table 5.4.   Comparing Means for Training Methods:
Items 1, 5, and 6 (One-Way ANOVA)**

Item	F	p
Item 1 (Russian system)	1.91	0.11
Item 5 (Sloyd system)	2.13	0.07
Item 6 (Arts and Crafts Movement)	1.18	0.38

and Crafts Movement training systems. Associated with mass production, the Russian training system seems to be more in line with "the more, the better" syndrome that dominated the minds of vocational educators during the Industrial Revolution. Today, student self-direction and initiative, aesthetics, creativity, and rotation of work seem to be buzzwords in vocational education in the United States. Another reason why the Russian system is not preferred may be that the training method takes place in an instruction lab rather than a construction lab; this formal class method of instruction provides little opportunity for self-expression or for recognition of individual differences. Because the Russian system is based on results from a series of graded exercises, it does not enhance the concept of learning by doing that is well accepted by vocational educators in the United States.

This study was designed to bring together the historical facts relating to three important and influential foreign teaching methods in the United States and to determine which one of the foreign training methods vocational educators prefer. There is no significant difference in preferences among the three methods; rather, all three, in combination, are still used. It is surmised that because of the length of time the methods have existed in the United States (i.e., over 100 years) and because educators regularly share successful teaching methods, the three training systems have made their way into mainstream vocational education and that teachers select the method(s) that best suits their needs.

Further research should include a qualitative component to find out why certain methods are preferred, and observations and interviews should be conducted to obtain a comprehensive understanding of which teachers prefer methods from each system (i.e., who teaches what and why). Another recommendation is to examine the influence of vocational educators' own training backgrounds to determine personal instructional preferences. Also, it should be noted that institutional objectives might require vocational educators to use certain approaches regardless of personal preferences. Further research should focus on institutional objectives to determine instructional approaches. Curriculum developers, teachers, students and their families, and industry all can benefit from information about instructors' preferences. Eventually, findings may be generalized to the general population in order to predict and clarify classes needed in secondary schools, community colleges, trade schools, technical schools, colleges, universities, and state employment development departments. Vocational education programs can be developed to instruct students how to make a smooth transition from school to work or to retrain in employment.

An increased understanding of teaching methods within their historical context, the purpose of these methods, and their relationship to present educational needs assists vocational education instructors in making decisions about how to improve teaching effectiveness and how to provide the workforce with skilled and knowledgeable students. It is our hope that readers of this research will find the information useful and that further research will continue.

REFERENCES

Bott, P. A., Slapar, F. M., & Wang, V. (2003). *History and philosophy of career and technical education*. Boston: Pearson.

Brehony, K. J. (1999). "Even far distance Japan" is "showing an interest": The Froebelian movement's turn to Sloyd. *History of Education, 27*(3), 279-295.

Chen, X. (1999). *The Industrial Revolution: It's affects and consequences*. Retrieved April 15, 2003, from http://members.tripod.com/xuchen/ indusrevolt/

Crawford, A. (1997). Ideas and objects: The Arts and Crafts Movement in Britain. *Design Issues, 13*(1), 1-7. Retrieved April 11, 2003, from EBSCOHost Academic Search Elite database http://www.ebscohost.com/

Cumming, E. (2001). The Arts and Crafts Movement. *British Heritage, 22*(4), 1-5. Retrieved April 11, 2003, from EBSCOHost Academic Search Elite database http://www.ebscohost.com/

Finch, C. R., & Crunkilton, J. R. (1999). *Curriculum development in vocational and technical education: Planning, content, and implementation* (5th ed.). Needham Heights, MA: Allyn & Bacon.

Fish, M. (1997). Assessing recent interpretations of the Arts and Crafts Movement. *Art Journal, 56*(3), 90. Retrieved April 11, 2003, from EBSCOHost Academic Search Elite database http://www.ebscohost.com/

Grubb, W. N. (1998). *Preparing for the information-based workplace: Pedagogical issues and institutional linkages*. Retrieved April 11, 2003, from http://mitsloan-MIT.edu/iwer/papers.html

Oklahoma State University. (n.d.a.). *Progressive discourses: Revisiting the purpose of OCED*. Retrieved April 12, 2003, from http://home.okstate.edu/ homepages.nsf/toc/oced5313_links!OpenDocument&Expand-Section=2#_Section2

Oklahoma State University. (n.d.b.). *Snedden & Prosser vs. Dewey: The great debate*. Retrieved April 12, 2003, from http://home.okstate.edu/homepages.nsf/toc/oced5313_links!OpenDocument&ExpandSection=4#_Section4

Roberts, R. W. (1965). *Vocational and practical arts education: History, development, andprinciples* (2nd ed.). New York: Harper & Row.

Roche, J. F. (1995). The culture of pre-modernism: Whitman, Morris, & the American Arts and Crafts Movement. *The American Transcendental Quarterly, 9*(2), 1-12. Retrieved April 11, 2003, from EBSCOHost Academic Search Elite database http://www.ebscohost.com/

CHAPTER 6

PERSPECTIVES OF A HEALTHY WORK ETHIC IN A 21st CENTURY INTERNATIONAL COMMUNITY

Gregory C. Petty and Ernest W. Brewer

Traditionally, we have attributed the development of the work ethic to historic and ancient values and mores spawned by religious and socially acceptable beliefs. The twenty-first century, however, is creating a world society based on instant communication and global competition. Young people in developing countries are rapidly catching up with their peers in industrialized countries with regard to their use and adaptation of technology and their expectations for leisure and luxury and better safety and health practices on the job. We need to explore these perspectives and the dynamics of developing a work ethic in a modern world.

Innovations in Career and Technical Education: Strategic Approaches Towards Workforce Competencies Around the Globe, pp. 119–131
Copyright © 2008 by Information Age Publishing
All rights of reproduction in any form reserved.

INTRODUCTION

The nature of work and the manner for which young people develop a healthy work ethic is changing (McCortney & Engels, 2003; Pogson, Cober, Doverspike, & Rogers, 2003). Changes in the global nature of jobs, diversity in the workplace, unemployment, and possibly even changes in personalities of individuals themselves are creating work ethic havoc. Today we are a world market economy. With instant (and sustained) communication, prevalent outsourcing of jobs, and international competition, all of us are tied to an international workforce community (Hudelson, 1992; McCortney & Engels). Worldwide recognition and response to the disaster of the Asian Tsunami, events of September 11, 2001, and the recent corporate ethics failures of Enron and Martha Stewart and others has altered the landscape of working-class citizens (Baker, Jacobs, & Tickle-Degnen, 2003). Perhaps what we have adopted and have known as the Protestant Work Ethic as first recognized and identified by Max Weber is an ideal not acceptable to twenty-first century workers (Baker et at., 2003; McCortney & Engels, 2003; Niles & Harris-Bowlsbey, 2002).

Today it is important for us to reflect on the forces affecting workers from all parts of the world. To better understand the complex nature of how a positive work ethic is developed, many professionals, particularly baby boomers, need to change their perspective of the world of work (McCortney & Engels, 2003). The concerns of business leaders and workforce educators alone are not enough to improve a young worker's work ethic (Clark, 2003; Petty, 1997).

To better prepare young people for work, it seems proper to review why we work, the value and meaning of work, and how we can foster and develop a positive work ethic. With a view to the history of vocational education and training and the work ethic and to the roots of our profession, perhaps we can improve the future.

WHY WE WORK

People work because they need to work. This observation seems to be a commonly held tenet for work. For some, work provides an important sense of achievement and belonging. It brings meaning to the day and provides some level of self-efficacy. For others, work is a means to an end. People work to earn money and to accumulate property. The need may be driven by several factors, foremost of which is economic.

However, economic needs do not explain the emotional needs expressed by the increasing numbers of retirees who return to work to fulfill intrinsic, even therapeutic needs (Brewer, Campbell, & Petty, 2001). This is but one of the issues regarding the value and meaning of work that complicates its study.

SEVEN VIEWPOINTS ON WORK

An overview and analysis of work reveals seven basic tenets of work. Everyone has a different viewpoint toward work. If the task is pleasurable or is performed among friends and family, work becomes an enjoyable experience. However, if work is drudgery providing little or no emotional satisfaction, it can pose a negative impact for the worker. Seven viewpoints toward labor relations and workforce education and development suggest that: (1) work is continuous and leads to additional activity; (2) work is productive and produces goods and services; (3) work requires physical and mental exertion; (4) work has sociopsychological aspects; (5) work is performed on a regular or scheduled basis; (6) work requires a degree of constraint; and (7) work is performed for a personal purpose (intrinsic or extrinsic).

WORK RATIONALE

For our discussion we will start with the basic premise in life: Everyone must work. Philosophers have argued that the purpose of work is to distinguish leisure time from other forms of personal time. Some may work because they must make a living whereas others work to maintain a lifestyle or to fulfill obligations. Work can bring great personal pleasure as well as help other people in the process.

One perspective of work comes from Fedorov (1990), a Russian philosopher, who spoke primarily of the learned and the unlearned and that human property (extrinsic rewards) and human dignity (morality and happiness) is the inner spiritual life given power of work itself. This perspective implies the dichotomy of work-it is both extrinsic and intrinsic.

Karl Marx, the German philosopher, did not believe that all people worked the same way, or that how one works is entirely personal and individual. Instead, he argued that work is a social activity, and that the conditions and forms under and through which people work are socially determined and change over time (Whelan, 1999).

Looking at the literature over time may reveal some insight into our own beliefs about work. Indeed, we are not the first to explore the value and meaning of work. The ancient Greeks were reported to have published much on the subject.

THE MEANING OF WORK IN EARLY CIVILIZATIONS

Greeks

How did individuals from early civilizations come to view work? From Homer, who we learned much about human development, archaeological as well as sociological, we can explore early ancient Greek culture. Homer recorded the Greek belief that the gods hated humankind and out of spite and condemned humanity to toil (Bennett, 1926; Mosse, 1966/1969). To the ruling classes of ancient Greece, work was a curse. Tilgher (1930) quotes Xenophon as calling work the painful price that the gods charged humankind for living (Hill, 1996).

The early Greeks, whose political organization was structured around the city-state, believed that the citizens should own businesses or supervise their own agricultural efforts (Seaford, 2004). Farming, being a necessary factor for the survival of society, became exempt from the stigma attached to other forms of work (Borow, 1973). They deplored the mechanical arts, which they thought brutalized the mind because the mind would be unfit for the thinking of great truths or the practicing of virtue (Bennett, 1926; Brewer & Marmon, 2000; Mosse, 1966/1969). Free artisans and craftsmen were scorned and the mechanical and menial tasks were done by slaves. Slavery itself, in the classic civilization, was not regarded as wrong, morally or otherwise. In fact, slavery was considered to be in the same vein as using beasts of burden such as donkeys and was a means of getting the bulk of the heavy, undesirable labor done (Dougherty & Kurke, 2003; Kazanas, Baker, Miller, & Hannah, 1973; Konstan & Rutter, 2003).

Romans

The Romans conquered the Greeks and as a consequence learned much from them. The Romans assimilated most of the Greek's attitudes about the arts, science, and social values into their own culture. Cicero, a notable Roman philosopher and statesman, recited two occupations worthy of a free man. The first was agriculture and the second was commerce, with all other pursuits (of work) being vulgar and dishonoring. Handcraft, the work of artisans, and the crafting of material goods were held in low-esteem (Ermatinger, 2004; Tilgher, 1930).

Hebrews

In the Western world we know much about the Hebrews, who like the early Greeks, considered work to be a painful drudgery. However, whereas the Greeks could see no reason why humanity should be condemned to labor other than at the whim of the gods, the Hebrews felt that work was necessary to make amends for the original sin committed by Adam and Eve in their earthly paradise (Bennett, 1926; Tilgher, 1930).

Early Christians followed the Hebrew belief that not only was work necessary to provide expiation and the existence of many of the necessities, but it was a means for accumulating enough to share with one's fellow human being (Borow, 1973; Brewer & Marmon, 2000). Upon work, then, was reflected some of the divine light that stems from charity. Riches shared with the poor were considered to bring God's blessing upon the giver (Tilgher, 1930).

Early Christians

Early Christian doctrine recognized no separation between mental, bodily, or physical work. To work and share the products of work with others (charity) was desirable. To eliminate the middleman and to allow the recipient of the sharing to share directly in the work was even more desirable. Thus, it became the duty of the Christian brotherhood to give work to the unemployed so that no man need remain in idleness. A refusal to work resulted in the offender being cast out of the community for the good of both the community and the offender (Kazanas et al., 1973; Tilgher, 1930). Despite these foundations, no intrinsic value was yet recognized in work. Therefore, work remained a means to a worthy end (Borow, 1973; Tilgher, 1930).

Artisans and craftsmen were not tied to the land; therefore, they were free to sell their services to the highest bidder. By keeping the processes and methods highly guarded secrets of their trade, they were able to control, to an extent, the commerce and the trades. Early Christian leaders generally held a low opinion of physical labor. Thus, greater diligence led to a degree of wealth that enabled a middle class to form about commerce and the trades (Mosse, 1966/1969; Tilgher, 1930).

THE PROTESTANT ETHIC OF WORK

The first great Protestant reformer, Martin Luther, believed that work was both the universal base of society and the real distinction between social classes. It is said he had little sympathy with commerce because it was a means of using work to pass from one social class to another. Luther believed that to rise in the social hierarchy was against God's laws (Borow, 1973). But, Luther believed there was just one best way to serve God, and that was to do most perfectly the work of one's calling (Borow, 1973; Tilgher, 1930). To promote this concept, Bennett (1926) portrays Luther as having promoted formal schooling in religious matters for all classes.

Calvinism adopted a new attitude toward work. They borrowed from Luther's concept of religion and believed that it was the will of God for all, including the rich and noble, to work. Further, it was their belief that it was man's obligation to God to extract the maximum amount of wealth from his work. Sweat and toil only had value as a means to establish the kingdom of God on earth (Tilgher, 1930). In addition, no one should lust after the fruits of their labor-wealth, possessions, or luxurious living. The element of profit was therefore added to the Protestant ethic (Hill, 1996).

In a short time, Calvinists discovered that the principles of profit could produce for the secular arm great wealth, position, and other desirable things. These concepts also pleased non-Calvinists and subsequently modern business began. From the religious convictions of the protestant merchant was spawned the businessman who was strong-willed, active, austere, and hard working. According to Hill (1996) it was common to shun idleness, luxuriousness, prodigality, and other extravagances that resulted in the softening of either the muscles or the soul.

The Protestant work ethic developed during this era was a foundation to the success of the modern factory. The diligent application of humanity's energy, regardless of the project on which the efforts were spent, was an essential ingredient of the Industrial Revolution (Tilgher, 1930).

THE PROTESTANT ETHIC OF WORK IN THE WEST

In the western hemisphere, particularly in America, several conditions existed that were beneficial to the establishment and strengthening of the work ethic and became a powerful concept in society. The colonies (America) were largely peopled by those who had everything to gain and comparatively little to lose. These individuals (primarily immigrants) had strong feelings regarding the benefits of diligent work and prosperity that were ingrained in both their moral and religious fiber (Ringer, 2004). Another factor was the vast opportunity in land and natural resources that could enable almost anyone to succeed who was willing to put forth the effort (Barlow, 1967). Even the concept of indentured servitude was but a postponement of the probability of ultimate success. It provided a means of getting to the land where success was so probable (Barlow, 1967).

In America, however, another factor entered into the evolving work ethic. This was the factor of education and training. Partly because of the availability of wealth, the established Protestant ethics, the ingrained social attitudes and regard for diligent work, and the social mobility possible in a culture without distinct and traditional cultural castes, many colonists wished for their sons and daughters better training and education than they had received (Barlow, 1967; Bennett, 1926). Colleges, universities, mechanics institutions, and other forms of formal education appeared throughout the colonies (Bennett, 1926). Education and wealth were the means to social ascension (Barlow, 1967). This upward mobility was impossible in other societies, but was made possible in America. Therefore, the American working class achieved what no other working class had achieved in history. The working class became the middle class and the more they worked, the more and greater success and upward mobility they enjoyed (Balmer, 2002; Eby, 1952; Ringer, 2004).

THE EFFECTS OF THE INDUSTRIAL REVOLUTION AND AUTOMATION ON THE VALUE OF WORK

In the Western world large factories were established where labor could be divided so that semiskilled individuals could perform repetitive elements of a job using apprentices. This led to the development of a working class. With the advent of the Industrial Revolution and the vast flooding of the metropolitan areas with unemployed rural population, the old values (such as the lord of the land exhibiting a degree of kindness and care) were eliminated. Bennett (1926) and Tilgher (1930) indicated that with the money economy, factory lords found a way to get around the traditional burden of responsibility through the payment of wages.

The factory-dominated society led to the metamorphosis of serfs to workers creating a lower class (workers). Culturally, this complemented the middle class, which was composed largely of artisans and merchants, and an upper class composed of the landed and titled nobility and the wealthy. However, through hard work, luck, and diligence a worker could move, by virtue of accruing wealth, from the lowest class to within the limits of the upper class (Bennett, 1926; Runes, 1951; Tilgher, 1930).

A number of authors have pointed out that one of the results that affected working during the Industrial Revolution was the intensification of the division of labor (Brewer et al., 2001; Venn, 1964). The implications of the intense division of labor for the purpose of increasing production were to bring specific work processes to an ever-increasing fragmentation. This removed the worker further and further from participating in the final product (Venn, 1964). This factor resulted in the change in work attitudes from those that existed in the sixteenth, seventeenth, and eighteenth centuries to the emerging new work attitudes of today. Ironically, those very changes that have increased our potential for work productivity, such as mass production, automation, cybernation, and occupational technology, have resulted in making the work ethic, in its classic form, less meaningful and seemingly less appropriate for the individual worker. It is easily observed from a comparison of the production processes of the early seventeenth century and modern procedures that work has changed; however, the extent and the type of change in the work ethic is not as easily seen.

As work and society changed, the work ethic also changed. Decreased manual labor and reduction in the hours of work contributed to the increased prosperity and freedom from toil experienced by most workers. However, depriving workers of both their involvement in the total production process as well as the possibility of self-realization through work has presented problems far beyond those imagined by the people who felt they were freeing the worker for more honorable labors.

The erosion of the traditional work ethic began with the willingness of immigrants to provide cheap labor and ultimately advance in a new society (Dowd, 2003; Jardine, 2004). Immigrants from countries undergoing political revolution, famine, or vast social pressures in the seventeenth, eighteenth, and nineteenth centuries would literally sell themselves into servitude, oftentimes with their entire families to move to the new world (Barlow, 1967; Bennett, 1926; King, 2001; Timmins, 2000). These immigrants gladly lived in crowded tenements, worked for substandard wages and worked under less than desirable conditions for the sole purpose of providing themselves a means of transportation to the new world (Petras & Veltmeyer, 2003). Even today, this trend continues with recent immigrants from third-world countries (including Mexico) who move to America to participate in our economic marvel.

STAGES OF HUMAN DEVELOPMENT AND THE WORK ETHIC

So, how does the work ethic develop today? Some researchers think that instilling professionalism is one way of accomplishing this difficult task. It is believed that professionalism leads to a positive value and meaning of work, ergo a positive work ethic. These investigators studied learning and psychological development by exploring thought and behavioral processes within a chronological system (Haines, 2003). Researchers such as Benjamin Bloom, Jean Piaget, and Erik Erikson linked behavior to age cycles (Bloom, 1956; Brewer et al., 2001; Erikson, 1964).

To better explain human development, researchers have divided the human life cycle into periods or stages. It is thought that these different levels may offer some ideas of how behavior or physical characteristics, even cognitive and affective development, affect a person's work ethic. The five stages of life suggested in Table 6.1 I demonstrate how a chronology of life in years reflects in specific changes in men and women what might affect our work ethic.

CONCLUSIONS

So, where are we today with the struggle to develop and instill meaning and value to work, ergo the work ethic? Surely, global competition has created a lot of pressure for establishing and sustaining a positive work ethic. Traditionally, a person's work ethic was related to production and historically has been established during the postindustrial revolution period and the change from an agrarian society to an industrial society. Workers in developed countries were engaged in the making of something of value and learned to develop their work ethic from this basis.

Table 6.1.   Effects of Five Stages of Life on Work Ethic

Stage	Age	Effects Related to Work Ethic
1	Growth (birth to 14years old)	Child moves from sensory and tactile, identity is established and the child explores interests related to future career potential, and later develops adult motor and critical thinking skills.
2	Exploration (15-24 years old)	Psychosexual identity matures as young man/woman develops goals and career objects, moving from early adulthood, man or woman develops work ethic and pursues career objectives and experiences psychosexual and career development.
3	Establishment (25-44 years old)	Represents a period of domestication and settling down, with planning for future, retirement, and long-term needs/goals with career advancement, change, and renewal; continued planning and long-term goal assessment.
4	Maintenance (45-64 years old)	The apex of worker achievement; family development in flux, workforce advancement is stifled; some anxieties from aging process with preretirement and income reduction concerns, some identity problems for workers in transition from work to retirement.
6	Decline (65+ years old)	Period of worker retirement, financial, and health concerns with some quality of life disruption and anxiety over health issues, family dislocation, and mortality.

When a worker creates a product or delivers a service the intrinsic satisfaction resulting from this professional endeavor leaves a feeling of satisfaction and a positive work ethic. Unfortunately, though, production work is being outsourced from so-called first-world countries to developing third-world countries where labor is cheaper. Outsourcing is leaving the preponderance of jobs to a more educated, technologically skilled workforce. This global transfer has created new fields of work that are not directly related to creation satisfaction. This transfer lends credence to Marx's position that work is a social activity and changes over time (Whelan, 1999). Perhaps this can partially explain the changing work ethic.

Another factor that is causing a change in the work ethic is the great rise of service workers in such fields as teaching, police and fire protection, medical assistance, as well as many others. These jobs have a recognized place in our society and as a result of modern technology have become very specialized. Service workers also include the areas of convenience, leisure, and entertainment. In the western world this transference of jobs from industrial production to service has resulted in increased productivity along with an increased standard of living and pay rate. This change, however, carries with it the baggage of decreasing the personal involvement of the worker in earning a living (Petty, 1995a). Consequently, the situation has been established to gradually erode the traditional work ethic by lessening the personal involvement and commitment to work. Work then becomes more and more a means of financing entertainment, a high standard of living, and other nonwork activities (Miller, Woehr, & Hudspeth, 2002). This changes our perception of the work ethic.

The traditional work ethic, is undergoing a radical transformation, especially in the minds of young workers. Changing attitudes of young people in conjunction with changing economic times and conditions are presenting greater demands for change. Herzberg, Mausner, and Snyderman (1959) supported the concept of change 4 decades ago. However, they also felt that for industrial workers, in which work is a means of providing the way of life rather than the thing desired in itself, the traditional work ethic is being replaced by an avoidance ethic. Today these thoughts are not supported by others, who contend that although there are differences in the work ethic of young people and adults, there is no conclusive evidence supporting the erosion of the work ethic (Miller et al., 2002; Petty, 1995b; Pogson et al., 2003).

By most indications the work ethic is changing and is being challenged by several forces of modern society (McCortney & Engels, 2003). Some studies (Csikszentmihalyi, 2003; Petty 1995b, 1997) indicate that many workers in the industrialized western world appear to reject the notion that work is good in and of itself and has intrinsic value. Evidence of this is that more and more people are retiring early in both the blue-collar and white-collar categories. More emphasis is being placed on nonwork or leisure activities as a distraction to the drudgeries of work. Today we are experiencing increased rates in standards of living. Personal health and job safety have come to the forefront of concerns expressed by today's workers. Although these immediate concerns of workers are a manifestation of a progressive, modern society, they may jeopardize the heritage of the traditional work ethic, which states that work in itself is important and has value (Csikszentmihalyi, 2003).

REFERENCES

Baker, N. A., Jacobs, K., & Tickle-Degnen, L. (2003). A methodology for developing evidence about meaning in occupation: Exploring the meaning of working. *Occupation, Participation and Health, 23*(2),57-66.

Balmer, R. H. (2002). *Protestantism in America.* New York: Columbia University Press.

Barlow, M. L. (1967). *History of industrial education in the United States.* Peoria, IL: Charles A. Bennett.

Bennett, C. A. (1926). *History of manual and industrial education up to 1870.* Peoria, IL: Charles A. Bennett.

Bloom, B. (1956). *Taxonomy of educational objectives; The classification of educational goals, by a committee of college and university examiners.* New York: D. McKay.

Borow, H. (Ed.). (1973). *Career guidance for a new age.* Boston: Houghton Mifflin.

Brewer, E. W., Campbell, A. C., & Petty, G. C. (2001) *Foundations of workforce education.* Dubuque, IA: Kendall/Hunt.

Brewer, E. W., & Marmon, D. (2000). *Characteristics, skills, and strategies of the ideal educator.* Boston, MA: Pearson.

Clark, R. (2003). Fostering the work motivation of individuals and teams. *Performance Improvement, 42*(3), 21-29.

Csikszentmihalyi, M. (2003). The evolving nature of work. *North American Montessori Teacher's Association Journal, 28*(2), 87-107.

Dougherty, C., & Kurke, L. (Eds.). (2003). *The cultures within ancient Greek culture: Contact, conflict, collaboration.* New York: Cambridge University Press.

Dowd, D. F. (2003). *Capitalism and its economics: A critical history.* Ann Arbor, MI: Pluto Press.

Eby, F. (1952). *The development of modern education, in theory, organization, and practice.* New York: Prentice-Hall.

Erikson, E. H. (1964). *Childhood and society.* New York: Norton.

Ermatinger, J. W. (2004). *The decline and fall of the Roman Empire.* Westport, CT: Greenwood Press.

Fedorov, N. F. (1990). What was man created for? In E. Koutiassov & M. Minto (Eds.), *The philosophy of the common task: Selected works* (pp. 12-36). Lausanne, Switzerland: Honeyglen/L'Age d'Homme.

Haines, A. M. (2003). Work. *North American Montessori Teacher's Association Journal, 2,* 49-58.

Herzberg, F., Mausner, B., & Snyderman, B. (1959). *The motivation to work.* New York: Wiley.

Hill, R. B. (1996). *Historical context of the work ethic.* Retrieved March 4, 2005, from http://www.coe.uga.edul-rhill/workethic/hist/htm

Hudelson, D. (1992). Roots or reform: Tracing the path of workforce education. *Career and Technical Education Journal, 67*(7), 28-29, 69.

Jardine, M. (2004). *The making and unmaking of technological society: How Christianity can save modernity from itself.* Grand Rapids, MI: Brazos Press.

Kazanas, H. C., Baker, G. E., Miller, F. M., & Hannah, L. D. (1973). *The meaning and value of work* (Information Series No. 71). Columbus, OH: The Center for Vocational Education. (ERIC Document Reproduction Service No. ED 091 504).

King, S. (2001). *Making sense of the Industrial Revolution.* New York: Manchester University Press.

Konstan, D., & Rutter, N. K. (2003). *Envy, spite, and jealousy: The rivalrous emotions in Ancient Greece.* Edinburgh, Scotland: Edinburgh University Press.

McCortney, A. H., & Engels, D. W. (2003). Revisiting the Work Ethic in America. *The Career Development Quarterly, 52*(2), 132-40.

Miller, M. J., Woehr, D. J., & Hudspeth, N. (2002). The meaning and measurement of work ethic: Construction and initial validation of a multidimensional inventory [Monograph]. *Journal of Vocational Behavior, 60,* 451-489.

Mosse, C. (1969). *Le Travail en Grece et a Rome* [The ancient world at work] (Janet Lloyd, Trans.). New York: Norton. (Original work published 1966)

Niles, S. G., & Harris-Bowlsbey, J. (2002). *Career development interventions in the 21st century.* Upper Saddle River, NJ: Prentice Hall.

Petras, J., & Veltmeyer H. (2003). *A system in crisis: The dynamics of free market capitalism.* New York: Zed Books.

Petty, G. C. (1995a). Adults in the work force and the occupational work ethic. *Journal of Studies in Technical Careers, 15*(3), 133-140.

Petty, G. C. (1995b). Vocational-technical education and the occupational work ethic. *Journal of Industrial Teacher Education, 32*(3), 45-58.

Petty, G. C. (1997). Employability skills. In C. P. Campbell (Ed.), *Best practices in workforce development* (pp. 122-145). Lancaster, PA: Technomic.

Pogson, C. E., Cober, A. B., Doverspike, D., & Rogers, J. R. (2003). Differences in self-reported work ethic across three career stages. *Journal of Vocational Behavior, 62*(1), 189-201.

Ringer, F. K. (2004). *Max Weber: An intellectual biography.* Chicago: University of Chicago Press.

Runes, D. D. (1951). *The Hebrew impact on Western civilization.* New York: Philosophical Library.

Seaford, R. (2004). *Money and the early Greek mind: Homer, philosophy, tragedy.* New York: Cambridge University Press.

Tilgher, A. (1930). *Homo faber: Work through the ages* (D. C. Fisher, Trans.). New York: Harcourt Brace.

Timmins, G. (2000). *Understanding the Industrial Revolution.* New York: Routledge.

Venn, G. (1964). *Education for work: Postsecondary career and technical and technical education*. Washington, DC: American Council on Education.

Whelan, F. (1999). *Karl Marx (biography of Marx)*. London: Fourth Estate.

CHAPTER 7

FRAMING STRATEGIC PARTNERSHIPS GUIDED BY ADULT LEARNING

Bridging the Education Gap With CTE

Kathleen P. King

This case study research examines the use of several adult learning principles in career and technical education for the purpose of extending them to secondary and other career and technical programs to help bridge the compulsory education vs. higher education (K-16) educational gap. The focus is on the National Center for Career and Technical Education (NCCTE) exemplary and promising award program standards and a sampling of programs that have received this designation. Findings include the frequency of use of identified adult learning principles, trends in their use, and examples. Additionally, a related emphasis on softskills and recommendations for applying these experiences and findings to secondary education are offered.

Innovations in Career and Technical Education: Strategic Approaches Towards Workforce Competencies Around the Globe, pp. 133–165
Copyright © 2008 by Information Age Publishing

INTRODUCTION

In the midst of the Post-Information Age, vocational education now includes high schools, postsecondary education, trade and technical schools, and other career-to work programs. While high schools are often dominated by concerns related to competition for admissions to the best higher education institutions, this field has developed over the years to be a valuable option for both college and non-college bound students. The rising costs and extended timeline of pursuing a college education is not always available to young adults and they may need to move into the workforce more rapidly, thereby making career-to-work programs indispensable (Delci & Stern, 1997; Scott & Bernhardt, 1999). These conditions, and others, have contributed to a gap that vocational, or more recently named "career and technical education" has been attempting to bridge (Kerka, 2000; Levesque, Lauen, Teitelbaum, Alt, & Librera, 2000).

With career and technical preparation including a post-high school time frame, the characteristics and needs of students as adults become more urgent as adults of all ages attend such programs (Brown, 1999; Castellano, Stringfield, & Stone, 2002; Wonacott, 2002). To facilitate a smooth, effective transition from high school to the workplace or postsecondary education, administrators, educators, trainers, and career counselors can then examine the field of adult learning to further support both our CTE efforts in high schools in our adult education, vocational, and technical programs. One strategy to do this is to not just refer to theories and principles of adult learning, but also examine best practices among career and technical education to see how they already use adult learning to bridge the gap.

This chapter addresses questions that also emerge from educational and socioeconomic trends, including: What teaching and learning issues need to be addressed among learners as they continue in their adult years? What theory, research, and best practices in adult and vocational education can allow us to address this trend? And, how can program and curricular planning in career and technical education on both ends of the continuum—secondary and postsecondary—benefit from or incorporate this knowledge base? Specifically, the chapter explores how adult learning principles (e.g., active learning, immediate application of knowledge, and building on the experience of learners) are and can be used further to guide and shape programs in career and technical education in secondary and postsecondary settings.

Building upon a review of the literature, this research analyzes the NCCTE's exemplary and promising program standards of outstanding practice and several member programs. This analysis is an extended case study that includes both a national scope and individual specificity

(Creswell, 1998; Yin, 2003). The NCCTE standards, and multiple examples within the case, are examined across selected programs. The results are presented based on the theoretical propositions of the study rather than as a case study descriptive narrative to more fully articulate the findings and their meaning based on our framework of examining the compulsory education vs. higher education (K-16) gap (Yin, 2003).

This research entailed five major research questions. First, through a survey of the literature, how is career and technical education addressing the compulsory education versus higher education (K-16) gap within our current economic, political, and educational settings? Second, what insights does the adult learning literature provide into salient characteristics of adult learners relevant to career and technical education settings? Third, how do the NCCTE standards for exemplary programs demonstrate these adult learner principles, or not? Fourth, what do four sample programs from the NCCTE awards program reveal as they are analyzed for their possible illustration, operationalization, and maximization of adult learning principles? Finally, what recommendations for secondary, postsecondary, and career and technical education research and practice can be made based on the application to and further development of adult learning in this context?

CAREER AND TECHNICAL EDUCATION FILLING THE COMPULSORY VERSUS HIGHER EDUCATION (K-16) GAP

As I surveyed the literature of the CTE field regarding theory, research, practice and program planning, specific trends became and some emerged as standing out more than others. Over the past 30 years this educational movement has transitioned from a remedial and vocational school often less highly valued, but duly provided service to school systems to become a clearly recognized valuable alternative for preparing young adults for trade, technological, and professional careers with or without postsecondary study as part of their future. No longer solely serving a marginalized population, career and technical education is providing valuable preparation and career alternatives for a wide-range of students (Bragg & Reger, 2002; Kerka, 2000; Wonacott, 2002). During a time when the costs of higher education have skyrocketed, many adults cannot pursue that pathway, or if they do, they pursue it over an extended period of time. These economic factors have increased the value of career and technical education that prepares secondary and postsecondary learners in shorter, work-oriented, hands-on programs of study.

Very often these programs are also based on local occupational needs and federal or independent occupational forecasts such as the U.S. Department of Labor's *Occupational Outlook Handbook* (2006) (Kerka, 2000). The field of career and technical education has similarities and differences across its many applications. From computer-aided graphics to welding, from culinary arts to agriculture, and from early childhood education to emergency medical technicians, one is impressed by a sampling of the vast expanse of programs and careers included in this field (Bragg & Reger, 2002). Certainly different content areas, but also different expectations, philosophies, and requirements compose the constellation of programs included in career and technical education.

Throughout its history vocational education, and now career and technical education, (CTE) has consistently addressed the needs of young and older adults who are examining their formal education. It has also attempted to match it immediately to their careers.

Based on interviews with program leaders, which we will describe shortly, frequent questions and concerns of these learners include,

- How can my education build upon my interests and abilities to prepare me for a valuable occupation?
- How does what I am learning in the classroom apply to real life?
- What is the value of what I am learning?
- How can this area become not only a job, but also a career for me?
- How can I prepare to continue my learning into the future?
- And how can I learn the many things I need to know to succeed in the workplace?

Rather than stopping at a credential, career and technical education has increasingly become a platform from which to explore and build perspectives and skills in understanding learners' ongoing educational and professional needs (Brown, 2002; Wonacott, 2002).

Today career and technical education is more prominently providing a bridge from requisite secondary education to a lifelong opportunity for education and development. The research reported in this paper begins to explore how we can learn from successful career and technical education programs and bring these approaches into secondary and postsecondary education so that our learners and curriculum might benefit from a stronger bridge and smoother transition of purpose and practice.

THE VIEW FROM ADULT LEARNING

As educators and trainers consider career and technical education, we are examining it from the perspective of adult learning principles. In this

light, the literature of adult education provides insight into salient characteristics of adult learners relevant to career and technical education settings. While the adult learning field is vast and diverse, over the years
many common principles have consistently emerged (Caffarella, 2002;
Cooper & Henschke, 2007; Imel, 1998; Lawler & King, 2000). While I
recognize that different learning theories have and continue to emerge,
the focus here is on overarching learning principles that have been identified in the literature including, involving learners in planning, cultivating
self-directed learning, involving learners in active learning, learning for
application, building on learner's experience, building a climate of
respect, and cultivating collaborative skills (Lawler & King, 2000).

The principle of *involving adult learners in planning* is one that closely
links to cultivating self-directed learning. As we work with learners to
include them in needs assessment, content selection, assignment selection, and/or evaluation decisions, we are providing opportunities for them
to learn how learning can be planned. Whether the learners are college
students, employees, or literacy students, participating in planning learning builds ownership of, motivation for, and relevance of educational initiatives (Caffarella, 2002; Lawler & King, 2000). As recommended by
Caffarella (2002), "A second strategy for building learner support [of
adult learning programs] is to actively involve current and potential
learners in planning and conducting the programs" (p. 86). This principle has never been an easy one to integrate into traditional organizations
or curricula and distinctly challenges a teacher-centered and authoritarian model. However, when learners are involved in the planning of learning it promotes powerful results to support and extend learning
experiences and qualitatively change learners' and teachers' perspectives.

These experiences in planning can also be a basis for building patterns
and skills for *self-directed learning*. By educators not keeping the planning
process exclusive or invisible, learners who engage in planning begin to
see themselves increasingly as able to make decisions about learning
(Caffarella, 2002; Vella, 2002). Programs can demonstrate their
involvement in cultivating self-directed learning when learners determine
needs, set goals, and evaluate their own performance, among other tasks.
Rather than depending on an outside authority/teacher to lead the way,
learners experience the freedom, autonomy, and power of leading the
way for themselves. The locus of power in educational decisions shifts
from the outside, to the learner. Merriam and Caffarella (1999) state that
this structure much more closely resembles how learners face many
learning opportunities in their adult years, "this form of learning can take
place both inside and outside institutionally based learning programs. For
the most part, however, being self-directed in one's learning is a natural
part of adult life" (p. 293). Shifting the control and direction of learning

from teacher to learner in the formal classroom opens the door to a natural transition when the learner encounters formal and informal lifelong learning opportunities.

Such involvement in self-directed learning sets the stage for *involving learners in active learning*. These learners cannot be passive recipients of knowledge that comes from an authority. Learners must be engaged in seeking and experiencing learning as recognized by Lawler (1991), "Adults learn more effectively and efficiently when they actively participate in the educational activity" (p. 39). Hands-on activities, small groups, and project-based learning are examples of how learners can become active participants (Caffarella, 2002; King, 2005; Lawler & King, 2000). Demonstration techniques are examples of how hands-on experience can be clearly illustrated in the area of technology learning. When a course in word processing consists of lectures about how the program works and then transitions to working through lessons in the program in the computer laboratory, new information is more fully and vividly understood through active learning and experience. Adult learners overwhelmingly respond positively to experiences that enable them to interact with, critically examine, and experience new information, skills, and ideas (Caffarella, 2002; Merriam & Caffarella, 1999; Vella, 2002). Active learning techniques can transform a once quiet classroom to one humming with activity, inquiry, and learning.

This active learning can be easily meshed with *learning for application* among learners as project-based learning, case studies, and group projects are used. Rather than memorizing content, when adult learners engage in using information for a specific application, it takes on new meaning and urgency. Indeed, from the beginning, adult learners continually ask why material is being taught and how they will use it (Vella, 2002). As we build on this need and interest in our educational programs, we capture intrinsic needs and motivation (Caffarella, 2002; Cochran, 2007; King, 2005; King & Wright, 2007; Lawler & King, 2000). An example from faculty development reveals that faculty, as adult learners, exemplify the need to see application, "If there is a prevailing attitude that this new learning will not enhance their professional life or that there is little support, affirmation, or reward, the faculty [adult learners] may see little or no need to attend or learn" (Lawler & King, 2000, p. 11).

In formal educational settings this emphasis on motivation is often seen as an optional approach; however in informal educational settings, such as independent and avocational learning, application often becomes the purpose of learning. Without the need to use the learning, many informal educational pursuits would not even be started. In their busy and complex lives, adults need to see the usefulness, and the application, of any learning within which they might invest themselves. Cultivating a vision for application of learning introduces adult learners to valuable strategies for lifelong learning.

Adult learners do not learn in a vacuum. Instead their learning is scaffolded on prior, and many times extensive, experience. When educators unleash many opportunities for understanding, application, and extension they *build on learners' experience* (King, 2005; Lawler & King, 2000). Caffarella (2002) succinctly states this point, "Adults have a rich background of knowledge and experience and learn best when this experience is acknowledged and new information builds on their past knowledge and experience" (p. 29). Rather than teaching content in isolated fragments, if we can bring learning into learners' webs of experience, we know they will more quickly understand and more successfully retain the learning (Vella, 2002).

Building on learners' experiences includes assessing prior learning and experiences. Providing opportunities for class discussions, small group activities, and reflective practice all cultivate the activity of drawing out past experiences that apply to new learning. As learners wrestle with how new learning fits together with prior understanding, they open the door to not just learning subject matter, but also to integrating learning into their understanding and perspective in fundamental ways. Much like the old lesson plan mnemonic—"Hook-Took-Look"—prior experience can be an invaluable "hook" into learners' understanding, validation, motivation, and context for learning.

Within a learning environment that builds on experience, *a climate of respect*, encouragement, and support is necessary to ensure learners' personal, professional, social, and emotional safety. Vella (2002) describes this vividly as she relates,

> Safety is a principle that guides a teacher's hand throughout planning, during the learning needs and resources assessment, in the first moments of the course. The principle of safety enables the teacher to create an inviting setting for adult learners. People have shown that they are not only willing but also ready and eager to learn when they feel safe in the learning environment. (p. 8)

If learners feel their prior experience is open to harmful criticism by others, or if they sense that their experience may be devalued, then they cannot take the risks involved in investing themselves genuinely into the learning experience. Educators therefore need to consider how to communicate and cultivate respect, encouragement, and support in their relationships with the students, their classrooms, and their programs. Such an environment is often explicitly identified by ground rules for communication, appreciation for diverse opinions and experiences, and confidentiality (Caffarella, 2002; Merriam & Caffarella, 1999; Vella 2002). However, other adult learning principles also integrate with this positive climate. For instance, students quickly recognize respect, encouragement, and support when they participate in planning their learning and valuing their experience.

Finally, *cultivating collaborative skills* through small groups is an adult learning principle that prepares learners for the workplace and personal life as it builds teamwork, leadership, communication skills, and interpersonal understanding (King, 2005; Scribner & Donaldson, 2001). Much of our experience as adults involves working with other people; and developing collaborative skills will help learners to succeed in these circumstances. Collaborative skills may be developed in adult learning settings through many forms including working in small groups, on team projects, group presentations, and role-playing (Caffarella, 2002; King, 2005; Vella, 2002). Vella effectively illustrates benefits of collaborative learning as she discusses teamwork,

> In a team, learning is enhanced by peers. We know that peers hold significant authority with adults, even more authority than teachers. Peers often have similar experiences. They can challenge one another in ways a teacher cannot. Peers create safety for the learner who is struggling with complex concepts, skills, or attitudes. I have seen significant mentoring go on in teams: peers helping one another, often with surprising clarity, tenderness, and skills. (p. 23)

As adults explore relationships with others, they gain new strategies for learning that include communication, appreciation, cooperation, negotiation, and conflict resolution. Such activities can release the power of collaborative skills for lifelong learning and ongoing professional development that are encountered through living and learning in adulthood.

This overview of adult learning principles from the literature provides a context for determining if and how the principles are implemented in NCCTE standards and the related exemplary and promising career and technical education programs.

CASE STUDY–NCCTE PROGRAM—PHASE ONE

NCCTE Program Background

The NCCTE is a nonprofit organization that represents leaders of some of the nation's premier providers of career and technical education and their instructors, administrators, and counselors. Additionally, the consortium includes a national advisory council of leading experts, internationally recognized consultants, and other collaborating institutions, agencies, and organizations. The vision of the NCCTE's national research and dissemination centers states, "as primary sources of research-based information, [the Centers] will significantly affect the quality of knowledge and understanding necessary to advance career and technical education in the United States" (NCCTE, 2003, para. 1).

METHOD AND ANALYSIS

Method

This research was pursued as a qualitative case study. It examines the prevalence of specific categories, or principles, within the NCCTE program. The method of document review and interview of a lead administrator was selected in order to provide a baseline and context of data for the alter study in which several exemplar CTE programs would be studied. Rather than just study the schools, the research deemed it important to gain fuller background about the values, mission, goals and perspectives of the organization.

Procedures

The NCCTE documents and interview of the co-director of the organization were used to collect data about the NCCTE program. Documents were obtained via mail after the interview and others were available on the Internet and were reviewed and analyzed prior to the interview. These documents described the NCCTE organizational program's mission, purpose, reports, publications, and history. They were obtained from NCCTE to examine the awards program in general, and most specifically the standards, or outstanding practices, upon which prospective career and technical education program applications are assessed.

The interview with one of the codirectors of the program was prearranged, and while certain questions were predetermined for the discussion, the follow-ups were also expected. The interview was conducted by phone. Purposes of the interview included: (1) to gather more first hand perspectives in-depth background about NCCTE, (2) to determine the basic educational orientation of the NCCTE program, (3) to gain an overview of the awarded programs and (4) check the categories of adult learning principles, which the researcher had identified from the literature with the interviewee. Results of this interview would guide the final development of categories to be used in the school CTE program leader interview protocol and coding protocol for school CTE program documents.

Analysis

The researcher gathered, examined, categorized, coded, and tabulated the data using these protocols (Yin, 2003). In these ways the coding was created through a process grounded in both the literature of adult learning and the context of NCCTE Exemplary and Promising Programs initiative. This process provided a focused, or bounded, approach to examining the vast possibilities of data collection and analysis for the stated research questions (Creswell, 1998; Yin, 2003).

FINDINGS: STANDARDS AND ADULT LEARNING

The NCCTE's outstanding standards for exemplary and promising status in career and technical education include 15 categories: access and inclusiveness, align with standards, certification and credentialing, curriculum reform, evaluation and continuous improvement, placement and retention, partnerships, professional development, program and instructional delivery, program and institutional leadership, technology enhancements, transition options, student development and leadership, sustainability and finances, and systematic and whole school reform (NCCTE, 2002). While nearly half of these standards are organizationally oriented, many also address the planning and delivery of teaching and learning. It is from among these guidelines that the linkages with adult learning principles become evident.

The adult learning principles were not present in every one of the NCCTE practices. This finding confirms expectations that the NCCTE program review has additional purposes while also exemplifying adult learning principles. Table 7.1 provides a matrix of the principles and practices determined in this analysis and this section describes how the NCCTE program demonstrates each principle within the 15 NCCTE categories.

Learning for Application

Direct linkages from the following NCCTE practices to learning for application are evident. *Alignment with standards* by the NCCTE's definition is based on what is effective in the workplace. *Certification and credentialing* make concrete the purposes of career and technology programs to

**Table 7.1.   Principles and Practices Identified Among
NCCTE Exemplary and Promising Programs
Outstanding Practices Standards***

Learning Principles**	NCCTE Outstanding Practices Standards*
Learning for application	• Align with standards • Certification and credentialing • Curriculum reform • Placement and retention • Technology enhancements
Involving learners in active learning	• Curriculum reform
Building on learners' experience	• Program and instructional delivery
Cultivating self-directed learning	• Curriculum reform • Student development and leadership
Cultivating collaborative skills	• Partnerships
Building a climate of respect, encouragement, and/or support	• Partnerships
Involving learners in planning	• Student development and leadership
**Adult learning principle identified as parallel CTE principle- based on interview with NCTE interview and Dr. King's expertise of adult education learning (King, 2005)	* Selected from, the 15 NCCTE practice standards categories are: access and inclusiveness, align with standards, certification and credentialing, curriculum reform, evaluation and continuous improvement, placement and retention, partnerships, professional development, program and instructional delivery, program and institutional leadership, technology enhancements, transition options, student development and leadership, sustainability and finances, and systematic and whole school reform (NCCTE, 2002)

develop skills that are directed to application in the designated area. *Curriculum reform* specifically encourages problem-based learning that is one example of learning for application. *Placement and retention* makes explicit the close coordination of curriculum and student learning for preparation for the workplace. And finally *technology enhancements* demonstrate learning for application as they ensure that students can experience and gain proficiency in using current technologies.

Involving Learners in Active Learning

The emphasis of *curriculum reform* supports problem-based learning. Such activities can incorporate several modes of active learning as learners engage in problem solving, critical thinking, collaborative learning, research, and planning. Rather than an archetype, authoritarian, teacher-centered classroom, students should participate actively in discovering, interacting, analyzing, and applying their learning.

Building on Learners' Experience

This principle is evident in developing *program delivery, instructional delivery,* and *transition options* when learners' experience, knowledge, and skill are assessed to plan their learning. This emphasis is seen not only in current programs of study, but also for the purpose of effectively moving among educational programs and institutions where applicable. Building on learners' experience reduces redundant learning experiences, wasted time and resources, and validates and further progresses learners on continuous pathways toward their educational and vocational goals.

Cultivating Self-Directed Learning

The standard for *student development and leadership* articulates the goal of learners developing experience and confidence as leaders of their own learning and among their peers. *Curriculum reform* also supports this principle as learners engage in problem solving much like they will in the workplace and further cultivates self-directed learning perspectives and experience. The independence and confidence the learners gain within their learning, organization, and field lay the practical groundwork for taking charge of their own learning as they continue to grow within their professional and personal skills in the future.

Cultivating Collaborative Skills

Organizational partnerships provide the opportunity to demonstrate collaboration within professional settings to the learners. Such collaboration can demonstrate effective and appropriate communication, collegial support, negotiation, and problem-solving within and among groups.

Building a Climate of Respect

Partnerships also provide learners experience with prospective employers in real-life environments. Professional respect may be demonstrated in the classroom and reinforced with peers and superiors in work placement assignments. These experiences can have important results in guiding learners in how to recognize and facilitate respect and support.

Involving Learners in Planning

Opportunities for *student development and leadership* engage learners in planning their education and careers. Even when learners do not have much choice among courses in a closely specified program, these development and leadership experiences can afford participation in other aspects of their educational planning for a class, the organization, and/or themselves. Gaining experience in planning one's career and including ongoing professional development in it are important gains from participating in such programs.

In addition to these principles being evident in many of the specific NCCTE standards, standard number nine, *program and instructional delivery*, is a major guideline that supports "program and instructional approaches that have been proven to work" (NCCTE, 2002). Certainly the adult learning literature can provide a valuable, rigorous, and reputable resource of educational philosophy, curriculum theory, learning theory, program planning, and assessment and evaluation to build program, classroom, and student learning experiences. This standard can provide an overarching rationale for using adult learning principles in career and technical education.

Standard number 12, *transition options*, articulates the need to build "linkages between secondary and postsecondary education" so that barriers will not arise and remediation will not be needed (NCCTE, 2002). This standard explicitly states the thesis of this research and demonstrates that high standards for career and technical education represent the need and benefits of bridging the compulsory education vs. higher education (K-16) gap. Indeed, the twelfth standard indicates that programs should plan to bridge this gap directly through organizational and curricular planning.

Based on how the adult learning principles are represented in the NCCTE standards, a perspective of "bridging the compulsory education versus higher education (K-16) gap" is evident in this program. Looking to career and technical programs for examples and recommendations in pursuing both of these points is consistent with their purposes. In these ways the fundamental framework of the research problem and questions is confirmed in these data.

CASE STUDY-INDIVIDUAL NCCTE PROGRAMS—PHASE TWO

Individual Programs Background Now Being Studied

As stated, this study also examined career and technical programs that had been cited by NCCTE as *exemplary* or *promising* based on the NCCTE's stated standards. Programs submitted applications to apply for this status and NCCTE examiners made site visits to the finalist programs. Such programs included both secondary and postsecondary programs. They are representative of programs across the U.S.A. and include awardees for the years 2000 and 2001. Materials about the programs were gathered via NCCTE documents and their Web site.

CTE School Program Participants

Participants in the study included both individuals who were interviewed and programs that were studied. Four interviews were conducted. All of these participants were instructors in their programs, while two were also directors. Three of the programs represented in the interviews were from the exemplary category and one was from the promising category. The programs were located in Virginia, Phoenix, and two were in Oklahoma. These programs ranged in the number of students from 23 to 2,500 and faculty numbering from 1 to 49. All of the programs had postsecondary learners, while two also had secondary learners enrolled. Three specific programs of study were identified: certified network administrator (CNA), database management, and graphic design. The remaining program had many career and technical areas including: auto body, banking/retail, computer technology programs, computerized office programs, facilities and maintenance, food preparation, medical assistant, machine trades, meat cutting, nursing, printing trades, and welding.

Data regarding 30 programs were reviewed via program documents, with 23 programs for the year 2000 and 7 for 2001. Additionally, among these programs 7 had been awarded exemplary status and 23 awarded promising. Several of these programs served more than one constituency of learners so that the distribution was secondary learners, 20 (66.7%), adult learners, 10 (33.3%), and postsecondary learners, 10 (33.3%). Occupational areas of these 30 programs were many and represent the following categories: automotive, business and marketing, construction, culinary arts, education, finance, health services (e.g., nursing, EMT, surgical technician), hospitality and tourism, industrial maintenance, interior design, technical computer-related, manufacturing, office technologies, and transportation,

METHOD

Selection for Phase Two

The programs included in the initial review included for this study were all of those receiving awards in 2000 and 2001 for which sufficient data were available. Regarding the phone interviews, these were conducted with one of the codirectors of the NCCTE program to confirm and extend the initial assessment and analysis of the award program and purposes. These interviews also provided further insight into programs that had both secondary and postsecondary programs. Recommendation by the codirector concurred with the preliminary findings to indicate four programs to be interviewed in-depth in the *second phase of the study.* Purposely the selection of interviewees was not random, as the aim was to determine best practice from which to build recommendations.

Data Collection Phase Two

Data was gathered through published documents, questionnaires, and interviews. Following preliminary evaluation of these NCCTE published documents, the interview with the NCCTE program codirector was conducted, and semistructured interviews were conducted with each of the four career and technical education programs. All interviews were transcribed.

These interviews and questionnaires not only address whether programs used adult learning principles, they also asked for examples of how they are used. In addition, realizing that these programs represented valuable experience in the field of secondary and postsecondary education, the interviewees were asked directly what they perceived as similarities and differences among such learners. Additionally, rather than solely relying on the "outside" researcher to determine recommendations, building upon best practice and educational expertise, those questioned were also asked for recommendations. In this way the case study included self-analysis and reflective practice and could be substantially rooted in not only adult learning theory, but also grounded in career and technical education experience.

Data Analysis Phase Two

Qualitative analysis of this case study included coding by themes of adult learner characteristics and principles developed from the literature (Creswell, 1998). Additionally, the limited quantitative data were evaluated for frequencies, and other basic descriptive statistics. As with many case studies this research included examining, categorizing, tabulating, and recombining the qualitative and quantitative data (Yin, 2003) to build an understanding of both the NCCTE program and a selective sample of program awardees.

FINDINGS AND DISCUSSION–INTERVIEWS—PHASE TWO

Through the interviews it was again evident that the adult learning principles that had been identified in the literature and recognized in the NCCTE standards were also evident within the individual programs. Four basic trends were recognized in the interviews and program documents. First, in-depth discussions revealed that these four programs used the learning principles frequently. Second, the postsecondary programs indicated use of more of the learning principles than the secondary. Third, programs with classes where secondary and postsecondary learners worked together demonstrated the viability of using the adult learning principles with secondary students in this context. Finally, the emphasis in career and technical education programs on softskills was recognized and found to be consistent with the use of adult learning principles. Each of these observations will be discussed in this section.

Use of Adult Learning Principles

The interviews offered the opportunity to learn whether program leaders recognized the same principles in their programs and if so, how these principles were operationalized. Table 7.2 presents these findings with the mean rating and standard deviation on a 1-5 Likert scale in which 1 is "Never" and 5 is "Always."

Application

The interviews revealed that all of the programs, 100%, used "learning for application" as a major theme of their learning experiences and rated

Table 7.3. Frequency of Learning Principles Used Based on Interviews

Learning Principles	M	SD	Examples
Learning for application	5.00	.00	• Build network from donated computers • Do work for companies • Project-based assignments • Simulate the work environment and culture • Real-life case study examples to apply their learning
Involving learners in active learning	4.875	.25	• Hands-on • Simulations • Create projects • Field trips • Case studies
Building on learners' experience	4.75	.50	• Build on previous courses • Assess technology skills upon entrance • Evaluate skills. • Determine what learners need
Cultivating self-directed learning	4.75	.50	• Self-paced program • Monthly progress reports by the students • Critical thinking skills used to solve problems • Self-paced with parameters as guides
Cultivating collaborative skills	4.50	1.00	• Team projects • Critique and help one another constantly • Teams solve case studies • Some communication workshops
Building a climate of respect, encouragement, and/or support	4.50	.58	• Emphasize respect in the classroom and workplace • Collaboration and work as peers-colleagues • Taking into consideration interests and needs of learners throughout courses • Monthly presentations by students in which they support and encourage one another • Celebration of certification awards
Involving learners in planning	4.25	.50	• Students set target dates • Students review course objectives and suggest assignments, special speakers, and content • Student suggestions regarding the curriculum • Students identify their progress and needs

Note: ($N = 4$ individuals each representing a program of more than 15, therefore the group characteristics are indicative of approximately $n = 60$).

it as "5/Always." Indeed, adult, vocational, and career education has been grounded in this principle in the literature. Many initiatives have emerged from the need to explicitly integrated into application. However, it was confirmation and validation to see that these programs incorporated learning for application through simulated environments, true-to-life projects, and actual commerce through either program/school-based services or work in conjunction with local businesses.

Several quotes demonstrate the primary role of application in these programs.

> I use a lot of project based [activities]. That's how I test my students' project based tests. For example, you may have noticed on the Web site, we are dealing with web design. We actually take on Web sites that need to be developed as community service for nonprofits or some businesses and they pay or donate money to the student organization. But the students actually develop a real project as their test project, instead of taking a written test, and they do take online certification tests for certification in the software. But I use projects to assess them and to help them build their portfolios at the same time.

> Several of our programs also are used for trade. That is, you see people coming in here to pick up their meat orders. In our meat-cutting program they actually work on taking and filling orders. So the students get to see what it is really like.

> I think one [recommendation] is that at least having someone in the faculty who has come from that industry, rather than just from the academic [realm]. Simulate the business environment as closely as possible. This is applied learning, so everything needs to be tied back [to application].

> In this program they might be sent by their employer or a government agency to obtain certain skills and proficiencies. So what we do in the classroom has to be directly connected to application.... All the training is hands-on, from making posters in printing to simulations of other work assignments.

Active Learning

Regarding "involving learners in active learning," the programs again scored this very high on the scale ($M = 4.875$) and with little variation in scores ($SD = .25$). Examples of active learning illustrate that common teaching methods used in career and technical settings include several of these learning principles simultaneously. Respondents cited hands-on projects, simulations, project development, case studies, and field trips as opportunities for active learning. This practice is seen in the following quotes:

> For example, one of the things that the students here just finished [demonstrates active learning.] We had 30 donated computers and what the

students did was based upon previous things that they had learned and throughout the last year and a half. They had to build the network from the computers, make the computers work, create the network cables, you know, make the whole thing come together.

I try to do questioning and elaboration types of things as we're kind of exploring. Again, I have the luxury of having a small enough class. I only have 16 students in a session. I can have a personal rapport, it's hard to do that if you have 200 students. I can question them as to their understanding, but also take it a step farther with elaboration and say, "How would you apply this?" So those are two active learning techniques. Obviously they do hands-on and practice and things. We have a guest speaker or take a tour and they get to see the application of the technology toward particular business objectives.

Learner Experience

Regarding "building on learners' experience" three out of the four interviewees rated this item "5/Always" and found it to be an integral part of their program. Programs were consistent in evaluating the students' skills when coming into the programs and at least one program allowed students to "place out" of requirements or take course substitutions if learners demonstrated knowledge and proficiency. As illustrated in the following quotes, these program directors did not mention the use of techniques to draw out experience from the learners as some adult education techniques employ, but instead mostly mentioned course placement.

And so I try [to] employ different learning strategies that are appropriate for them and one of the things that I try to use the most in that respect is the use of analogies. [Based on] what kind of background that they have, if their background is business, then I might try to use a different analogy than if their background is science or engineering. As much as I, because some of the time I can't help them with an analogy.... I also try to give them case studies where the technology would be used. If they're coming from a different discipline then I will try to think of case studies or examples where the technology that they're learning would be applied to the profession that they came from. I've had everything from retired teachers to school counselors, to new college graduates with degrees in mathematics and physics to engineering, and I've had kind of a wide variety of students, so I try to relate it in that respect to maybe the discipline they are coming from.

Primarily what I just try to use is that I sit down with each student when they begin the program and kind of ascertain at least a little bit about what their motivation is for entering the program and what their background is, both professional and personal.

A lot of high schools here do what is called keyboarding or IS programs, where they're kind of introduced to desktop applications, like the (MS) Office programs. So what we really do is that we take that as the starting point. The students that come into my program generally don't come in without any background at all. So I'm taking what computer work they have already learned and we go from there [identifying]…standards of learning, plus [what they have learned] from high school.

Self-Directed Learning

Respondents rated "self-directed learning" at the maximum, "5/ Always," three out of four times. More importantly the ways that they worked to cultivate this characteristic were insightful. Some programs were entirely based on a self-paced format, used self-paced methods for some activities, and combined this approach with providing parameters and guidelines for the learners to be able to judge their own progress. While another program had the students provide a monthly-progress report of all of their work. One respondent also recognized that their work in developing critical thinking skills to solve problems was in fact cultivating self-directed learning. This area especially leads toward building patterns for lifelong learning. While they may not always be in formal classroom learning settings, adults are continually engaged in learning across the lifespan in both professional and personal arenas. Building strategies and a mindset about learning that incorporates self-directedness certainly lays the groundwork for lifelong learning perspectives and habits. The following quote from one interviewee illustrates self directed learning in the career and technical education context,

> [Ours is a] self-directed, self-paced program, so I don't have students in the same place at the same time. [For instance,] 5 in Photoshop, 2 in HTML, it depends on the student and how quickly they learn. They are required to keep a calendar that shows what they complete each day which they submit to me at the end of each month for a grade. That's like a time card for them; it helps them set a target date on that, helps them keep on track. [The] student sets the target date, based on my outline for them, a plan of study which shows them how many hours or weeks for each unit that they have to complete that.

Collaborative Learning

Most of the programs used "collaborative learning" in significant ways. One program however volunteered that they had plans to do more in this area. This fact primarily contributed to the large variance evident in the standard deviation of 1.00. In the following interview excerpt, one participant reveals how important collaborative learning is for her program's setting and plans to incorporate more in it,

> That's something [collaborative groups] in which we could stand to do some improvement. And in fact, it's interesting- that's one of the things I have felt. Having individualized instruction, sometimes that makes group projects more difficult. They do already attend formalized, professional workshops in concepts like teamwork and resume writing ... and communication workshops, but all students attend that. They attend in-house resume writing workshop and job interviewing workshops and also attend customer service workshops which is also in-house from a variety of sources.... This semester I am going to require every student to participate in a group project that's related to the learning that they are doing. So this is a pilot semester for that because I feel like that is something that has really been missing. So we do have that with a couple of the projects that we're running now, and by the end of the semester, every student will have had an opportunity to participate in a group project, and they will last anywhere from 4 weeks to 8 weeks depending on the project.

Team projects and small groups appeared in each program as techniques. However, one program articulated the strategy that they used to have learners constantly responsible to critique and assist each other; this practice was embedded within the concept parallel to field functions in the workplace. Additionally, one program had special workshops on communication and team building activities; again this formal approach simulates workplace experiences of human resources activities. Certainly, these programs had identified the need for collaborative experience and skills in the workplace and were incorporating them in the learning experiences. The following quotes clearly illustrate this connection,

> In the auto body program students are assigned to groups that they work in on a continual basis. This provides realistic experience of how they will work in their careers.

> Constant collaboration in the classroom, standing over another, critiquing their work, helping someone with something they've already learned, suggesting different ideas, they work on a lot of different projects together.

> I have them set up in groups of 4 so that they can actually work as a team in certain situations we try to do building the network-they were assigned groups-that was a group project. They have to work in teams to figure it out. I'll give someone an example of a problem I worked on or someone else had

and I say to the team, OK you need to figure this out. So they work in small groups or groups of 4 and occasionally with the class as a whole.

Climate

The practice of "building a climate of respect, encouragement, and/or support" was originally intended to capture the relationship among instructors and learners. Instead many of the respondents highlighted the cultivation of respect among the learners and upon further examination they had brought forth a valid point. Teachers and learners create the learning environment; therefore, the relationships, interactions, and communication among the learners can be very instrumental in setting the tone. Examples of working toward such a climate included conducting coursework in teams and small groups, having monthly presentations in which students could gain skill and confidence as the class supported their efforts, and celebrating the achievements of learners. The respondents revealed a real sense of individuals' needs in this area.

> I think that one [example of respect and support among] the students is when they present their monthly technology reports to each other, they don't really critique at the end of that; it's more about getting people to relax and so we all clap at the end of that. Regardless of how good or bad it was. They are encouraged to work with each other. So that if I'm not available, because I'm working with somebody else. They are encouraged to work with each other so that everybody kind of knows everybody, even on a personal level.... When students pass their certifications; an important point nearing the completion, they are treated to lunch. We try to support and reward as well.

Learners in Planning

Regarding "involving learners in planning," the respondents indicated this had the lowest score ($M = 4.25$, $SD = .50$). While students participated in setting personal target dates and goals, it was not customary for them to directly contribute to the curriculum decisions. A striking exception to this observation is evident in one program in which the learners review objectives for the courses and make suggestions about content, activities, and assignments. The autonomy of the learners in this format really represented a different level of their involvement in and responsibility for their learning. It may be observed that such learner-centered planning is again providing a basis from which learners may easily develop lifelong learning skills. The two quotes provided here illustrate ways that programs are incorporating learner participation in planning.

> They went in there as a team and collaboratively [decided] what assignment could they be given this year. And what things did they want to know about that they think would help them. And they actually came up with homework assignments and I said don't be afraid that I am going to overload you; I would rather give you a relevant assignment than give you busy work. So they actually came up with suggestions about assignments and also kinds of companies that they would like to see speakers come from and things like that.

> We provide for custom planning of their education. Their plan might be based on a learning disability or it could be on employer's goals for them. So although they are not involved in curricular planning, they are involved in instructional planning for themselves.

FINDINGS AND DISCUSSION–PROGRAM DOCUMENTS

The evaluation of the program description documents revealed similar rankings of the learning principles (see Table 7.3.) "Learning for application" was certainly the predominate characteristic identified from the descriptions of the programs as 86.7% of the programs highlighted it. "Active learning" was also a prominent characteristic closely followed by "collaborative learning skills" and "self-directed learning." Many of these programs described careers and skills learners gain from the programs. In addition, they described how the learning proceeds. It is expected that these purposes may have brought some principles to light more frequently than others. However, it is noticeable that learners' planning and

Table 7.3.   Frequency of Learning Principles Used Based on Documents

Learning Principles	*N yes*	*%*
Learning for application	26	86.7
Involving learners in active learning	10	33.3
Cultivating collaborative skills	8	26.7
Cultivating self-directed learning	7	23.3
Building a climate of respect, encouragement, and/ or support	4	13.3
Involving learners in planning	4	13.3
Building on learners' experience	3	10

$N = 30$

experience, where they would be more fundamentally involved in the direction of the on-going learning experience, were less often mentioned. It must also be remembered that these principles were identified in documents that publicly described the programs in contrast to the interviewer being able to query respondents regarding responses to specific inquiries. This difference certainly accounts for the wide difference in citation of items, however remarkably the ranking of them remained nearly constant. This fact likely speaks to the likelihood that these principles are indeed consistent within career and technical education as it is currently practiced.

Postsecondary and Secondary Comparison

Regarding the identification of adult learning principles postsecondary and adult programs averaged 2.50 indicators per program compared to secondary programs averaging 1.85. The distribution of the principles was also insightful as they followed nearly the same ranking order as the previous data (see Table 7.4.).

Consistent with the evaluation across all programs, "learning for application" was the clear leader at 90% in secondary programs and 80% in adult programs. The next tier of responses included active learning, self-directed learning, and collaborative learning competing for second, third, and fourth rankings. Following fourth place, there was much variation. In the adult and postsecondary programs, "involving learners in planning" was 30% and "building a climate of respect" and "building on experience"

Table 7.4. Comparison of Frequency of Adult Learning Principles Comparing Programs

Learning Principles	Adult and Postsecondary Programs (N = 10)		Secondary Programs (N = 20)	
	N yes	%	N yes	%
Learning for application	8	80	18	90
Involving learners in active learning	5	50	5	25
Cultivating collaborative skills	4	40	4	20
Involving learners in planning	3	30	1	5
Building a climate of respect, encouragement, and/or support	2	20	2	10
Building on learners' experience	2	20	1	5
Cultivating self-directed learning	1	10	6	30

N = 30

were 20% with "self-directed learning" coming in last at 10%. In contrast, secondary programs rated "climate of respect" 10%, and both "involving learners in planning" and "building on learners' experience" 5%. Clearly the biggest variations were the greater percentage range of the principles being indicated in the adult and postsecondary programs and the higher ranking for "self-directed learning" in the secondary programs.

FINDINGS AND DISCUSSION–ADDITIONAL FINDINGS

Application to Secondary Students

In the interviews, the programs that merged both secondary and postsecondary learners in the same classroom explicitly demonstrated the viability of using adult learning principles with secondary students in this context. As documented in the following quote, those program representatives stated that the presence of the adults in the classroom raised the level of professionalism and seriousness about studies.

> It's [having adults and secondary together] an advantage instead of a disadvantage, and the reason why is because adults help to stabilize the classroom and my younger students are able to learn from them -I guess a lot of "adult" characteristics. And the adults pick up a lot of creativity from the high school students as well. They'll be working on a design that is specifically for a younger audience, and so they will go to the high school students and get tips on what is hip; [they get] input from them. It's impressive when you watch them interact. There's no division at all as far as adults and high school students are concerned. It is a learning experience for both. I always think adults come with a lot more baggage than high school students, but that's not always true, because of the harsh environments that the high school students are being raised in. They don't have family stability and this offers a stability that they can come to each day. I have real high attendance, very few problems with absences.

> I think in many situations there is a great advantage to having the high school and adult students mixed. We see that a lot. Most of our programs have high school students. High school students can learn a great deal from the adult students, in mentor-type relationships. Sometimes the high school students get on the adult students' nerves. They work well together; by and large it's beneficial to have a mixture.

The greater emphasis on learning for application, success in the workplace, and learner responsibility and involvement that we are accustomed to identifying with postsecondary career and technical education can be used with benefit among secondary learners. Rather than having a traditional teacher-centered learning environment throughout secondary studies, it may well benefit the learners by moving them toward perspectives and practices that will more closely resemble postsecondary career and technical education. Instead of a disjuncture as learners exit one system and enter the next, a more seamless transition could easily benefit learners immediately and in their future studies and work.

Softskills

It also became evident that these programs not only emphasized technical workplace skills, but also "soft skills," variously defined as workplace basic skills, employability skills, or generic skills, "the general skills that most workplaces require" (Brown, 2002) include communication skills, appropriate workplace behavior and dress, and project management, to name a few examples. Softskills are recognized as being instrumental in contributing to success in the workplace. These programs recognized this widely held perspective and incorporated them in many different ways-some programs did this more formally than others by having formal lessons and workshops on softskill topics. Other programs used relationships as a primary way of communicating softskill learning as instructors coached learners about etiquette, appropriateness, habits, protocol, and expectations through conversation, modeling, mentoring, and discussion. The learning principles that were recognized in this research also are consistent with softskills in that learning for application, collaborative learning, self-directed learning, and respect are all characteristics that do not just include technical knowledge. As the following quotes demonstrate, softskills were emphasized as a characteristic of these successful career and technical programs.

> Softskills are integral; our student organization-Skills USA [is conducted] every Wednesday-VICA-in my program and 20 percent of their grade is tied to their involvement in that. I require every one of my students to compete in a leadership contest and then those who qualify for the leadership contest (5) compete at the national level and it's considered a privilege. It's additional too. We placed in nationals last year - 10 students to nationals who placed first at state, 1 placed 5, and others in the top 3. They work so closely in teams with that. [They] also work with developing resumes. Guest speakers come in and speak and talk to them about what it takes to be a good employee. I have a video library that I use and give them a sheet of paper when they go to watch it and they have to fill it in at the end on time management. Teamwork skills and "How to succeed in job interviews" complement that. [They also use the] Professional Development Plan-5

different books that help them assess career goals and help them reach those goals.

One of the things we focus on is softskills and in computer networks that is customer service. So in order to know [technical skills] by the end of the two years and work with customers I expect them to treat each other in that manner. They are not allowed to cuss and they aren't allowed to put anyone down. We work on that very, very hard. They have dress up days; every Tuesday where they speak and they have to be not only respectful to the speaker, they have to turn off their monitors while the speaker is speaking. Also, if someone runs into trouble, they are expected to help bail each other out. We're not going to fail an individual; we are all going to fail. So we work on that a lot.

You could go to a store or restaurant, and it's the same in business- if people don't understand you, can't read you work, or you don't treat them respect-fully, you are not going to get or will have trouble keeping a job. You can be a great technician and super smart, but if you don't come to work on time, dressed appropriately [you will have problems]. I don't let tardies go, [these are] big etiquette issues.

STUDY LIMITATIONS

Case study limitations often include small sample sizes, potentially highly individualized settings, and the limited extent to which they may be generalized (Creswell, 1998; Yin, 2003). With this understanding, this study presents a basis to promote further discussion and research about how adult learning principles can be beneficially used in second-ary and postsecondary career and technology education settings based on the success of these programs. The concepts presented are an extended example of the use of adult learning principles within these specific contexts and settings and are not intended to be generalizable to all settings. These findings provide a basis for further consideration, discussion, and research.

IMPLICATIONS FOR A COMPULSORY VERSUS
HIGHER EDUCATION (K-16) BRIDGE

What does this research show us about the composition and construction of a compulsory vs. higher education (K-16) bridge based on the strength of career and technical education? As we compare the adult education lit-erature and the other findings of this study, what is the meaning for spanning the compulsory vs. higher education (K-16) gap? This research helps inform and delineate a framework for addressing these questions and relevant teaching and learning issues and trends.

Embedded in a grounded set of adult learning principles from the literature, this research study demonstrates several major implications that are connected: (1) principles of adult learning that can be contextually applied, (2) a vision of lifelong learning and ongoing professional development that can be cultivated earlier in learners' education, and (3) a focus on softskills in addition to technical or academic knowledge and skills.

Adult Learning

Regarding the adult learning principles, a clearly prominent emphasis is placed on application of learning and a tandem simulation of the workplace that emerge as major themes over and again in the NCCTE standards and programs. These data remind us that we need to point young or older adults toward how their learning fits into their learning and career needs and their world. Other programs can benefit by engaging their learners in active learning and simulations of and active participation in workplace projects and environments.

Vision

Closely ranked to these major points are the needs to build on learners' experience, cultivate self-directed learning, and learn collaborative skills. These strategies may be seen as laying groundwork for ongoing professional development and lifelong learning. As learners experience the freedom, ownership, and motivation of learning that meets their needs and includes autonomy and collaboration at various times, a wider spectrum of learning possibilities are experienced. The emphases and curriculum of these programs result in a vision or expectation of ongoing professional development, and more broadly, lifelong learning. Secondary education programs can benefit by introducing this perspective earlier to young adults so they begin to see the vast extension and application of learning into their futures. Revealing the relevance and continuity of their current learning to their adult lives can likely have powerful possibilities for other secondary learners like it does for career and technical education learners.

Softskills

Finally, not just technical skill and knowledge were needed, but also "softskills" were incorporated in these programs. In an age of standards-based teaching and learning, we need to consider how we are accounting for valuable softskills in these standards and in our evaluation of learning. So often our secondary education becomes focused on achievement tests and college placement, but career and technical education provide us with some new considerations. How are we guiding learners in integrating their technical and content knowledge and skill with their perspective, attitudes, behavior, and work? Career and technical education programs provide a vivid lesson that softskills can be interwoven into the curriculum and extracurricular activities alike. By bridging content knowledge with the learner's attitudes, behaviors, and other affective attributes, these programs and learners can experience many benefits including increased learner motivation, an elevated, "professional" classroom climate, increased transfer of learning, more successful work placement assignments, development of leadership and teamwork skills, and development of perspectives of a career rather than a more short-sighted "job."

RECOMMENDATIONS FOR BUILDING A STRONGER COMPULSORY VERSUS HIGHER EDUCATION (K-16) BRIDGE

As we consider the implications of this research, several recommendations emerge regarding how career and technical education can inform and strengthen a compulsory vs. higher education (K-16) bridge. Three areas of recommendation may be identified, those for educators, curriculum, and learners. These recommendations apply not only to secondary schools and educators, but also to career and technical programs. The professional development of educators is the cornerstone to success in this process. Through professional development we have the opportunity to introduce adult learning principles and strategies to a constituency who may not have been exposed before to them in terms of how they apply to their learners. Such professional development could take the form of not just lecture style presentations, but instead, interactive discussions, case studies, problem and project-based activities, reflective practice, and modeling the intersection of adult learning practices across the contexts of CTE (King, 2002, 2005; Lawler & King, 2000). Professional development can provide opportunities to discuss the meaning of lifelong learning and determine how to introduce it to their learners; likewise educators can consider and develop strategies for integrating softskills into their class experiences. By engaging educators in discussing these findings, they can work toward assessing and reflecting on what their classes and programs currently do and what else is possible. Critical to implementation is that the element that they make plans to operationalize what they have learned through these activities and determine what needs to be done.

Regarding the curriculum, instructors and administrators can work toward not only learning about the principles and strategies, but also individually and collaboratively developing curriculum for their classes and across programs that reflect these findings. Even if an educational institution does not have a specialized career and technical program, their courses can be aimed to prepare students to become self-directed learners so that they can see application of their learning to contexts beyond the classroom. For instance, in our urban setting cultivating a vision of future "careers" for K-12 students is a critical shift from what they may have in their neighborhoods. Even without a CTE program, educators can integrate content into the traditional curriculum that discusses careers and activities build skills that provide pre-career foundations for these students (King, 2007). Specifically, educators can determine the best ways to add or enhance the use of learning for application, active learning, collaborative learning, self-directed learning, building on learner experience, lifelong learning, and softskills in their curriculum. They can explore new standards, new curricular materials, and new objectives and goals that might extend what they are already doing or bring them into new areas.

Finally, educators can also look at what may be accomplished regarding the students' involvement. How can they be involved in the planning process? For instance how can they begin to experience taking some responsibility for the planning of their learning? Such a step would open wider the door to self-directed learning, learner responsibility, and perspectives of lifelong learning. Recommendations to accomplish this could be programmatic: student representatives on program advisory boards, extracurricular: student participation and leadership in appropriate professional associations, or course specific: student participation in determining course goals, learning activities, and timetables. These are responsibilities that they will soon encounter as they cross the gap from secondary to postsecondary education and the workplace. The issue is how to best prepare them by building a bridge of learning experiences that reflects their need to shoulder these responsibilities successfully.

Each of these recommendations provides vibrant opportunities to reconsider "business as usual" and determine how secondary and postsecondary education might bridge the compulsory versus higher education (K-16) gap. Examining secondary and postsecondary education from the perspective of career and technical education through a lens of adult learning results in recommendations for educators, learners, and the curriculum. Educators today have the opportunity to refine or redefine their educational objectives based on these findings. Educational institutions hold the possibility of creating a compulsory versus higher education (K-16) transition that is smoother so that learners' gains have the potential to be magnified and enduring. Beyond test scores and job placement, what are we doing to introduce learners to a culture of self-directed learning and a perspective of lifelong learning? These recommendations can help us addresses this critical question.

FUTURE STUDY OF THE COMPULSORY EDUCATION VERSUS HIGHER EDUCATION (K-16) GAP

Many more questions for research emerge as we continue to consider how career and technical education can assist in bridging the compulsory vs. higher education (K-16) gap. Further research can focus on, how effectively do these principles and practices transition to the secondary context? How can these findings further inform practice in technical education, workplace learning, higher and further education? What adaptations work in different contextual and content areas? What additional benefits emerge as learners engage in taking increased responsibility for their learning? What impact does a perspective of lifelong learning and ongoing professional development have on learners immediately and as they progress in their work and learning through their adult years? What other challenges in secondary and postsecondary education might be addressed by bridging the compulsory vs. higher education (K-16) gap in these ways? As secondary education implements some of these changes, what complementary responses do we learn are needed in technical education, workplace learning, and postsecondary education? The desire is to continuously move ahead educational practice, theory, and research so that we can address the challenges facing our learners and our institutions. Addressing this gap through lessons learned from career and technical education does not provide final, definitive answers; instead it outlines a research-based framework for our efforts and reveals many more opportunities for us to explore.

REFERENCES

Bragg, D. D., & Reger, W. (2002). *New lessons about tech prep implementation.* St. Paul, MN: National Research Center for Career and Technical Education.

Brown, B. L. (1999). *Vocational certificates and college degrees, ERIC Digest No. 212*. Columbus, OH: ERIC Clearinghouse on Adult, Career, and Vocational Education. (ERIC Document Reproduction Service No. ED 434 248) Retrieved May 1, 2007 from http://eric.ed.gov/ERICDocs/data/ericdocs2/content_storage_01/0000000b/80/2a/2e/c3.pdf

Brown, B. L. (2002). *Generic skills in career and technical education; Myths and realities, No. 22*. Columbus, OH: ERIC Clearinghouse on Adult, Career, and Vocational Education. (ERIC Document Reproduction Service No. ED 472 363) Retrieved May 1, 2007 from http://eric.ed.gov/ERICDocs/data/ericdocs2/content_storage_01/0000000b/80/28/12/9c.pdf

Caffarella, R. S. (2002). *Planning programs for adult learners: A practical guide for educators, trainers, and staff developers* (2nd ed.). San Francisco: Jossey-Bass.

Castellano, M., Stringfield, S., & Stone, J. (2002). *Helping disadvantaged youths succeed in school*. St. Paul, MN: National Research Center for Career and Technical Education.

Cochran, J. (2007). Reactions to Western educational practice: Adult education in Egypt. In K. P. King, & V. C. X. Wang (Eds.), *Comparative adult education around the globe* (pp. 85-112). Hangzhou, China: Zhejiang University Press.

Cooper, M., & Henschke, J. (2007). Expanding our thinking about Andragogy: Toward the international foundation for its research, theory and practice linkage in adult education and human resource development A continuing research study. In K. P. King, & V. C. X. Wang (Eds.), *Comparative adult education around the globe* (pp. 151-194). Hangzhou, China: Zhejiang University Press.

Creswell, J. (1998). *Qualitative inquiry and research design*. Thousand Oaks, CA: Sage.

Delci, M., & Stern, D. (1997). *Who participates in new vocational programs?* Berkeley, CA: National Center for Research in Vocational Education.

Imel, S. (1998). *Using adult learning principles in adult basic and literacy education*. Columbus, OH: ERIC Clearinghouse on Adult, Career, and Vocational Education. (ERIC Document Reproduction Service No. ED 425 336) Retrieved April 25, 2007 from http://eric.ed.gov/ERICDocs/data/ericdocs2/content_storage_01/0000000b/80/11/31/7d.pdf

Kerka, S. (2000). *Career and technical education: A new look*. Columbus, OH: National Dissemination Center for Career and Technical Education. (ERIC Document Reproduction Service No. ED 448319) Retrieved April 25, 2007 from http://eric.ed.gov/ERICDocs/data/ericdocs2/content_storage_01/0000000b/80/24/26/43.pdf

King, K. P. (2002). Testing the waters for distance education in adult education programs. *PAACE Journal of Lifelong Learning, 11*, 11-24.

King, K. P. (2005). *Bringing transformative learning to life*. Malabar, FL: Krieger.

King, K. P. (2007). Robotics—Prime opportunities for careers and student learning. In M. Gura, & K. P. King (Eds.), *Classroom robotics: Case stories of 21st century instruction for millennial students* (pp. 133-144). Charlotte, NC: Information Age Publishing.

King, K. P., & Wright, L. (2007). New perspectives on gains in the ABE classroom: Transformational learning results Considered. In K. P. King & V. C. X. Wang

(Eds.), *Comparative adult education around the globe* (pp. 231-252). Hangzhou, China: Zhejiang University Press.

Lawler, P. A. (1991). *The keys of adult learning*. Philadelphia: Research for Better Schools.

Lawler, P. A., & King, K. P. (2000). *Planning for effective faculty development: Using adult learning strategies*. Malabar, FL: Krieger.

Levesque, K., Lauen, D., Teitelbaum, P., Alt, M., & Librera, S. (2000). *Vocational education in the United States: Toward the year 2000. Statistical Analysis Report*. Washington, DC: National Center for Education Statistics.

Merriam, S., & Caffarella, R. S. (1999). *Learning in adulthood* (2nd ed.). San Francisco: Jossey-Bass.

National Centers for Career and Technical Education. (2002). *Exemplary programs: Outstanding practices*. Retrieved December 12, 2002, from http://www.nccte.org/programs/exemplary/Practices/definition.asp

National Centers for Career and Technical Education. (2003). *About: Vision*. Retrieved January 2, 2003, from http://www.nccte.org/about/aboutVision.asp

Scott, M., & Bernhardt, A. (1999). *Pathways to educational attainment and their effect on early career development*. Berkeley, CA: National Center for Research in Vocational Education.

Scribner, J. P., & Donaldson, J. G. (2001). The dynamics of group learning in a cohort: From nonlearning to transformative learning. *Educational Administration Quarterly, 37*(5), 605-636.

United States Department of Labor. (2006). *Occupational outlook handbook 2006-2007*. Indianapolis, IN: Jist Works.

Vella, J. (2002). *Learning to listen, learning to teach*. San Francisco: Jossey-Bass.

Wonacott, M. E. (2002). *The impact of work-based learning on students*. Columbus, OH: ERIC Clearinghouse on Adult, Career, and Vocational Education. (ERIC Document Reproduction Service No. ED 472603) Retrieved April 25, 2007 from http://eric.ed.gov/ERICDocs/data/ericdocs2/content_storage_01/0000000b/80/2a/38/b0.pdf

Yin, R. K. (2003). *Case study research: Design and method* (3rd ed.). Thousand Oaks, CA: Sage.

CHAPTER 8

TRAINING IN CHINA

Victor C. X. Wang

This chapter reports the results of a study designed to investigate the training preferences of Chinese trainers in light of the Western (i.e., United States) traditional trainer roles versus the performance consultant roles. Trainers from a Chinese Communist Party school and two training colleges in Beijing, China, volunteered to respond to a survey comprised of 13 statements about their training practices. Study results indicated that, while Chinese trainers agreed with Western trainers on the purpose of training, Chinese trainers clung to the role of a traditional trainer instead of that of performance consultant as preferred by Western trainers. Study results also revealed the characteristic of training in China, a finding that was consistent with reports in the literature of training in China.

INTRODUCTION

Few things have more amazed Western scholars, than the fact that China's real GDP has grown 9.7% a year for the past 2 decades (Vachhani, 2005). As a direct result of this high-speed economic development, China has become the so-called "world factory" in the early 1990s. More and more

Innovations in Career and Technical Education: Strategic Approaches Towards Workforce Competencies Around the Globe, pp. 167–179

multinational corporations have gained a foothold in China. Naturally, this has created a dire need for suppliers of training. Much training has been conducted in China's Party schools and training colleges. What is clear to Western scholars is that China does produce what the rest of the world needs in terms of daily commodities. China is a labor-intensive market for profitable foreign businesses.

What puzzles Westerners is how training is conducted in China to promote desired changes in political ideology, socioeconomic relations and human productive capabilities (Wang & Colletta, 1991). To Westerners, China is known as a strong ideological nation. First there was Confucius who emphasized moral cultivation and individual merit in training. Confucius' thinking has inspired generations of Chinese teachers and trainers. Then there were influential figures such as Marx, Lenin, and Mao who inspired Chinese to engage in class struggle. Under the guise of "politics takes command," training was virtually next to nonexistent in China during the Great Cultural Revolution, which lasted for 10 years between 1966 and 1976. After China opened its door to the outside world in the early 1980s, there was much talk on training such as "system theory" and "decision making theory" in China. However, the reality in China has been that political aptitude and connections are still the all-important prerequisites to promotion and a degree in training is no shortcut.

Chinese cadres and workers are trained by Party schools and training colleges. Chinese trainers have been arguing over the importance of two controversial issues concerning training of their employees: moral cultivation or individual merit. Outside China, trainers are beginning to make a transition from traditional trainers to performance consultants. The traditional roles of trainers are somewhat outmoded as organizations improve their overall performance capacity to compete in a global economy.

Although the general mode of Chinese trainers may be imaginable to Western scholars, the question remains unexamined as to whether Chinese trainers still cling to their age-old mode of training, revolving around moral cultivation and individual merit. Western trainers have been advised to assume the roles of performance consultants to customize training to fit the organization and to align training to organizational goals. Has this form of training penetrated into Chinese training as a by-product of China's continuous use of foreign capital to develop its economy? Western scholars argue China must reform its training in order to keep up with the fast development of its economy. Without a sound form of training for its largest number of trainees in the world, China's form of training may be an impediment to learning.

In the context of increasing globalization, it seems appropriate to undertake a study of training in China, so China may effectively improve its human productive capabilities and Western trainers may customize training to fit the particular requirements of China's organizations. It is commonly argued that trainers' roles may either facilitate trainees' performance or inhibit it. While the goal of training in China is to train personnel for socialist construction (Kaplan, Sobin, & Andors, 1979), the roles of the trainers are unclear to Western observers. Without a doubt, a study of the Chinese form of training may shed more light on the much-debated issues of traditional trainer roles versus performance consultant roles. With this purpose in mind, the researcher formulated the following research questions: What are the training preferences of Chinese trainers in light of the Western training preferences relative to:

1.   Learning needs versus performance needs;
2.   Structured learning versus formation of performance models;
3.   Measuring numbers of days and courses versus measuring performance;
4.   Evaluating participant reaction and learning versus performance change and cost benefit;
5.   Viewing training as a direct cost versus viewing training as an investment?

In addition, the researcher was interested in the following question that is closely related to the research topic under study: What is the characteristic of training given China's special social setting with a background of semi-communism?

THEORY AND PRACTICE OF TRAINING IN NORTH AMERICA

Training in the United States was primarily influenced by three foreign training systems: the Russian system, the Sloyd system (Originated in Scandinavian countries), and the Arts and Crafts Movement (Originated in England) (Bott, Slapar, & Wang, 2003; Brehony, 1998; Grubb, 1998, Roberts, 1965; Roche, 1995). While the Russian training reaches large groups of trainees in the least possible time, the Sloyd training system encourages trainee self-direction and initiative, and the Arts and Crafts Movement emphasizes the aesthetic and creative sides of work. Although these foreign influences are still felt to this day, training in the United States has gone in a different direction. First, the cost of training is high. According to Robinson and Robinson (1996), training in North America has become a $50 billion enterprise. If the cost of having employees attend training off the job is added into the equation, the total expenditure in formal training and development of employees may exceed well over $300 billion. Second, one in eight Americans receives training every year. The American Society for Training and Development (ASTD) specifies different training categories for American workers:

1. Executive and Supervisory;
2. Customer Service;
3. New Technology;
4. Basic Skills (Wang, 2003, p. 32).

As its overall purpose, training in North America must help organization improve its overall performance capacity so it can compete in a global economy (Gilley, 1998, p. 111). Caffarella (2002, p. 11) divides the purpose of training into three kinds of change: individual change related to acquisition of new knowledge, building of skills, and examination of personal values and beliefs; organizational change resulting in new or revised policies, procedures, and ways of working; and community and societal change that allows for differing segments of society.

Based on the purpose of training, trainers in North America have traditionally focused on identifying and addressing *learning* needs of employees. Training programs have produced *structured learning* experiences such as self-paced packages, and computer-based programs. Training has been viewed as *an end*; if trainees have learned, then the desired output from the traditional trainer role have been achieved. Measures concentrate on *number* of participant days, instructor days, and courses. The implication is "more is better." Training evaluations have focused on participant *reaction* and *learning*. Trainers have only identified the training needs of employees. Trainers have viewed training as a *cost* and training programs have been viewed as having a *limited, acknowledged* linkage to business goals.

As competition has become one of its survival skills for organizations in this global economy, organizational decision makers are demanding that trainers produce results that improve organizational effectiveness (Gilley, 1998). Trainers no longer assume the role of just being trainers. To bring about organizational change, trainers in North America are required to assume a new role of becoming performance consultants. The traditional role of trainers is still useful. However, the new role of becoming performance consultants requires more. Trainers in North America need to make the transition from trainers to performance consultants. In contrast to its traditional trainer role, performance consultants identify and address *performance* needs of people. Performance consultants provide services that result in changing or improving performance.

Training programs should include formation of performance models and guidance in addressing work environment obstacles. Training is viewed as a *means* to an end. Employees learn to transfer what they learn to their jobs. Consultants learn to establish and maintain partnerships with managers and others in the organization. Measures focus on performance of people in the organization. The results and non-training actions are measured for *performance change and cost benefit*. Assessments focus on determining performance gaps and the reasons for these gaps. The work environment is required to support required performance. Training is seen as producing measurable results. Training programs and services have a *high* linkage to the organization's goal.

To make a successful transition from trainers to performance consultants, training leaders advocate that trainers in North America must learn to do the following:

- Develop thorough knowledge of organizations.
- Foster critical consulting skills.
- Learn a cross-cultural perspective of training.
- Adopt and adapt the responsibilities and roles of performance consultants.
- Apply the consulting skills.

HISTORY AND PRACTICE OF TRAINING IN CHINA

Although the Chinese pioneered the system of education and training for public service as early as the tenth century A.D. (Paltiel, 1992), this entire tradition disappeared by the 1960s as a result of the Great Cultural Revolution launched by Mao as a result of power struggle. Since then, the Chinese authorities have had tremendous difficulties in establishing even the minimal standards of training for public officials. Starting in the early 1980s, the educated elite of China began to reestablish the same intimacy with prestige and power that training had in traditional times. However, training in China has been revolving around two priorities: professionalism and moral competence as advanced by Confucius. Although Confucius suggested selecting members of the ruling class on the basis of individual merit, Chinese officials nowadays have tended to favor moral cultivation in training. Traditionally, Mao rejected formal training as the basis of his new hierarchy, but insisted on individual cultivation of moral worth as a means of inculcating revolutionary solidarity in a collective setting. The task of training Chinese cadres rested with the trainers in Moscow. The Soviets, interested in indoctrinating Chinese youth with revolutionary spirit in China, tapped the hunger for training among Chinese youth by establishing training colleges for Chinese on Soviet territory. Later, a Marxist-Leninist Training Academy was established on Chinese territory. These training academies were later known as "May Seventh Cadre Schools." Training in these schools took the form of reading a Party document or texts of Marx, Engels, Lenin, and Mao. After the reading, the trainees were sent down to gain practical experience in lower-level line positions. Mao's trainers argued that Western training focused on narrow utilitarianism. Instead, Mao made "redness," that is, political motivation, a priority in recruiting and promoting cadres.

After the hiatus of the Cultural Revolution, the industrialized West became the model for Chinese reformers. Priority was given to induce older, less-educated cadres from the Party's guerrilla days to retire and yield their place to younger, better-trained personnel. The purpose of training has begun to attach importance to educational background and academic record as well as to experience and achievements in work. All Party schools and training colleges must revise their teaching plans and shoulder the regular training of cadres for socialist modernizations. In addition to systematic training in Marxist theory, trainees should receive training in economics, management, law, and scientific leadership methods. Professional training should constitute 70% of the curriculum in these Party and training schools.

Although Chinese training programs have been expanded, all the long and short-term training courses are prescribed by the Ministry of Education. The trainers, normally teachers from universities with no real world experience, are expected to teach experienced employees. Textbooks and training programs conveniently repeat abstract generalizations and manipulate buzzwords like "system theory" and "decision making theory." Although trainers and trainees in China argue that training is a matter of technical competence rather than political commitment to the Party and the people, political aptitude and connections are still the all-important prerequisites to promotion and a degree in training is no shortcut. Numerous Chinese graduates of MBA programs at the institutions of American higher learning have difficulty finding appropriate positions in China. Some have taken the jobs of teaching English as a foreign language for Chinese universities.

As far as expenditure is concerned, Chinese trainers view training as a direct cost. Virtually no employers are willing to offer high costs to train their employees. As more and more foreign enterprises and joint ventures have gained a foothold in China, terms such as performance consultants are used more and more frequently to refer to human resource development professionals. However, the question remains unanswered as to whether training in China is comparable to the traditional focus or the current focus of training in North America (i.e., the United States).

METHODOLOGY

The site of this study was comprised of a small Party school (enrollment 900) and two training colleges in Beijing, China, with a population of well over 10 million. Since the Chinese communists came to power in 1949, these Party schools and training colleges throughout China have shouldered the responsibilities of training China's cadres and workers. Trainers in these schools are tenured teachers or teachers from other universities. They have been using training methods prescribed by either the Ministry of Education or other higher authorities. To make their training popular, these trainers like to use Western terms such as "system theory" and "decision-making theory."

During June 2005, 49 participants (100%) were contacted and volunteered to return questionnaires. Thirty were male trainers and 19 were female trainers. Of these trainers, 95% were between the ages of 45 and 65.

Data were collected by means of a questionnaire containing 13 items. The instrument was developed using the well-accepted traditional trainer roles versus the performance consultant roles by Robinson and Robinson (1996) in an easily understood format with a 1-7 Likert continuous scale: (1) strongly disagree and (7) strongly agree. All information used in this analysis was derived from the questionnaire data. This questionnaire had been developed by the researcher and tested at one institution of higher learning in the United States before its use in Beijing, China. It proved to be content-valid. The reliability of the questionnaires was alpha .92, N of cases = 49, N of items = 13.

Data collected in this study were analyzed using SPSS (12.0 for Windows) software. High mean scores on statements 1, 2, 3, 4, and 5 represent support for the traditional trainer role. High mean scores on statements 6, 7, 8, 9, and 10 indicate support for the performance consultant role. For statements 11-13, high mean scores reflect support for the traditional Chinese mode of training. Low mean scores show support for a different mode of training.

FINDINGS

In Table 8.1, statements 1, 2, 3, 4, and 5 dealt with the traditional trainer role specified by Robinson and Robinson (1996). In Table 8.2, statements

Table 8.1.   Mean Responses: Traditional Trainer Role

	Statements	*M*	*SD*
1.	Trainers should identify and address learning needs of trainees.	4.31	1.69
2.	Trainers should produce structured learning experiences such as training programs, self-paced packages, and computer-based training programs.	4.73	1.18
3.	Trainers should measure number of participant days, instructor days, and courses.	5.11	1.38
4.	Training evaluations should be completed for participant reaction and learning.	4.25	1.34
5.	Training reflects a direct cost. Therefore, training programs and services have a limited linkage to business goals.	5.21	1.47

Note: $n = 49$; $N = 49$.

6, 7, 8, 9, and 10 represented the performance consultant role based on Robinson and Robinson (1996). In Table 8.3, statements 11, 12, and 13 reflected the characteristic of Chinese training. The standard deviation scores for these trainers are also provided in Tables 8.1, 8.2, and 8.3.

Table 8.1 indicates that Chinese trainers had high scores on all five statements that make up the traditional trainer role. Their scores in statements 3 and 5 were highest. These results suggest that Chinese trainers favored the traditional trainer role over the performance consultant role. Neither their training nor their training evaluations focused on performance. They viewed training as a direct cost. They did not view training as an investment. They believed that the linkage between training and business goals was limited.

Table 8.2 describes the trainers' responses for the performance consultant role. It illustrates that Chinese trainers had low scores on all five statements that make up the performance consultant role. These results

Table 8.2.   Mean Responses: Performance Consultant Role

	Statements	*M*	*SD*
1.	Trainers should identify and address performance needs of trainees.	3.31	1.29
2.	Trainers should formulate performance models for trainees.	3.73	0.28
3.	Trainers should measure performance of trainees.	3.41	0.18
4.	Training evaluations should be completed for performance change and cost benefit.	3.05	1.34
5.	Training reflects an investment. Therefore, training programs and services have a high linkage to business goals.	2.01	0.47

Note: $n = 49$; $N = 49$.

Table 8.3.   Mean Responses: Characteristics of Chinese Training

Statements	*M*	*SD*
1. The Ministry of Education should prescribe training courses.	4.11	1.35
2. Moral cultivation and connections are important prerequisites to promotion in China.	5.73	1.36
3. The purpose of training is to improve one's record and achievements in work.	5.11	1.38

Note: $n = 49$; $N = 49$.

suggest that Chinese trainers did not assume the performance consultant role. Their training or training evaluations focused on the traditional trainer role. They viewed training as a direct cost. They did not view training as an investment. They did not believe that the linkage between training and business goals was high. These results verified the results from Table 8.1.

Table 8.3 contains the trainers' responses for their mode of training in China. The table shows that Chinese trainers had high scores on all three statements that make up the characteristic of training in China. These results indicate that Chinese trainers believed that moral cultivation and connections were prerequisites to promotion in China, although they agreed with Western trainers on the purpose of training. These results also show that training in China was top-down.

DISCUSSION

The purpose of this study was to determine Chinese trainers' training preferences in light of the Western traditional trainer roles versus the performance consultant roles. An additional purpose of the study was to determine the characteristic of training in China. The findings showed that trainers in China surveyed supported the traditional trainer role. In other words, Chinese trainers identified and addressed learning needs of trainers and produced structured learning experiences such as training programs, self-paced packages, and computer-based training programs. They measured number of participant days, instructor days, and courses and their evaluations were completed for participant reaction and learning. Above all, Chinese trainers viewed training as a direct cost. They did not see a high linkage between training and business goals. The findings also indicated that these Chinese trainers viewed moral cultivation and connections as important prerequisites to promotion, although they did believe that the purpose of training was to improve human capabilities.

These Chinese trainers relied on the Ministry of Education to prescribe training courses to them in China.

These findings confirmed Wang and Bott's (2004) research concerning Confucian heritage cultures. According to Wang and Bott, Chinese trainers or educators prefer a liberal philosophy in training. Wang's (2005) research on teaching philosophies of Chinese vocational education instructors further confirmed the liberal philosophy in training. Trainers are regarded by their trainees as an unchallengeable authority. Trainers focus on structured learning experiences in which they serve as directors or coaches, whereas trainees assume the submissive roles of simply following their trainers. Chinese trainers provide less hands-on experience because they view training as a direct cost. The fact is if these Chinese trainers have to follow directives from the Ministry of Education, it is really hard for them to make the transition from the traditional roles of trainers to the current Western roles of performance consultants because their roles have been predetermined by higher authorities. Numerous studies have suggested that compliance with authority is highly valued in the Chinese culture (Pratt, 1988, 1993).

What is wrong with the traditional roles of trainers is that structured learning does not offer trainees freedom to transfer what they learn to their jobs. Both trainers and trainees need to be aware that performance is needed to achieve business goals. To have such desired performance outcomes, trainees need to be given the Western trainee-centered learning approach in which trainees become responsible for their own learning. Naturally, trainees are in a position to transfer what they learn to their jobs. This is not to say that trainees under the traditional mode of training cannot perform their jobs. Rather, the current Western roles of performance consultants may lead to maximized performance needed by businesses. For example, performance consultants measure the contribution to improving the performance of people in the organization. They measure performance change and cost benefit. Above all, they identify performance gaps. All of these roles point in one direction—performance of the trainees. To remain competitive in this globalization, human productive capabilities are equally as important as political ideology and socioeconomic relations.

The United States of America cannot remain the only superpower in the world without its highly trained scientists, engineers in Silicon Valley and its well-trained career and technical workers elsewhere in the country. In training, U.S. trainers have adopted and adapted a series of foreign training methods (Wang & Redhead, 2004). It seems for now that the performance consultant role has become more pronounced in the Western hemisphere because Western trainers believe that success in the training world is determined by job performance (Rossi, 2005). The traditional trainer role seems to have become outmoded in the new context of globalization. That Chinese trainers view training as a direct cost is shorted sighted in light of the Western performance consultant role. Although China's economic development is impressive, China cannot remain competitive unless its trainers believe that completed work has a high linkage to the organization's goal. To put this in more concrete terms, China needs to make training a multi-billion dollar enterprise just like its American counterpart. And the Western role of performance consultants cannot be neglected in the context of globalization. In the years that follow, the relation between performance professionals and consultants will increase in importance in the training world (Suleiman, 2004).

IMPLICATIONS

This study was designed to determine the training preferences of Chinese trainers in light of the Western training preferences of being performance consultants in the new context of globalization. The Western preferred training methods have evolved from foreign training methods such as the Russian, the Sloyd and the Arts and Crafts Movement (Bott, Slapar, & Wang, 2003). Over the years, American trainers have adopted and adapted a series of foreign training methods to help organizations improve their overall performance capacity, so its organizations can compete in a global economy.

However, this beautifully, well-reasoned performance consultant role meets with resistance from an authoritarian culture. For Western suppliers of training to be successful in China, particular attention must be given to local social contexts. Most importantly, social norms and type of government predetermine whether Chinese trainers need to cling to the traditional role of training or the Western performance consultant role. Since training in China is seen as training from above, for Western trainers to be successful in China, it is best to convince Chinese higher authorities of the effective performance consultant role before they try to persuade Chinese trainers to buy into their training mode.

This chapter supports a fresh look at the traditional trainer roles versus the performance consultant roles through the lens of Chinese trainers. The study implies that social norms, the type of government in which training takes place, cannot be ignored. An ideological country like China with approximately 1.3 billion people needs to realize that training to improve human productive capabilities is just as important as political ideology and socioeconomic relations. Training should be viewed as a means to an end. It is the performance of trainees that needs to be evaluated. Performance is needed to achieve business goals.

Further research is necessary, especially in the area of why Chinese trainers prefer the traditional trainer role to the performance consultant role. In-depth observations and interviews may facilitate such an undertaking in the future.

REFERENCES

Brehony, K. J. (1998). "Even far distant Japan is showing an interest": The English Froebel Movement's turn to Sloyd. *History of Education 27,* 279. Retrieved May 21, 2005, from EBSCOHost Academic Search Elite database www. ebscohost.com/

Bott, P. A., Slapar, F. M., & Wang, V. (2003). *History and philosophy of career and technical education.* Boston: Pearson.

Caffarella, R. S. (2002). *Planning programs for adult learners* (2nd ed.). San Francisco: Jossey-Bass.

Gilley, J. W. (1998). *Improving HRD practice.* Malabar, FL: Krieger.

Grubb, W. N. (1998). *Preparing for the information-based workplace: Pedagogical issues and institutional linkages.* Retrieved May 22, 2005, from http://mitsloanMIT.edu/iwer/papers.html

Kaplan, F. M., Sobin, J. M., & Andors, S. (1979). *Encyclopedia of China today.* New York: Harper & Row.

Paltiel, J. (1992). Educating the modernizers: Management training in China. In R. Hayhoe (Ed.), *Education and modernization: The Chinese experience* (pp. 337-357). New York: Pergamon Press.

Pratt, D. D. (1988). "Andragogy as a relational construct." *Adult Education Quarterly, 38,* 160-181.

Pratt, D. D. (1993). "Andragogy after twenty-five years." *New Directions for Adult and Continuing Education, No. 57.* San Francisco: Jossey-Bass.

Roberts, R. W. (1965). *Vocational and practical arts education: History, development, and principles* (2nd ed.). New York: Harper & Row.

Robinson, D. G., & Robinson, J. C. (1996). *Performance consulting moving beyond training.* San Francisco: Berrett-Koehler.

Roche, J. F. (1995). The culture of pre-modernism: Whitman, Morris, and the American Arts and Crafts Movement. *ATQ, 9*(2), 1-12. Retrieved May 20, 2005, from EBSCOHost Academic Search Elite database www.ebscohost.com/

Rossi, J. (2005). Putting performance into practice. *Training & Development, 59*(5), 18.

Suleiman, A. (2004). Consultants: the trainer's friend. *Training & Development, 58*(11), 4.

Vachhani, A. (2005). *India and China-a game of one-upmanship.* Retrieved May 1, 2005, from http://www.blonnet.com/2005/04/04/stories/2005040400090800.htm

Wang, J. L., & Colletta, N. (1991). Chinese education problems, policies, and prospects. In I. Epstein (Ed.). *Chinese education problems, policies, and prospects* (pp. 145-162). New York: Garland.

Wang, V. (2003). *Principles of adult education*. Boston: Pearson.

Wang, V. (2005). Teaching philosophies of Chinese vocational education instructors. *International Journal of Vocational Education and Training*, *13*(1), 7-21.

Wang, V., & Bott, P. A. (2004). Modes of teaching of Chinese adult educators. *Perspectives*: *The New York Journal of Adult Learning*, *2*(2), 32-51.

Wang, V., & Redhead, C. K. (2004). Comparing the Russian, the Sloyd, and the Arts and Crafts movement training systems. *International Journal of Vocational Education and Training*, *12*(1), 42-58.

CHAPTER 9

REFORMS IN EDUCATION AND TRAINING CURRICULUM AS A STRATEGIC APPROACH TO WORKFORCE DEVELOPMENT COMPETENCIES IN KENYA

Fredrick Muyia Nafukho

INTRODUCTION

The issue of youth unemployment and other vulnerable members of society in Kenya like in many low and middle income countries need urgent attention. Kenya's government efforts to address the issue have included reforms and diversification of the education and training of the school curriculum. In addition, policies designed to increase the number of young people entering vocational and technical training institutions as preparation for self employment have been started. An intended outcome of the current school curriculum reform in Kenya is to create awareness among school and college graduates that there are opportunities for self employment in the informal sector (Republic of Kenya, 1986, 1992).

Innovations in Career and Technical Education: Strategic Approaches Towards Workforce Competencies Around the Globe, pp. 181–192
Copyright © 2008 by Information Age Publishing
All rights of reproduction in any form reserved.

Despite the introduction of vocational and technical subjects in the school curriculum, unemployment persists even among those with technical skills and knowledge. This situation has led to the introduction of entrepreneurship education to develop entrepreneurial skills among graduates from vocational and technical training institutions.

This chapter examines the development of vocational, technical, and entrepreneurship education and training in Kenya as a strategic approach to workforce development competencies. It is shown in the chapter that the development of workforce competencies should be a lifelong process and should involve learning how other countries around the world prepare students for the competitive world of work. Specific examples of successful uses of entrepreneurship to address unemployment from the United States of America are cited.

DEVELOPMENT OF VOCATIONAL AND TECHNICAL EDUCATION IN KENYA

Before examining the development of vocational and technical education in Kenya, it is important that we define the term vocational and technical education. United Nations Educational, Scientific and Cultural Organization (UNESCO) (1984) defines technical and vocational education as

> a comprehensive term referring to the educational process when it involves in addition to general education, the study of technologies and related sciences and the acquisition of practice skills and the knowledge relating to occupations in various sectors of economic and social life. (p. 23)

This definition assumes that vocational education and technical education refer to similar programs. To make a distinction between the two terms, UNESCO (1984) further defines vocational education as; "education designed to prepare skilled personnel at lower levels of qualifications for one or a group of occupations, trades or jobs" (p. 23). While technical education is defined as "education designed at upper levels to prepare middle level personnel such as technicians and at university level to prepare engineers and technologists for higher management positions" (p. 23).

Kerre (1991) observed that the notion of vocational education is not new to Africa since it was central to the important task of preparing an individual for mature adult life. In African and by extension Kenyan context, vocational education was concerned with life and work. A vocation included what a person did for a living. This for example, included hunting, singing or carving. In this chapter, vocational education refers to the kind of education that develops key workforce development competencies in the individual and enables the individual to be flexible and meet the demands of the changing economy. Thus, the introduction of vocational and technical subjects in the Kenyan school and training institutions were intended to ensure that students are equipped with key competencies required by both the informal and formal sectors of the economy. In the traditional Kenyan economy, the survival of the tribe depended on vocational skills such as hunting, cookery, pottery, and the ethics and norms peculiar to a given tribe, clan and family. During the colonial period, Africans mainly did manual work. There existed racial segregation in the education system. The Africans trained at low levels of vocational education. It was during this period that vocational education earned its low status as compared with academic education among Africans (Sheffield, 1971).

The colonial government developed several reports that supported racial segregation in education. The Fraser Report of 1949 emphasized the type of education that would make the African a better laborer and that would suit them to their immediate environment. Phelps-Stokes Report of 1924 stressed the need to preserve the best African traditions and prepare students for the world of work (Kenya Colony and Protectorate, 1925). Sheffield (1971) pointed out that in 1925 the first African Jean School modeled after the Jean schools in the United States of America was established at Kabete. The school was set up to train Africans who would then teach fellow Africans. The Beecher Report of 1949 recommended the need for Africans to learn agriculture in schools (Kenya Colony and Protectorate, 1960). It also called for vocational training to instill the dignity of manual labor among the Africans. During the colonial period, vocational education was viewed by the colonial administration, missionaries and settlers as necessary for Africans. Sifuna (1976) argues that Africans rejected vocational education then because of the rationale behind its introduction. They considered vocational education as having been designed to keep them politically and economically behind.

VOCATIONAL EDUCATION AFTER INDEPENDENCE

On attainment of independence in 1963, the Kenya government set up an education commission that developed the Ominde report of 1964 (Republic of Kenya, 1964). This report recommended the abolition of racial segregation system of education. In addition, the Ominde report recommended and implemented the removal of agriculture in the school curriculum. The report developed an education system intended to meet the country's human resource needs especially at professional and technical levels. There was need to develop skilled personnel who would fill vacancies for the departing expatriates. Thus, a highly academic curricu-lum was implemented by all Kenyan public schools.

The problem of unemployment among school leavers was not experi-enced. It was not until 1968 that an unemployment problem was noticed especially among primary and secondary school leavers with purely aca-demic education. In fact the school leavers with technical and vocational background never experienced an unemployment problem (King, 1977). The vocational education curriculum and agriculture gave less emphasis on attainment of independence started gaining value in the early 1970s. As of 1966, the government set up technical schools with a vocational bias. These schools addressed youth unemployment problems that had become evident among those with purely academic education. In this manner, Village Polytechnics (currently referred to as Youth Polytechnics) were established. In addition, Harambee Institutes of Research Science and Technology were established through similar efforts.

The Gachathi report of 1976 (Republic of Kenya, 1976) and the Mackay report of 1981 (Republic of Kenya, 1981) are the two major com-missions which have influenced the development of vocational and tech-nical education in post-independence Kenya. The Gachathi report recommended the need for a practical system of education. The one existing then was purely academic and theoretical and helped in acceler-ating the unemployment problem among primary and secondary school leavers. The Mackay report recommended the change from 7-4-2-3 sys-tem of education to the 8-4-4 system (Republic of Kenya, 1981). The cur-rent 8-4-4 system introduced in January 1985 had 8 years of primary (elementary) education, 4 years of secondary education and a minimum of 4 years of university education (Republic of Kenya, 1984). The 8-4-4 system of education borrowed heavily from the American system of edu-cation while maintaining the positive aspects of the British system of edu-cation such as a centralized school curriculum and a nationally administered examination after 8 years of primary education and 4 years of secondary education.

VOCATIONAL AND TECHNICAL EDUCATION IN THE CONTEXT OF 8.4.4 SYSTEM OF EDUCATION

Because of the unemployment problem and many technological changes at the work place, vocational and technical education, once resented in the pre-independence period has now become very popular. The curricu-lum is now offered by all public and private Kenyan schools.

All school children enrolled in more than 13,500 primary schools are exposed to vocational programs (Kerre, 1991). The subjects studied include music, arts and craft, agriculture, business education, and family and consumer sciences. The vocational education component also exists at secondary school level. Business education is compulsory in forms one and two. In forms three and four students are required to choose one vocational subject from a list of subjects such as agriculture, commerce, keyboarding, power mechanics, building and construction, metal work, technical drawing, electronics, and home science.

Besides the introduction of technical and vocational subjects into the school curriculum, the government has tried to respond to the problem of youth unemployment by setting up specialized vocational and technical training institutions. There are more than 600 youth polytechnics, 20 technical training institutes, 19 Harambee Institutes of Research Science and Technology and 4 national polytechnics. These technical training institutions are government funded and offer technical and vocational skills and knowledge to the students who do not go on to universities. The institutions could be compared to vocational and technical training institutions in the United States of America.

DEVELOPMENT OF ENTREPRENEURSHIP EDUCATION IN THE UNITED STATES AND IN KENYA

In the United States of America, it has been observed that entrepreneurial capacity and behavior are the prime drivers of economic growth and job creation (DeVol, Koepp, & Fogelbach, 2002). Thus in the United States, entrepreneurship has been recognized as one of the secrets behind economic growth (Christensen. Johnson, & Rigby, 2002; Kirby, 1983; Schumpeter, 1950). Acs, Carlsson, and Karlsson (1999) argue correctly that entrepreneurial vitality is one of the factors explaining the superior performance of the U.S. economy in generating innovation and employment.

Vesper (1982) observed that at the end of the 1970s the curricula in the U.S. universities with one or more courses in entrepreneurship were approximately 130, which is more than ten times what it was in the 1960s. Vesper and Gatner (1997) observed further that during the 1980s and 1990s curricula with entrepreneurial courses rose steadily from 250 in 1985 to 370 in 1992 and to approximately 400 in 1995. In recognition of the importance of entrepreneurship studies, in 1997, there were 160 permanent chairs in the United States in the area of entrepreneurship. Katz (2003) noted that by the late 1990s there was a well established education infrastructure in the United States in the field of entrepreneurship with more than 300 endowed faculty positions, more than 100 centers of entrepreneurship, more than 40 refereed journal articles and several professional organizations. Thus the field of entrepreneurship education in the United States is better recognized than in any other country of the world. It is a dynamic field that is rapidly growing. In addition, a plethora of research studies in the field of entrepreneurship education exists in the United States. Outside the United States only Canada and the United Kingdom (UK) have the highest number of courses and programs in the field of entrepreneurship education.

When it comes to the critical role of entrepreneurship education in opportunity identification and new business venture creations, it is not just in the United States where entrepreneurship is valued. In many low and middle income countries such as Kenya, entrepreneurship has been considered the panacea to unemployment problem. The development of entrepreneurship education in Kenya can be traced to the Ominde report of 1964, Ndegwa report of 1971 and International Labor Organization report of 1972 (International Labor Organization, 1972). These three reports emphasized the importance of teaching business education in schools. The Mackay report of 1981 which led to the introduction of 8.4.4 system of education had notable effects on the development of entrepreneurship education in the country's educational institutions (Republic of Kenya, 1981).

The Kamunge report of 1988 recommended the introduction of entrepreneurship education in all levels of training programs to promote self-employment among graduates from these institutions (Republic of Kenya, 1988). In response to this recommendation, the Ministry of Technical Training and Applied Technology aimed at creating awareness and providing entrepreneurial skills necessary to enhance productivity and profitability of the self-employed by introducing entrepreneurship education in all vocational and technical training institutions. Mburugu and Thiong'o (1991, p. 4) note that by teaching technical and entrepreneurial skills that are compatible with market realities, a training system is able to influence youth in the formative years of growth to acquire appropriate business habits and to use later in life.

The entrepreneurship education program which was initially funded by United Nations Development program and executed by the International Labor Organization was introduced as a compulsory course in all vocational and technical training institutions in 1990 (Mburugu & Thiong'o, 1991). The students enrolled in entrepreneurship courses were required to produce a business proposal outlining the business venture to be started on graduation from technical training institutions. The entrepreneurship education program is intended to develop positive attitudes among students toward self employment. The program also aims at ensuring high success rates among graduates who become self employed in micro and small business enterprises. It has been realized that small business enterprises that have been in existence for some years and have growth potential, may require a special focus for management training, business counseling and extension services (Republic of Kenya, 1992).

LIFELONG LEARNING MODEL OF ENTREPRENEURSHIP

In Germany, it has been observed that in order to prepare students to survive in today's world, students must be taught to acquire information on their own (Goal, 2006). In the United States, Goal observed further that schools must address three important issues as a strategy to prepare the workforce needed in the twenty-first century and beyond. (1) They must provide a strong academic foundation in the cognitive domain with a major focus on language, math, social studies and science skills (2) schools must emphasize the affective domain of knowledge with a focus on soft skills such as teamwork, creative thinking and problem solving skills while emphasizing the need for values and ethics and (3) schools must provide opportunities for students to exercise and develop psychomotor skills and encourage them to make, repair, and destroy things, as noted "We live in a material world, and to reduce a student's school experience to solely mental activities divorces the student from the real world" (p. 38).

Schools systems in low and middle income countries such as Kenya may need to adapt some positive aspects of school curriculum reforms being implemented in high income countries such as Germany and the United States. Ashmore (1990) noted that the National Center for Research in Vocational Education developed the Lifelong Entrepreneurship Education Model to explain what entrepreneurship education means to different audiences at different stages of educational development. In fact, the Kenyan education system adapted the lIfelong Entrepreneurship Education Model.

The model is based on the premise that skills and attitudes necessary for successful small business developments are not learned at any one place of time (Ashmore, 1990). The model further proposes that the earlier young people begin to learn such skills, the more likely they are able to become successful entrepreneurs. One approach to enhancing entrepreneurial activity and enterprise growth in developing countries like Kenya is to encourage the development of an entrepreneurial spirit among the youth of the country (Nafukho, 1998). By focusing on the youth while they are still in school, this approach may provide long term solution to the problem of job creation and business growth (Nelson & Scott, 1997).

According to Ashmore (1990), the lifelong learning model of entrepreneurship education has five stages. The first three stages are school and college based. Stage one starts at a very early age and is offered from primary (elementary) level of education upwards. Stage two is mainly designed to teach an understanding of the management skills in subjects such as business education, commerce and accounting at secondary level of education. Stage three provides a more in depth understanding of the competencies needed for one to become a successful entrepreneur. It is offered by vocational and technical training institutions in Kenya. Students are required to prepare a business plan before graduation. The emphasis here is for one to look for a business opportunity related to one's skills. Owano's (1988) study among self employed youth who were polytechnic graduates revealed that those in self employment lacked management skills. This observation led to the introduction of entrepreneurship education by all vocational and technical training institutions. In the fourth and fifth stages, entrepreneurship venture development and long term expansion and redirection respectively address the continuing need for helping entrepreneurs to start a business and to successfully sustain it. In stages four and five, nongovernmental organizations such as Kenya Management Assistance Program (K-MAP) and Kenya Institute of Management target those individuals already in business and require entrepreneurial skills. This management support is done through seminars, workshops, focus groups, business counseling and visits to the premises of the entrepreneurs.

GOVERNMENT ROLE IN THE PROMOTION OF THE ENTREPRENEURIAL SPIRIT

Rao and Wright (1991) and Nafukho (1998) note that entrepreneurship concerns not only the way individuals operate in the sphere of economic activities but also the way in which the government manages the economy. In order for efforts to be successful, the government should facilitate and not stifle entrepreneurial spirit. The existing political establishment in Kenya has a major role in ensuring that entrepreneurial spirit is fostered among graduates of vocational and technical training institutions.

While the government considers the informal sector the major employer of the graduates from vocational and technical training institutions (Republic of Kenya, 1986), there is need for a more conducive business environment. Ikiara (1991) highlights the fact that a conducive business environment is lacking for self-employed entrepreneurs in the informal sector in major urban centers in Kenya. As stated by Gichira and Nelson (1997), this trend needs to be corrected, "Government policies regarding the small enterprise sector should be reviewed to identify changes which are needed to make the external business environment more conducive for small enterprise development" (p. 107).

The government should also ensure that important sectors of the economy such as agricultural and industrial sectors are well managed to support the self employed in the informal sector to promote entrepreneurial spirit. The increased trend in Kenya of using vocational and technical training institutions for entrepreneurial skills development is due to strong government belief that entrepreneurship can indeed be taught. This calls for a systematic build up of knowledge to make entrepreneurship a rich and valid curriculum. Thus, all efforts of teaching entrepreneurship education to create an enterprise culture should place a high premium on experiential learning (Nafukho, 1998). Also required is research to determine the effects of entrepreneurship training on the management of small businesses enterprises operated by graduates from vocational and technical training institutions. This research should be sector specific and should focus on businesses in a particular sector (Gichira & Nelson, 1997). Besides government role in promoting entrepreneurship, empirical research shows "that in many instances people are indeed born with ambition, motivation, and a willingness to take risks, but encounter barriers that erode this spirit of adventure" (Rabbior, 1990, p. 54), therefore, a well designed entrepreneurship education program should aim at removing some of the barriers that have eroded self-confidence and self-esteem in people. According to Rabbior (1990) and using a Canadian example he provides key elements of a successful entrepreneurship education program. Such a program should:

1. Not solely focus on right answers.
2. Be highly participatory with hands on focus.
3. Be goal and achievement-oriented.
4. Encourage short-term accomplishments.
5. Focus on challenges to the status quo.
6. Have a community orientation focus.
7. Utilize a variety of approaches and teaching styles.
8. Have elements that surprise the student and present the unexpected.
9. Present familiar information in unfamiliar contexts.
10. Be easily amended and augmented by each individual teacher.
11. Provide focus for entrepreneurial ventures and initiatives.
12. Be fun and exciting.
13. Enable frequent and unanticipated feedback.

14. Entail approaches and activities that seek to build self-confidence.

15. Enable students to apply their knowledge and skill to a particular endeavor.

16. Build to a potential launch point for the endeavor.

17. Enable and encourage group and team activities.

18. Alert students to the common pitfalls and reasons for failed initiatives.

19. Place a heavy emphasis on opportunities, what gives rise to them, and how to evaluate them.

20. Expect the teacher to be entrepreneurial.

21. Link entrepreneurship to innovation.

22. Focus on the consideration and examination of disequilibrium as opposed to equilibrium.

23. Provide direction and guidance regarding the design of a conducive learning environment.

24. Utilize case studies that are varied in terms of the nature of the entrepreneur, the type of the initiative, and the degree of success.

25. Address behavioral dimensions of learning as opposed to just content (Rabbior, 1990, pp. 56- 65).

We find Rabbior's elements above relevant to any entrepreneurship program whether in low, middle or high income countries.

CONCLUSION

It is shown in this chapter that vocational and technical education in Kenya was resented by Kenyans during the colonial period because of its roots in racial segregation (Republic of Kenya, 1964; Sifuna, 1976). On attainment of independence, the government abolished agriculture, a practical subject from the school curriculum. This was quite ironical given that the development of the newly independent state entirely depended on agriculture.

The chapter shows that due to an unemployment problem among school leavers with purely academic education in the late 1960s, vocational and technical education started gaining value. In the early 1970s, most vocational and technical institutions were established on "Harambee" (self help) basis. In 1985, a new education system 8.4.4 was introduced. The system put greater emphasis on a diversified school curriculum with technical subjects being offered. Besides vocationalization of the school curriculum, postsecondary vocational and technical training institutions have been established. To make graduates from these institutions successful entrepreneurs, entrepreneurship education has been introduced. The chapter finally looks at the role of the government in promoting entrepreneurial spirit among graduates from vocational and technical training institutions as a strategy to develop workforce competencies. In addition, it provides key elements of a successful entrepreneurship education program.

REFERENCES

Acs, Z. J., Carlsson, B., & Karlsson, C. (1999). *Entrepreneurship, small and medium-sized enterprises and the macroeconomy.* Cambridge, MA: Cambridge University Press.

Ashmore, C. M. (1990). Entrepreneurship in vocational education. In C. A. Kent (Ed.), *Entrepreneurship Education: Current developments, future directions* (pp. 211-229). New York: Quorum Books.

Christensen, C., Johnson, M., & Rigby, D. (2002). Foundations for growth, *MIT Sloan Management Review, 43*(3), 22-32.

Devol, R., Koepp, R., & Fogelbach, F. (2002). *The state technology and science index: Comparing and contrasting California.* Santa Monica, CA: Milken Institute.

Gichira, R., & Nelson, E. R. (1997). Training needs perceptions of Kenyan entrepreneurs. *Journal of Industrial Teacher Education, 35*(1), 89-108.

Goal, J. (2006, January). International workforce development perspectives: Germany and the United States. *Techniques, 82*(1), 36-39.

Ikiara, K. G. (1991). Policy changes and the informal sector: A review. In P. Coughlin & K. G. Ikiara (Eds.), *Kenya's Industrialization Dilemma* (pp. 309-318). Nairobi: Heinemann.

International Labor Organization (1972). *Employment, incomes and equality: A strategy for increasing productive employment in Kenya.* Geneva: International Labor Organization.

Katz, J. A. (2003). The chronology and intellectual trajectory of American entrepreneurship education 1876-1999. *Journal of Business Venturing, 18*(2), 283-300.

Kenya Colony and Protectorate of. (1925). *Education in East Africa.* London: Edinburgh House Press.

Kenya Colony and Protectorate of. (1960). *African education in Kenya.* Nairobi: Government Printer.

Kerre, B. W. (1991). Vocational and technical education and training in Kenya: The past, present and future prospects. *Kenya Journal of Education, 5*(1), 18-45.

King, K. (1977). *The African artisan: Education and the informal sector in Kenya.* London: Heinemann Educational Books.

Kirby, P. (1983). An entrepreneurship problem. *The American Economic Review, 73*(2), 107-111.

Mburugu, J. B., & Thiong'o, J. M. (1991). *Entrepreneurship education in Kenya: Promoting entrepreneurship education in technical training institutes.* Nairobi: Government Printer.

Nafukho, F. M. (1998). Entrepreneurial skills development programs in Africa: A second look. *Journal of Small Business Development, 36*(1), 100-103.

Nelson, E. R., & Scott, D. J. (1997). Entrepreneurship education as a strategic approach to Economic Growth in Kenya. *Journal of Industrial Teacher Education, 35*(1), 7-21.

Owano, A. (1988). *Education for employment: The contribution of the Youth Polytechnic Program to youth employment in Kenya.* Unpublished doctoral dissertation, Kenyatta University, Nairobi, Kenya.

Rabbior, G. (1990). Elements of a successful entrepreneurship/economics/education program. In C. A. Kent (Ed.), *Entrepreneurship education: Current developments, future directions* (pp. 53-65). New York: Quorum Books.

Rao, T. V., & Wright C. (1991). *Entrepreneurial skills development programs in fifteen Commonwealth countries.* London: Commonwealth Secretariat.

Republic of Kenya. (1964). *Education commission report.* Nairobi: Government Printer.

Republic of Kenya. (1976). *Report of the national committee on education objectives and policies.* Nairobi: Government Printer.

Republic of Kenya. (1981). *The presidential working party on the second university in Kenya.* Nairobi: Government Printer.

Republic of Kenya. (1984). *8.4.4 system of education: Ministry of Education Science and Technology.* Nairobi: Government Printer.

Republic of Kenya. (1986). *Sessional paper No. 1 on economic management for renewed growth.* Nairobi, Government Printer.

Republic of Kenya. (1988). *Report of the presidential working party on education and training for the next decade and beyond* (Kamunge Report). Nairobi: Government Printer.

Republic of Kenya. (1992). *Small scale Jua Kali development in Kenya* (Sessional Paper No. 2). Nairobi: Government Printer.

Schumpeter, J. A. (1950). *Capitalism, socialism, and democracy* (3rd ed.). New York: Harper & Row.

Sheffield, J. R. (1971). Kenya. In the *Encyclopedia of Education* (pp. 294-297). New York: MacMillan & Free Press.

Sifuna, D. N. (1976). *Vocational education in schools: A historical survey of Kenya and Tanzania.* Nairobi: East African Literature Bureau.

United Nations Educational, Scientific and Cultural Organization. (1984). *Terminology of technical education.* Paris: Author.

Vesper, K. H. (1982). Research on education for entrepreneurship. In C. A. Kent, D. L. Sexton, & K. H. Vesper (Eds.), *Encyclopedia of Entrepreneurship* (pp. 321-343). Englewood Cliffs, NJ: Prentice-Hall.

Vesper, K. H., & Gartner, W. B. (1997). Measuring progress in entrepreneurship education. *Journal of Business Venturing, 12*(5), 403-421.

CHAPTER 10

WORKFORCE COMPETENCIES

A Comparison of U.S. and
Jamaican Experiences

Henry O'Lawrence

INTRODUCTION

*The future of Manual Training is to introduce handwork as the principal factor in
the first four years' work, to be continued in the four years of the grammar grades,
and to be correlated with all other subjects. Indeed, the ideal is to introduce Manual
Training in all courses of study inclusively from Kindergarten to University. Manual
Training gives true dignity to labor; it calls attention to the place of handwork in
human progress, and as civilization goes on, it will have a higher and still higher
place in the hearts of the people.*

—as cited in Ham, 1900, pp. xii-xiii.

Career and technical education in the United States has had an impact on
many developing countries, especially Latin American and the Caribbean
countries. Specialists from the United States have been employed by such

*Innovations in Career and Technical Education: Strategic Approaches Towards
Workforce Competencies Around the Globe*, pp. 193–217
Copyright © 2008 by Information Age Publishing
All rights of reproduction in any form reserved.

agencies as the International Labor Organization (ILO) of the United Nations, United Nations Educational, Scientific, and Cultural Organization (UNESCO), U.S. Agency for International Development (USAID), the Peace Corps, and other various private agencies that espouse today's global competitive workplace. Thus, career and technical education (formerly known as vocational education) focuses on developing and training to the fullest extent, the moral, physical, and intellectual skills that people need to flourish in the global workforce.

The field of career and technical education seeks to dignify labor, generate power, and contribute to the harmony of development. It must be where the brain reforms muscle, where thought directs every blow, where the mind, eye, and hand constitute an invincible triple alliance (Ham, 1900). Workforce education of the twenty-first century must be established as the natural center of public schools, secondary schools, and the higher educational systems. The terms career and technical education and workforce education training and development are used interchangeably in this chapter.

It appears necessary, before setting forth the nature and positive value of career and technical education in a scheme of general education, to point toward the new trends and characteristics of the prevailing system of workforce education and development. Therefore, at the outset, this chapter specifies the role of career and technical education in developing a nation's wealth. It also discusses the historical background of vocational education in the United States and across the globe. In addition, discusses the importance of workforce development education and provides evidence from the Caribbean nations, especially Jamaica.

Workforce education is a professional endeavor. Professions are practices related to the central life-giving, life-sustaining, life-fulfilling events of human existence, coupled with four ethical obligations: to promote learning, to ensure health and safety, to protect the public or private trust, and to promote the transfer of learning (Gray & Herr, 1998). As noted

> The mission of workforce education is to promote individual opportunities by making students more competitive in the labor force, thus allowing them to pursue personal career goals, and to make a nation economically strong and firms internationally competitive by solving human performance problems of incumbent (i.e., already employed) workers. (p. 4)

Workforce education includes human resource development (HRD) efforts for all types of incumbent workers, including professionals.

THE VOCATIONAL EDUCATION MOVEMENT AROUND THE GLOBE

The programs of vocational education in the United States have influenced vocational education programs in many countries. Apprenticeship programs were brought from Europe to colonial America. The schools of Pestalozzi and Fellenberg from Switzerland were used as models in the United States for the work-study schools in the early nineteenth century; later, industrial education was influenced by the Russian system of manual training and the Scandinavian Sloyd system. France and Italy influenced instruction in the Arts and Crafts Movement and Germany contributed the idea of continuation schools to the vocational education programs of the United States (Roberts, 1965). Vocational education expanded rapidly in Italy during the postwar years, and the Ministry of National Education in the Republic of France was responsible for the administration of national vocation secondary schools and technical secondary schools, while apprenticeship training centers financed by public funds provided training for youth 14-17 years of age who were not attending school full time.

In Scandinavian countries, vocational education is divided among various ministries. For instance, in Norway, the vocational schools of agriculture are under the ministry of agriculture, the ministry of fisheries is responsible for schools for fishermen, the ministry of commerce and shipping controls schools for seamanship, and the ministry of family and consumer affairs controls nursery schools. Denmark vocational schools are similar to those of Norway, and apprenticeship schemes are used in Demark to provide vocational education in various trades. In Sweden, the board of vocational training manages responsibility for much of the vocational education. The board is composed of 15 representatives, including management and labor in various vocational fields concerned with business schools, schools of domestic education, technical high schools, and trade schools. The Swedish Employer's Association and the Confederation of Swedish Trade Unions also established a joint council to deal with matters affecting training in industry. In Finland, graduates of elementary schools may enter various types of vocational schools supervised by various ministries of the national government; and 4-year technical institutes admit students who are 18 years of age or older (Roberts, 1965). The Finish system of vocational education and training is currently being reformed. Until 1995 vocational education and training led to the same qualification whether preceded by the comprehensive school leaving certificate (9 years of school), or the matriculation examination (12 years of schooling). Higher vocational qualifications have traditionally been called postsecondary qualifications. Postsecondary vocational education and training provide students with broad practical skills as well as a solid understanding of the underlying theoretical substance (Bergstrom et al., 1997).

In view of the context and status of career and technical education, each European country varies in the analysis of its national reforms in terms of the four post-16 strategies: the national enhancement strategy (enhancement of vocational education programs), the linkage strategy (developing linkages between academic and vocational programs), the mutual enrichment strategy (encouraging mutual enrichment between academic and vocational programs), and the unification strategy (developing a unified educational provision to replace educational systems based on academic/vocational division). Overall, the European model is a form of social action and reform of the workplace to benefit the worker and on the other hand, approaches in the United States and Taiwan tend toward the development of human resources for strong economic growth (Heidegger, 2000; Hwang, 2000)

In Russia, the Russian vocational and technical education is supply driven, rigidly structured and slow to adapt to economic change, and it is known for its wide coverage of specializations and its relevance to employment. Russia's vocational training institutions confounded Western experts with signs of adaptability and creativity in the face of massive economic and social change. They have expanded in response to new demands and have demonstrated vigor that had been largely unanticipated (Heyneman, 1996).

The Russian system of education established four general types of vocational programs lower than college level for the education of its workers:

1. Basic elementary vocational schools for industry, popularly known as labor reserve schools, train youth for semiskilled or skilled work in industry.

2. For more technical applications, 1- and 2-year vocational schools are designed to train junior technical workers for employment in metallurgy, chemistry, construction, communications, mining, and other industries.

3. State and employer operated schools and courses provide on-the-job training for new employees, and this level of education is known as individual-brigade training designed to train new and unskilled workers in the process of production.

4. Formal and informal on-the-job and job-related training programs educate what are called semiprofessional technicians who are trained in technicums for agriculture and industry. The ministry of higher education has the responsibility for the operation of

semiprofessional programs for the training of technicians in industry and agriculture. These training programs are more advanced than the trade technical programs and less advanced than the professional programs for engineers and agriculturalists.

In German, there are three major types of vocational schools. These include:

1. Part-time vocational schools designed primarily for apprentices, who must continue their general education until age 18. The curriculum consists of about two-thirds technical and one-third general education.

2. Technical trade schools which are full-time vocational schools designed to replace all or part of the apprenticeship training, and the school program is from 1 to 3 years in length. The technical trade schools for women include curricula in homemaking, training children's nurses and household assistants, and women's trades and crafts. Some technical trade schools specialize in the education of welfare and social workers, kindergarten teachers, business or commercial subjects, and home economics.

3. Technical schools which offer full-time programs for the education of workers for technical occupations in such fields as building construction, chemistry, textiles, agriculture, commerce, and industry; the course of study combines practical training with theoretical instruction.

The German education system has been praised for its ability to provide quality general education combined with excellent specific training for a profession or skilled occupation. In 1992, about 65% of the country's workforce had been trained through vocational education. In the same year, 2.3 million young people were enrolled in vocational or trade schools. The German vocational education system also has more than 400 occupations offering apprenticeships, and is structured around nationally standardized curricula and examinations administered by external bodies (such as chambers of crafts). About 75% young Germans seek apprenticeships and the remaining 25% enter universities. In 2002, German firms offered more than 570,000 apprenticeship positions and roughly the same numbers of job seekers were placed into those positions (PortJobs, 2004).

In China, vocational education is conducted in vocational schools attached to and operated by industrial and business enterprises, and in on-the-job training programs. More students are enrolled in on-the-job and spare-time training than in organized schools, with the tendency for all students to engage in some productive work and all workers to enroll in some type of school.

Before the economic reform in China, only a state-owned economy existed, and there was no form of private ownership. Since the reform and an opening up of Chinese society, the economic system has gradually transformed from the traditional planned economy to the market economy. This transformation constituted a different influence on aspects of Chinese society. The establishment of the market economy led to innovation in China's system of vocational education, and the transformation of operational mechanism became the focus of this stage of development. The problems associated with an idle population and the varying quality of human resources within the labor force and the training market impact vocational education both externally and internally (Wang & Shieh, 2006).

In Japan, there are a broad range of vocational education programs for both boys and girls. Vocational education in agriculture, fisheries, trade and industry, commerce, homemaking, and technical education is provided in lower-secondary schools (Grades 7, 8, and 9), upper-secondary schools (Grades 10, 11, and 12), special schools, and in industry. Many of the upper-secondary schools in rural districts are vocational schools with emphasis on vocational agriculture, and the curriculum is somewhat similar to that of vocational agriculture in the United States. They also maintain part-time and evening schools for employed youth and adults, and most part-time schools are administered by the secondary schools while vocational technical education of a terminal nature is provided in some of the junior colleges. Most Japanese upper secondary schools offer academic programs that prepare students for higher education, but do not offer vocational courses, so those students who participate in vocational courses do so in vocational schools; in 1990 school year, about 26% of upper secondary school students were enrolled in vocational education classes (Murata & Stern, 1993).

In the Caribbean, vocational education is operated by the various ministries through tertiary institutions, with the governments financing the entire cost, selecting the teachers, and establishing curriculums and courses of study. The nations of the Caribbean affiliated with European countries, Canada, and the United States have developed educational plans in collaboration with the Caribbean commission to improve the economy of the area. In addition to the postprimary vocational and technical schools, which have been in existence for some time, some new technical institutes have been established (Roberts, 1965).

During Jamaica's colonial era for example, the teacher training colleges were always virtually the only avenue for advanced training in agriculture and other technical areas, and those trained in these colleges pursued careers in almost every field imaginable. The only other occupation comparable in numbers with teaching in Jamaica was that of government civil service—in 1861, there were 448 teachers and 624 civil servants compared with 1921, when there were 2,178 teachers and 2,521 civil servants. Together with other professional groups, these made up only 3.3% of the working population. Teacher training continues to be one of the most common forms of higher education available on the island and it also remains the least expensive path for students. In 1982, about 48% students would prefer having done something else besides teaching but the point remains that 42% students in Jamaica do not anticipate a career in teaching. Teaching training is free in Jamaica, including boarding accommodation for most trainees (Brandon & Moriah, 1988).

In a 1989 meeting of the Jamaican Council of Ministers of Education, the ministers decided that the territories should embark on a program of technical and vocational training to prepare the regional workforce to deal with the effects of deregulation, liberalization, and globalization. The ministers decided that the workers should be trained to meet a common set of standards that were globally competitive. The council mandated different territories to form training agencies to oversee, govern, and regulate training and to make people competitive. Jamaica established the National Training Agency (NTA) in 1991 to carry out the objectives of the council. The Jamaican government also recognized that a separate body was needed to concentrate on quality management, accreditation, and certification of training agencies, and so the National Council on Technical Vocational Education and Training (NCTVET) was established as a department of Human Employment and Resource Training Trust (HEART/NTA). In 2005, a total of 18,125 people were certified to meet international standards, an increase of 36% over the previous year (Chaplin, 2006).

THE VOCATIONAL EDUCATION MOVEMENT IN THE UNITED STATES

The Vocational Education Movement in the United States began in 1906 with the report of the Douglas Commission to the Massachusetts Legislature and the organization of the National Society for the Promotion of Industrial Education. However, for 30 years prior to 1906, interest in practical education had been increasing. The manual-training movement had spread rapidly, causing instruction in the mechanic arts and woodworking at high schools or many schools of upper-elementary grade. It was further discussed that when well taught, manual training provided a foundation of industrial knowledge and habits of performance with tools that served as a basis for further instruction in a mechanical trade (Bennett, 1937).

A few trade schools and technical schools demonstrated what could be done in the training of skilled workmen. Some schools were developed as manual training schools, with the analysis of tool processes using exercises, after the manner of the Russian system of tool instruction, while others followed a modified apprenticeship method of instruction. The best of them combined these tools and added related mathematical, science, and technical information, which was handed down from engineering schools and industry. The major schools were:

1. The New York Trade School, opened in 1881, and established by Colonel Richard T. Auchtmuty, who had studied the problems of trade teaching and reached some definite conclusions, which he proceeded to put into practice. The school was later adopted by the trade-school department of Pratt Institute established in Brooklyn, New York, in 1887.

2. The Williamson Free School of Mechanical Trades, located about 16 miles outside of Philadelphia, Pennsylvania. Isaiah V. Williamson endowed the school and opened it by 1891. The school was designed to take the place of the old system of apprenticeship, in so far as any school could do that, and all boys (between 16 and 18 years of age with evidence of moral character and who could pass an examination in the common-school branches) admitted were bound as indentured apprentices to the trusties of the school for 3 years.

3. The Hebrew Technical Institute of New York. In 1883, thousands of Jewish immigrants reached New York as a result of tremendous hardships imposed upon them in Russia. In the autumn of that year, a few citizens of New York met to consider what might be done for these immigrants. It was decided to start a technical school for the immigrants' sons for the purpose of promoting industrial pursuits among Jews. In 1889, the director of the school, Dr. Henry M. Leipziger, said that the object of the school was educational and economic—educational, as it proposed to apply the best methods of teaching the principles that underlie the trades, and economic, as it proposed to equip its graduates for some special calling in life.

4. The California School of Mechanical Arts, established in San Francisco through the gift of James Lick. Beginning in 1895, under the principalship of George A. Merrill, this school provided a 2-year manual-training course, followed by a 2-year trade or technical

course in any 1 of 10 industrial occupations. The school also emphasized instruction in academic subjects taught in their practical relation to industrial subjects (Bennett, 1937).

During this period, evening schools for industrial workers flourished and the mechanics institutes were supplemented by such schools as Pratt Institute in Brooklyn, the Drexel Institute in Philadelphia, and a few apprentice schools were conducted by corporations and by public evening schools. Among the earliest of the apprentice schools was the school established in 1872 by R. Hoe and Company of New York City, manufacturers of printing presses, machinery, and saws. Instruction included mechanical drawing, arithmetic, algebra, and geometry; and for a short time beginning in 1885, the Baltimore and Ohio Railroad Company maintained a technical school for the apprentices in the company's service. In 1902, the Grand Trunk Railway opened a school at Battle Creek, Michigan. In 1905, a note of warning was sounded in a paper before the Railway Mechanics Association, and a plan was outlined for apprentice instruction to solve the problem of increasing the efficiency of shop workmen (Bennett, 1937).

The object of the evening trade schools was mainly to give men already employed in the trades, who knew at least a part of the trade in which they were employed, an opportunity to broaden their mechanical training and make themselves more efficient workmen. During the years preceding the vocational education movement, it was generally assumed, and usually without question, that the teaching of trades should not be done at public expense; yet, in the later years of that period, there was a growing minority of citizens who were questioning the validity of the old attitude toward such expenditure (Bennett, 1937).

THE NEW SCHOOLS TO MEET NEW CONDITIONS

Based on the increasing demands of manufacturers, labor leaders, and the public for more practical instruction in public schools and, with the lessening of the opposition to the expenditure of public funds to tech trades, a great variety of experiments in industrial education were developed. From this variety of experiments, a few more or less definite types of schools evolved or were further developed during the 10 years from 1907 to 1917. Among these were:

1. The Prevocational or Industrial School—These were the elementary or intermediate industrial or prevocational schools intended to help give direction to children between 14 and 16 and

to provide education with an industrial bias parallel to that education with an academic bias, which was prevalent in the seventh, eighth, and sometimes ninth grades.

2. The Continuation School—This was a school in which one who had left the full-time day school had to continue his education—evening schools have long existed.

3. The Part-Time Cooperative School—This was one in which the pupils spent alternate weeks in school and in a commercially productive shop—hybrid modes of delivery of education had existed since 1908.

4. The Day Vocational or Trade School—Under the influence of the Vocational Education Movement, and especially when state aid was available, the full-time trade schools under public-school administration began to increase in number and change somewhat in form. These gave more attention to the teaching of technical and other related subject matter and to education for citizenship.

5. The Apprenticeship or Corporation School—This school flourished under the vocational education movement between 1907 and 1917, and most of the schools of this type were maintained to give instruction in mathematics, mechanical drawing, and such elements of physical science, as were related to the particular industry they served.

The vocational education movement aimed to fit boys and girls for specific occupations, to train them for definite skilled trades, and for jobs brought about by the necessity of their choosing between occupations and, consequently, between courses to pursue. The report of the Massachusetts Commission of 1906 and the work of the National Society for the Promotion of Industrial Education were so effective in arousing interest in the problems of industrial education that several states followed the example of Massachusetts; state commissions were appointed by Vermont, New Jersey, and Maryland in 1908, by Michigan in 1909, and by Maine in 1910. In that same year, Wisconsin appointed a legislative committee to investigate industrial and trade education (Bennett, 1937).

The chief goal of the National Society for the Promotion of Industrial Education was to secure an adequate federal law providing national aid for industrial education, and it was through this law that Charles A. Prosser emerged as deputy commissioner of education for the State of Massachusetts to become the secretary of the society. After accepting the position, he went to Washington to help draft Senator Page's new bill. However, the general support of the Page bill did not prevent powerful interests that caused delays. Instead, other legislators insisted that the

Smith-Lever agricultural extension bill be given precedence over the vocational education bill. A legislative deadlock followed and the Smith-Lever bill finally passed in January 1914; although Congress received it on June 1, 1914, it was not brought forward for final action until the president urged its passage in January 1916. Then came a new bill presented by Representative Dudley M. Hughes and it included home-economics (currently known as family and consumer science) in addition to previously designated industrial education for women. The Smith-Lever bill led Congress to pass a resolution creating the commission on National Aid to Vocational Education. Five leaders in the movement, including Dr. Prosser, discussed (a) the need of vocational education, (b) the need of national grants to the states, (c) kinds of vocational education for which national grants should be given, (d) aid to vocational education through federal agencies, (e) the extent to which the national government should aid vocational education, (f) conditions under which grants for vocational education should be given., and (g) proposed legislation. To the discussion of these subjects were added supporting data, including hearings, statements from letters, and statistics. The commission recommended that national grants be made to the states (a) for training teachers of vocational subjects, (b) for paying part of the salaries of teacher of vocational subjects, and (c) that appropriations be made to a federal board for making studies and investigations that would be helpful to vocational schools (Bennett, 1937).

Another factor in shaping public sentiment was the work of the Vocational Education Association of the Middle West, which held large annual conventions in Chicago. Most of its discussions at that time focused on the various problems of relationships between vocational education and the public school system. Under the leadership of Mr. Bogan, and with the support of nearly every leader of thought on vocational education in the Midwestern states, this association provided a public forum for the discussion of vital topics on vocational training and its relation to public education. Leaders from the East as well as the West, and representing widely different points of view, were brought together in an effort to solve a great social-educational problem in the wisest way. An important climax was reached in the discussion of the Smith-Hughes act after the United States Chamber of Commerce took a nationwide referendum vote on the subject of vocational education in 1916. This resulted in what was approximately a seven-to-one vote in favor of the provisions of the Smith-Hughes bill. After another delay and then an urgent demand for early action from the President, the Smith-Hughes bill was passed and was signed by President Wilson on February 23, 1917 (Bennett, 1937).

The signing of the Smith-Hughes act, thereby creating a federal directing and reimbursing law with reference to certain types of vocational education, served as the beginning of a new era in manual and industrial education in the United States. Its signing ended the era with which this chapter is concerned and established today's workforce education and development in a global perspective.

THE NEW PERSPECTIVES OF CAREER AND TECHNICAL EDUCATION

The conception of vocational education has changed throughout the years, as it is now perceived as an integral and essential part of our education system. It is no longer realistic to measure people by the kind of work they do; rather, people are measured by the quality of performance of such work. Vocational education has always had a strong social conscience that is concerned with people who are going to become members of the labor force and with the people who produce the goods and services required by society.

According to Barlow (1965), vocational education was born of social and economic needs and is closely linked to the needs and behavior of the total population and to its economic well being. Vocational education identifies key trends in population growth, such as minority groups that strive for recognition; deals with urbanization and the general mobility of the population across a large geographical area; has concern for women in the labor force, the scope of their employment, and their entrance into new occupational fields; and in general, creates solutions for social development. The purpose and function of vocational education in contemporary public education since World War II is evident in the growing dependence of the American economy upon the vocational competence of the people.

Vocational education is unique in a number of ways. It treats students as practitioners, preparing them for skilled entry-level jobs that do not require a baccalaureate degree. It offers training in specialized skills in 2-year postsecondary schools and its success in placing students in jobs is highly dependent upon the economy. There is a notion that vocational schools should prepare students for work by introducing practical subjects designed to train the hand as well as the mind. There are three pieces of legislation critical in the development of vocational education: the Smith-Hughes Act of 1917 (P.L. 64–347), the Vocational Education Act of 1963 (P.L. 88–210), and the 1968 amendments (P.L. 90–576) to the 1963 Vocational Education Act. The Smith-Hughes Act provided federal aid for vocational education offered by public secondary schools to adults who wanted better jobs. The Vocational Education Act of 1963 authorized increased funding for vocational education and also encouraged vocational education to shift to broader goals related to the development of human potential and long-term employment. The 1968 Vocational Education Amendments continued to emphasize serving the needs of students with the aim of providing better service to the disadvantaged, the handicapped, post-secondary, and adult students. The legislation also provided support for the career education movement by stressing career planning as well as employment preparation of students (Barlow, 1965).

The National Research Council (1976) stated that the primary objectives of vocational education programs have been to prepare students for occupations and job training, using two complementary strategies of labor-market information and career guidance. Vocational educators use labor-market information to predict future demand for certain occupations and to adapt programs to meet the demands. While labor-market demand forecasts attempt to take into account the extent to which wages and working conditions will change depending on how many workers are trained, program planners and researchers should recognize that labor-market information from various vocational education districts must be coordinated in some way because workers move from place to place. Since macroeconomic or institutionally oriented employment policy affects total demand for labor, it should be taken into account in labor-market forecasts. Career development and guidance strive to meet the needs of individual students while they are enrolled and after graduation. The overall goal of career guidance is to improve the ability of students to make career decisions.

The philosophy and interests of Dewey, Snedden, and Prosser had points of similarity as well as differences, as each wanted the schools to change and be directed toward preparation for occupations, more democratic, and to play a more significant role in preparing a larger segment of the population for a democratic society. However, all had the view that vocational education was an important part of America's schools (Miller, & Gregson, 1999).

REFORM AND VOCATIONAL EDUCATION

The implications of the following US national reports not only raised and echoed critical concerns that will be identified immediately below, but recognized vocational education as a means for improving the workforce, and academic achievement.

- 1983 Nation at Risk
- 1991 Secretary's Commission on Achieving Necessary Skills (SCANS)
- 2000 America's Choice: High Skills or Low Wages, Workforce 2000

*Reports' Implications: Prompted Education Reform With the Focus on
Secondary Education*

1. Concern about our ability to be competitive in the international market
2. Poor performance of students on tests
3. Employers' frustrations with lack of basic skills of young people entering the workforce.

General Recommendations

1. Longer school day and year
2. Increasing graduation requirements in basic academics
3. Raising entrance requirements for state colleges and universities.
4. Adding to the basics and foreign language for the college bound.

Implications for Today's Global Workforce Education

1. Federal support for vocational education
2. Leadership and cost-effective information sharing
3. Federal legislation increasingly reflects the needs of:

   I. Students.
   II. Changing economy.
   III. Diversification of the workforce.

4. Sometimes more emphasis on:

   I. National activities
   II. States and localities

For America to be competitive in the global economy, the federal investment in vocational education must support the improvement of academic and occupational skills and the expansion of access for all students in the programs. The needs of students and the workplace are crucial to the development of workforce competencies, and it is imperative that integration of core academic and vocational education continues. To ensure emphasis on this priority, governance of vocational education must remain within the purview of education and not segregated from other education reform efforts (Gordon, 2003).

THE ROLE OF COMMUNITY COLLEGE IN
THE TWENTY-FIRST CENTURY WORKFORCE

Federal law defines vocational education as preparation for occupations requiring other than baccalaureate or advanced degree. In spite of the statutory definition, vocational education has been changing. Institutions such as community colleges have developed new courses of study that prepare or will prepare students for work as well as for further education to meet the competitiveness of the labor market trend in the twenty-first century (Gordon, 2003). Community colleges and other postsecondary institutions offering career and vocational technical training programs will continue to adapt existing programs and establish new programs to prepare a workforce and serve state policy initiatives and employers' needs to compete and survive in the twenty-first century global economy (Levin, 2001).

Career and technical education and the role of the community college have evolved beyond that of traditional entry-level workforce training to include training that will provide individuals with skill sets needed to pursue careers in high-wage, high-skill occupations. This metamorphosis brought about by changing needs and demands made by the federal government, the private sector, and the business world has created what is being referred to as new vocationalism. This new vocationalism is centered on five core principles:

- Career clusters that extend from entry-level positions through professional levels in fields considered integral to the new economy
- An integrated curriculum consisting of both academic and vocational elements
- More integration into the K-16 educational system and a broader base of economic and social structures
- Active teaching strategies, learner-centered instruction, constructivist theories, and project-based approaches to teaching, and
- More holistic instruction and a curriculum that is more meaningful in applicability

Inherent in each of these core principles is the input of business. Active participation by business allows for more comprehensive, tailor-made programs that are mutually beneficial to all parties—students, community college, and businesses (Hennigan, 2001).

The American labor market continues to be strong and resilient because its economy creates jobs, expands output, and rewards work with good compensation. Job growth started recovering in 2003 from the effects of the last recession, and the economy has tallied 34 consecutive months of job gains through June 2006. As the economy grows steadily, there remain some challenges; the United States and the rest of the world are experiencing a major economic transformation in the area of technology and it has accelerated the pace of change, as the United States is making the transition to a knowledge-based economy. The key here is that good jobs are being created in large numbers and the majority of employment growth during the past 5 years was in occupations with above-average compensation. A caveat is that most of the new jobs projected for the future are expected to be filled by persons with some kind of postsecondary education and who have gained knowledge and skills that are in demand, which is the key to success in America's dynamic labor market (U.S. Department of Labor, 2006).

With workforce education in the twenty-first century, the occupational training and advanced workplace literacy-skills strategy is important for developing skills needed to be competitive in a global economy. Educational institutions, especially community colleges, will continue to play a central role in developing skills and equipping people to fulfill their place in society, and in providing solutions to the agony and malaise caused by a rising unemployment rate, which is exacerbated by unskilled workers. It was suggested that the better our trained workers are, the stronger a nation will be economically, which will, therefore, lead to more competition, more employment opportunities, and decreased susceptibility to crime, violence, and riots to improve desperate situations. Educators in all educational institutions should recognize the need for such an immensely important professional undertaking that influences the economy and the lives, opportunities, and dreams of many job seekers (Van Der Linde, 2006).

America's economy is at the forefront of a national policy debate, with federal, state, and local leaders examining ways to keep the country at the top of international innovation as other countries make technological and economic gains. It is evident that the nation has evolved from an industrial economy to a knowledge economy; and since the early 1990s, the pace of change in the global economy has accelerated, global lines are blurring, and companies once associated with American innovation are just as prominent in Bangalore as in Silicone Valley. Economists reported that the global economy grew 4.7% in 2004 and Asia (excluding Japan) grew 8.2%, while Latin America grew 5.6% and the U.S. lagged behind at 4.4%, just below the global average. Europe, Canada, South Korea, and many other countries around the world launched ambitious competitiveness agendas to increase innovation, develop technology, and make it easier for business to invest in new research and development to spur economic growth (Association for Career and Technical Education [ACTE], 2003).

THE CARIBBEAN EXPERIENCE

Vocational training institutions (VTIs) in Latin America and the Caribbean countries are undergoing considerable changes, primarily in response to the profound transformations taking place globally in the world of work and production. In some sectors, corporations and companies are playing more active roles as investors and/or direct providers of training for their workers. New providers of work training have emerged; private companies, renovated in-company training organs, training institutions initiated by management, centers of technological development, non-government organizations, and many others are actively involved in the provision of varying forms of adult vocational education.

The government agents connected with work training have also diversified significantly. They no longer include only ministries of education and the VTIs, but also new agents such as the ministries of labor and social welfare, solidarity or social compensation funds, local government entities, etc., which have become public sources of finance, taking advantage of and/or stimulating the emergence of training markets that involve numerous public and private providers. With this evolution has come the need to incorporate work-training systems into the discussion of public education and employment policy. This also raises the question of what roles the public and private sectors should play in this field, both from the perspective of public economy when it differentiates between the functions of public good and private good, and from the perspective of social equity in the interest of guaranteeing access to equal training opportunities for the whole population.

Jamaica is the largest of the English speaking Caribbean islands, with a population of 2.5 million at mid-1997 and well connected to United Kingdom, Canada, and the United States in development of its educational system. Government agencies connected with work training have branched out to form new agencies such as the Human Employment and Resource Training Trust (HEART), established in 1982 by then Prime Minister Edward Seaga, and the National Training Agency (NTA), set up in 1991 by the Michael Manley government, which was the largest training agency in the country.

The primary objective of this agency is to create a labor-force competence able to compete in the twenty-first century global economy. It was well stated in its mission that it wanted to create a Jamaican workforce that is trained and certified to international standards, stimulate employment, create investments, and contribute to improved productivity, competitiveness, and prosperity of individuals, enterprises, and the nation. HEART/NTA trains and assesses while the National Council of Technical Vocational Education and Training (NCTVET), an arm of the organization, certifies the workforce to world standards and is responsible for quality management and accreditation. For Jamaica's workforce to be competitive for twenty-first century global economy, it must go through a certification program, meaning that employees must hold certifications for their jobs. A training program such as an apprenticeship type in which graduates could learn craft and other skills on the job is a key requisite for preparation for the world of work, since employers are reluctant to employ untrained people.

Recent relevant data from a study done by a Planning Institute of Jamaica (PIOJ) and an International Labour Organization survey on the characteristics of some 2,685 youth ages 15 to 24 years old revealed that 32% of employed persons in Jamaica have received some level of vocational training; also indicated in the study was the type of training received: hospitality skills, automotive skills, and beauty-care skills were the most common training students chose. The report also indicated that older persons are likely to be employed in the workforce and people are looking for workers with experience. There is a correlation between age and employment; however, having no suitable training opportunities, an unsuitable general education, no education, unsuitable vocation education, and not enough jobs available are the major obstacles for the workforce (Kerr, 2006).

Unlike the United States, where private postsecondary institutions and community colleges remain the major training institutions for career and technical education, Jamaica's postsecondary education and training is through tertiary education, which is provided in undergraduate and postgraduate programs. Public institutions account for approximately 86% of enrollment, while undergraduate, diploma, and certificate students account for 95% of enrollment, including community colleges that also offer vocational programs. According to Blank and McArdle (2003), 7.2% of 18- to 24-year-old students enrolled in tertiary-level education institutions in 2001, while 17% of the wealthiest quintile enrolled in postsecondary institutions, as compared with less than 2% of the poorest quintile.

HEART Trust/NTA is responsible for the public vocational training system in Jamaica and for financing and delivering most public preemployment training. The programs are financed through a 3% tax on wages, while some revenues are also realized from fees to trainees and/ or firms. Heart operates 10 academies and specialized institutions, with 16 vocational training centers and two on-the-job training programs: the School Leavers Training Opportunities Program (SL-TOPS) and the

Apprenticeship Program. Training is offered in 11 sectorial groupings, with the largest concentrations of learners in hospitality trades (20%), information and communications technology (20%), and building and construction skills (15%). Training programs correspond to skill levels of employment: Level 1 (semiskilled,) Level II (skilled), and Level III (skilled and technician/supervisory levels of training). Almost one half of enrollments are in Level I programs, with 12% in Level II programs, 7% in Level III. The absolute numbers of persons enrolled in higher-level training has increased; however, targets for increased enrollment in higher-level courses have not been met (Blank & McArdle, 2003).

On the other hand, eight community colleges provide pre-university, general education, professional, paraprofessional, and vocational training. They have introduced almost 40 different technical/vocational and continuing education courses, but only 4% of total enrollment in community colleges is in vocational areas. Table 10.1 lists a summary of education and training providers in other to understand the whole of the lifelong learning in Jamaica.

THE TWENTY-FIRST CENTURY WORKFORCE EDUCATION AND DEVELOPMENT

What has emerged significantly in this chapter is that the foundation of career and technical education and the postsecondary institution have formed a globalization theory of divergence and diversity from local to global patterns of behavior—economically, and socially. Globalization increases interdependence in cultural, economic, and political activities across borders as well as awareness of the reduction of temporal and spatial boundaries globally (Guillen, 2001). Indeed, the global forces since the start of the twenty-first century influenced all postsecondary institutions internationally to look into economically competitive orientation and higher-level programming to meet the needs of the new economic paradigm—workplace skills that prepare business and industry for favorable global positions and that prepare individuals to compete in the global economy.

If postsecondary institutions and all tertiary institutions across the globe are to succeed in preparing individuals for careers in the global economy of the twenty-first century, the career needs of 18- to 25-year-old adults need to be met. These young adults need to discuss career pathways with counselors and make conscious career choices or plans. Resourceful counselors who can help adults understand the new workplace, the relationship between family and work, andragogy, diversity of customers and coworkers, assessment tools, and global

**Table 10.1.   The State of Education and Training:
Lifelong Learning in Jamaica**

	Institutions and Providers	Relevant Examination	Oversight Body
Early Childhood Education	Infant Schools and Department Basic Schools Private Kindergartens	N/A	MOEYC National Council for Education
Primary Education	Primary Schools All Age Schools Primary and Junior High Schools Private Preparatory Schools	National Assessment Program	MOEYC National Council for Education
Secondary Education	Junior High Schools Primary and Junior High School All Age Schools High Schools Technical High Schools Vocational High Schools Private High Schools	Junior High School Certificate Level 1: Semi-skilled, entry-level workers	MOEYC National Council for Education
Tertiary Education	Community Colleges University of the West Indies University of Technology Edna Manley School GC Foster College Teachers Colleges Private and off-shore institutions	Academic Certification (Associate, Bachelor's, Master's and Doctoral) Level 5L Professional Level 4: Paraprofessionals Level 3: Supervisory	MOEYC University Council of Jamaica National Council on TVET HEART Trust/NTA Jamaica Council of Community Colleges
Adult Education	JAMAL Private Adult Education Institute Various Community Development Projects and Programs Various NGO Training Programs	High School Equivalency Program	MOEYC HEART Trust/NTA National Council on TVET
Vocational Training	HEART Trust/NTA (Academies, Institutes, VTCs, SL-TOPS, Apprenticeship, Special Programs) Community Colleges Private Training Institutes Public/Private In-Service Training Community-Based Programs NGO Training Programs	Level 4: Master Craftsman Level 3: Supervisory Level 2: Skilled workers Level 1: Semiskilled, entry-level workers	HEART Trust/NTA National Council on TVET University Council of Jamaica Jamaica Council of Community Colleges

Source: Building a Lifelong Learning Strategy in Jamaica: World Bank/HEART/Trust project.

cultural understanding need to be provided through these institutions (Walter & Farmer, 1999).

The new school has transcended today's community college system with its new mission to train the workforce for the global economy. America's dynamic workforce has been a result of technical education, corporate training, and developmental programs designed to prepare individuals and to expand their career opportunities in the fields of education and training, leadership, supervisory, and administrative positions in areas such as manufacturing, health care, business/financial services, and information technology. This has led to the United States having one of the lowest unemployment rates and one of the highest rates of job creation among industrialized nations.

The challenge of twenty-first century workforce is twofold: increasing flexibility of older workers and global competitiveness. Already the flexibility of the U.S. labor market has enabled older workers to participate in the labor force; it is such flexibility and range of choices available from both the private sector and public sector that make it easier for all Americans to participate in the labor force and further increase job security. Global competitiveness, indeed to be competitive, will require new forms of communication and more efficient mobility, which will make it easier to import and export goods and products to other countries. In March 2005, U.S. exports were at a record high $102.2 billion and were 7.1% higher than 2004; it was estimated, based on the Department of Commerce data, that U.S. firms outsource about 300,000 jobs a year, but foreign companies employ directly at least 6 million workers in the United States (Furchtgott-Roth, 2005).

While in the United States, 62% of the working-age population is employed, 57% of the working-age population in Japan is employed, and 52% is employed in the four major European countries. The higher proportion of Americans employed also work longer hours every year than their counterparts in other countries. Data from Organization for Economic Co-operation and Development in 2003 revealed that Americans worked on average of 1,792 hours per year, compared with 1,718 in Canada, 1,673 in United Kingdom, 1,591 in Italy, 1,453 hours in France, and 1,446 hours per year in Germany; only Japanese among major industrialized countries work more hours per year than Americans. It is interesting to note that the United States has a lower unemployment rate than any other major industrialized nation. Only 12% are unemployed for a year or more. However, the percentage of people unemployed for more than a year is 33% for Japan, 34% for France, 50% for Germany, and 58% for Italy; the only country with low unemployment rates that compare with the United States is Canada, for which only 10% are unemployed for more than a year (Furchtgott-Roth, 2005).

It is impossible to forecast the challenge of the twenty-first century, what new technology is going to be in the 10 years, or what will lead us into 2015 or 2025; however, one thing is certain, flexibility is key. As noted, "Career success belongs to those who recommit quickly when change reshapes the nature of their work" (as cited in Wang, 2006, p. 41). Both employers and employees are going to need to adapt to whatever that comes along and they will need tools to adapt. Intellectual property of inventors and entrepreneurs needs to be protected to keep other countries from stealing the ideas. Because the U.S. leads the world in creativity, theft of intellectual property has been estimated to cost the U.S. hundreds of billions of dollars (Furchtgott-Roth, 2005).

Even though Jamaica is a small country, it is important for it to gain status in a socioeconomic context. Adult literacy levels in Jamaica are 79.9%. This is lower than other lower income and middle income countries, which average 85.3%. During the period between 1990 and 2002, overall employment increased by approximately 6%, and employment growth occurred in all industries within the services sector, while employment growth occurred only within the services sector. The exceptions were construction and installation, while employment in the goods-producing sector declined. Unemployment rates hovered around 15% to 17% during this period, while unemployment among women was consistently twice that of men. Youth unemployment remains high. In 2002, unemployment among females in the 14- to 19- and 20- to 24-year-old cohorts was 61.9% and 39.5%, respectively. Young males fared better, with unemployment among males in these age groups at 37.0% and 18.7%, respectively (Blank & McArdle, 2003).

Globalization will continue to shape and redefine the structure and function of the world economy as it offers unprecedented opportunities for all countries, particularly for developing economies. Further, increases in international trade will improve resource allocation, enhance efficiency by increasing competition among firms, and induce learning and technology transfer, thus facilitating growth. Globalization requires training for society, and the need to adapt rapidly is changing global markets. Surviving in an increasingly competitive and unpredictable business environment is pushing firms to strive for higher productivity and continuous innovation, the achievement of which relies necessarily on a better educated and skilled workforce. There will be new learning, cutting-edge enterprises, and learning organizations, which will lead to more investment in the training of workers.

The key to globalization is to build a high performance workforce; the capable workforce is the main ingredient that guarantees a competitive economic future for those countries that are ready to be competitive in global economy. An abundance of natural and capital resources no longer can guarantee economic success unless human resources become the competitive edge in the high performance, and the global economy. It is important to develop a comprehensive school-to-work system which provides all students (including adult learners) a clearly identifiable, attractive, and accessible career pathway capable to accommodate the needs of students, employers, and the variety of local, and regional labor markets. A supplemental funding and organizational support must also be established to develop an effective school-to-work transition system for all in providing opportunities within the community college system to continue an open entry/exit education and training so that workers can readily obtain new skills demanded by increased job requirement (Ducci, 1998).

REFERENCES

Association for Career and Technical Education. (2003). *Career and technical education's role in American competitiveness*. Retrieved on January 8, 2007, from http://www.acteonline.org/policy/legislative_issues/upload/Competitiveness.pdf

Barlow, M. L. (1965). *A platform for vocational education in the future*. Chicago: The National Society for the Study of Education.

Bennett, C. A. (1937). *History of manual and industrial education 1870-1917*. Peoria, IL: Charles. A. Bennett.

Benson, G. S. (1937, April). American state and local government. *The American Political Science Review, 31*(2), 280-285.

Bergstrom, H., Katajisto, J., Kimari, M., Kyro, M., Rahikainen, E., Sulamaa, K., et al. (1997). *Vocational education and training in Finland*. Lanham, MD: Bernan Associates. (ERIC Document Reproduction Service No. ED 414 490). Retrieved May 21, 2007 from http://www.eric.ed.gov/ERICDocs/data/ericdocs2/content_storage_01/0000000b/80/23/98/8b.pdf

Blank, L., & McArdle, T. (2003). *Building a lifelong learning strategy in Jamaica. A case study report*. Retrieved January 11, 2007, from www.oecs.org/oeru/documents/caribForum/Jamaica_case_study.pdf

Brandon, E. P., & Moriah, S. J. E. (1988).Vocational Guidance for trainee teachers?: Some Caribbean evidence. *British Journal of Guidance and Counseling, 16*, 157–166.

Chaplin, K. (2006). *HEART beats faster*. The Jamaica Observer (Web ed.). Retrieved on January 9, 2007, from, http://www.Jamaicaobserver.com/columns/html/20060626T190000-0500_107840_OBS_H

Ducci, M. A. (1998). Training for employability. In M. Singh (Ed.), *The adult learning and the changing world of work* (pp. 39–46). Hamburg, Germany: UNESCO Institute for Education.

Furchtgott-Rott, D. (2005). *The challenges of the 21st century workforce: Testimony before the Senate Committee on Health, Education, Labor and Pension*. Washington DC: Hudson Institute.

Gordon, H. (2003). *The history and growth of vocational education in America* (2nd ed.). Prospect Heights, IL: Waveland Press.

Gray, K. C., & Herr, E. L. (1998). *Workforce education: The basics.* Needham Heights, MA: Allyn & Bacon.

Guillen, M. (2001). Is globalization civilizing, destructive or feeble? A critique of five key debates in the social science literature. *Annual Review of Sociology, 27,* 235–260.

Ham, C. H. (1900). *Mind and hand: Manual training the chief factor in education* (3rd ed.). New York: American Book Company.

Heidegger, G. (2000). Future trends in European vocational education. In M.-L. Stenstrom & J. Lesonen (Eds.), *Strategies for reforming initial vocational education and training in Europe* (pp. 266-282). Jyvaskyla, Finland: University of Jyvaskyla, Institute for Educational Research.

Hennigan, J. (2001). *The business of vocational education.* Retrieved on January 8, 2007, from http://www.ericdigests.org/2003-3/business.htm

Heyneman, S. P. (1996, September). *Education and economic transition.* Paper presented to the National Academy of Sciences, Washington, DC

Hwang, J. J. (2000).The reforms of educational systems and quality: The future of career and technical education reform. *Journal of Technological and Vocational Education, 57,* 10-14.

Kerr, J. (2006). *Thirty-two percent of employed persons have received vocational training.* Kingston: Jamaica Information Service. Retrieved on January 4, 2007, from http://www.jis.gov.jm

Levin, J. (2001). *Globalizing the community college: Strategies for change in the twenty-first century.* New York: Palgrave.

Miller, M. D., & Gregson, J. A. (1999). A philosophic view for seeing the past of vocational education and envisioning the future of workforce education: Pragmatism revisited. In A. J. Pautler, Jr. (Ed.), *Workforce education: Issues for the new century* (pp. 21-34). Ann Arbor, MI: Prakken.

Murata, S., & Stern, S. (1993). Technology education in Japan. *Journal of Technology Education, 5.* Retrieved on January 10, 2007, from http://scholar.lib.vt.edu/ejournals/JTE/v5nl/murata.jte-v5nl.html

Port Jobs. (2004). *The German Workforce Development System. Greater Seattle International Study Mission to Munich. Sponsored by the Trade Development Alliance of the Greater Chamber of Commerce.* Retrieved on January 8, 2007, from http://www.portjobs.org

The National Research Council. (1976). *Assessing vocational education research and development.* Washington, DC: National Academy of Sciences.

Roberts, R. W. (1965). *Vocational and practical arts education: History, development, and principles* (2nd ed.). New York: Harper & Row.

U.S. Department Labor. (2006, August). *American dynamic worforce: 2006.* Retrieved January 8, 2007, from http://www.dol.gov/asp/meida/reports/workforce2006/ADW2006_Full_Text.pdf

Van Der Linde, C. H. (2006). *The need for relevant workforce education for the 21st century.* Retrieved January 8, 2007, from http://www.findarticles.com/p/articles/mi_qa3673/is_200007/ai_n8890840

Walter, R. A., & Farmer, E.I. (1999). Postsecondary workforce education. In A. J. Pautler, Jr. (Ed.), *Workforce education: Issues for the new century* (pp. 171-180). Ann Arbor, MI: Prakken.

Wang, I. M., & Shieh, C. (2006). Development of mainland China's vocational education—Facing the pounding of the market economy. *National Social Science Journal, 25*(2), 99-104. Retrieved on January, 10, 2007, from http://www.nssa.us

Wang, V. C. X. (2006). *Essential elements for andragogical styles and methods: How to create andragogical modes in adult education.* Boston: Pearson Education.

CHAPTER 11

TEACHING PHILOSOPHIES OF CHINESE CAREER AND TECHNICAL INSTRUCTORS AND U.S. CAREER AND TECHNICAL INSTRUCTORS

Victor C. X. Wang

This chapter compares the teaching philosophies of vocational education instructors teaching in Chinese vocational agricultural universities and American land-grant universities. A researcher-made survey instrument called the Philosophies of Vocational Education Scale (PVES) was employed to measure which of six philosophical approaches drove the teaching of these instructors in a given situation. Data were collected from 64 (74%) of 87 randomly polled instructors at the Chinese vocational agricultural universities and 64 (74%) of 87 randomly polled instructors at the American land-grant universities to determine and compare their teaching preferences. The results of the study showed while the two groups of instructors were from different social settings, both groups were liberal, progressive, behaviorist, and somewhat

Innovations in Career and Technical Education: Strategic Approaches Towards Workforce Competencies Around the Globe, pp. 219–239
Copyright © 2008 by Information Age Publishing
All rights of reproduction in any form reserved.

humanistic and radical but not analytic in their philosophy of instruction.

INTRODUCTION

It is well known to educators in the field of career and technical education that manual training was first introduced in the United States in 1876 by the Russian educator Victor Della Vos, who was the director of the Moscow Imperial Technical School (Bott, Slapar, & Wang, 2003, p. 36; Roberts, 1965). Not only did Della Vos bring the method of manual training to the United States, but also he brought with it the notion of competency-based education (also known as performance-based education in the field of career and technical education). "Competency-based" education (CBE) has been synonymous with American Vocational Education since its early inception in 1876. The Russian version of CBE places great emphasis on the skills aspect of work, and it has been the basis of many curricula, including the "Modules of Employable Skills" developed by the International Labor Office, the Developing a Curriculum (DACUM) process initiated in Canada and the *serie metodica ocupacionis*, or shopwork methodological series, developed in Brazil and disseminated throughout South America (Wang & Redhead, 2004, p. 50).

Numerous U.S. secondary schools have integrated competency-based curricula in vocational education since the 1960s, as have schools in Australia and Great Britain (Grubb, 1998). The behaviorist philosophy has been playing a major role in making educators adopt CBE in the western hemisphere and the chief proponent of this philosophy was Skinner (1968) who advocated his behavior theory. Not surprisingly, behaviorism has become American and mirrors the turn-of-the twentieth century notion that all people could achieve great accomplishments given the opportunity (stimulus), individual initiative (response), and fair treatment (rewards) (Knowles, Holton III, & Swanson, 1998, 2005). Because CBE programs specify in behavioral terms the goals and objectives to be met, the learning experiences to be engaged in and the method of evaluation used to demonstrate achievement of the predetermined goals, CBE has been popular with American vocational education instructors (Elias & Merriam, 1995, 2005).

China began to adjust its economic and educational policies in the early 1980s in order to catch up with the developed countries in the world. Thus, vocational education has assumed the objective of providing the people of China with the skills required for rapid economic development. As Chen (1981) put it, the overriding aim of vocational education in the post-Mao era is to serve the needs of the modernization program

(p. 153). Toward this end, China began training hundreds of thousands of skilled workers. At the same time, vocational education was expected to develop an array of technical fields specially tailored to national development goals. According to Ministry of Education in China, China will invest 14 billion Yuan (1.75 billion U.S. dollars) during the eleventh 5-year-plan period (2006-2010) to develop technical and skills training for young workers (Xinhua, 2006).

In spite of the popularity of vocational education in China, however, the philosophies adopted by Chinese vocational education instructors, especially with regard to the six prevalent Western (U.S.) philosophies, have remained unexamined. Of particular interest is the question of whether vocational education in China is delivered using primarily liberal methods, given China's Confucian heritage. In the Confucian tradition, educators prefer didactic teaching and rote learning to critical thinking and are regarded by their students as an unchallengeable authority; Confucian educators rely on lecture and externally established examinations (Wang & Bott, 2004, p. 47). Another compelling reason to examine whether Chinese career and technical instructors have adopted the six Western philosophies is because outsiders are well aware that in addition to Confucianism, Marxism, Maoism, and Leninism had influenced Chinese teaching philosophies in general. Although China began to send hundreds of scholars and students to industrialized nations to study Western advanced science and technology and advanced notions of education in the early 1980s, the number of returning scholars and students has been very low. Those who have returned to work for China may not be in leadership positions. Therefore, to determine the teaching philosophies of Chinese career and technical instructors in light of those of U.S. career and technical instructors will assist career and technical educators in adopting and adapting appropriate teaching philosophies in the field of career and technical education according to their respective social settings. As globalization brings different cultures together, it is really hard to tell which philosophies are Western and which are Chinese. In spite of cultural integration, one's teaching philosophies should be clear and sound. Otherwise, instructional outcomes cannot be resulted from meaningful philosophies.

To address these questions, this chapter was designed to investigate the philosophical preferences of Chinese vocational educators and compare their preferences to those of U.S. vocational educators. Specifically, the purpose of this chapter was to carry out a comparison of teaching philosophies of Chinese vocational education instructors with those of U.S. vocational education instructors, particularly in light of Western behaviorism characterized by competency-based education or performance-based education. To determine the generally accepted philosophy of Chinese vocational education instructors, the following research question was formulated: What is the philosophy of Chinese vocational education instructors relative to *liberal* vocational education, *progressive* vocational education, *behaviorist* vocational education, *humanistic* vocational education, *radical* vocational education and *analytic* vocational education as practiced by Western vocational education instructors, particularly at land-grant universities?

PHILOSOPHIES OF VOCATIONAL EDUCATION IN THE UNITED STATES

According to Elias and Merriam (1995, 2005), philosophy inspires one's activities and gives direction to practice. They further pointed out that the power of philosophy lies in its ability to enable individuals to better understand and appreciate the activities of everyday life. On this basis, it can be argued that the philosophy adopted by vocational education instructors can be expected to lead to specific instructional outcomes. Elias and Merriam (1995, 2005) described how instructors' philosophies influence their modes of instruction as follows:

- Liberal vocational education has its emphasis upon liberal learning, organized knowledge, and the development of the intellectual powers of the mind. Therefore, instructors recognize the lecture method as an efficient instructional strategy.
- Progressive vocational education emphasizes such concepts as the relationship between education and society, experience-centered education and democratic education. Instructors with this philosophy may organize, stimulate, instigate, and evaluate the highly complex process of education.
- Behaviorist vocational education emphasizes control, behavioral modification, learning through reinforcement, and management by objectives.
- Humanistic vocational education emphasizes freedom and autonomy, trust, active cooperation and participation, and self-directed learning. Instructors with a preference for this philosophical approach may implement group dynamics, group relations training, group process, sensitivity workshops, encounter groups, and self-directed learning.
- Radical vocational education emphasizes an awareness of social action. Instructors with philosophical orientation may implement libertarian, dialogic, and problem-posing education.

- Analytic philosophy of vocational education focuses on clarifying concepts, arguments, and policy statements used in vocational education. Instructors with this philosophical orientation may attempt to eliminate language confusions.

American vocational instructors' preference for the behaviorist philosophy can be traced to industrial revolution. The Russian training method and the Sloyd system (which originated in the Scandinavian countries and was brought to the United States by Lars Erickson and Gustaf Larson, both of Sweden in the 1880s) both emphasize the skills aspect of work. These two approaches were adopted primarily in response to the sharply increased demand for skilled workers during the period of the industrial revolution (Wang & Redhead, 2004, p. 42). Roberts (1965) and Grubb (1998) argued that both the Russian system and the Sloyd system contributed to the remodeling of the U.S. vocational educational system and that the influence of these two approaches can still be felt to this day.

Competency-based education in vocational education is associated with behaviorist philosophy because instructors who prefer behaviorist philosophy to other philosophies design and implement programmed learning and behavioral learning objectives. Although CBE remains a buzzword in American vocational education, other philosophies successfully co-exist in American vocational education. For example, John Dewey (1961) popularized the progressive philosophy that occupations should be used as vehicles of instruction in vocational education (Bott et al., 2003; Roberts, 1965). Progressive education's emphasis upon vocational and utilitarian training, learning by experience, scientific inquiry, community involvement and responsiveness to social problems may account for the hands-on nature of vocational education.

Although vocational education literature suggests the dominance of the behaviorist philosophy in vocational education in the United States, other philosophies clearly play a role in American vocational education. These other philosophies often supplement and enhance the CBE approach preferred by American vocational education instructors. The present chapter was intended to investigate whether a similar dynamic operates in the context of a Confucian tradition such as China's and if Chinese vocational education has been shaped by the same Russian and Sloyd systems. It must be pointed out that the Russian and Sloyd systems never reached China because when the two systems were adopted in North America, China remained an agricultural country. On the other hand, Dewey lectured in China between 1919 and 1921 (Kaplan, Sobin, & Andors, 1979) and he produced numerous articles, addressing education in China. Although an outspoken proponent of progressive philosophy, it is questionable how much influence Dewey may have exerted on career and technical education in China (Wang, 2007a).

THEORY AND PRACTICE OF VOCATIONAL EDUCATION IN CHINA

Chinese education has been profoundly influenced by the ideas of Confucius, Mao, and Marx, so dialectical materialism is the preferred process for identifying the objective facts of any situation. Thus, both the methodology and subject matter of China's schools are expected to rely on a "scientific" (i.e., dialectical) approach. This mode of education is grounded on the value of seeking truth from facts, objective truth and the unity of theory and practice (Kaplan, Sobin, & Andors, 1979, p. 218).

A significant application of these values for vocational education, however, was an approach enunciated by Mao (1957) in chapter 4 in *Selected Works of Mao Tse-tung*, "On the Correct Handling of Contradictions Among the People." According to Mao, formal education was to be combined with vocational education in order to produce a cultured, Socialist-minded worker (Cheng & Manning, 2003). It was Mao's intent that China's educational system would be open to the masses.

In December 1949, Liu Shih, head of the Supervision Department of the Ministry of Education, stated that the country's new educational system "will guarantee that all working people and their children will have the opportunity to enjoy educational facilities, thus enabling the country to cultivate more effectively every type of constructive talent from among the people" (Kaplan et al., 1979, p. 218). With regard to vocational education, the school system took special care to enroll children of worker-peasant backgrounds, as well as to provide a wide range of spare-time programs and short-course primary and middle schools for adults (Wang & Colletta, 1991). Because of this favorable educational policy initiated since the founding of China, vocational education developed rapidly. During the years when politics took precedence over education, vocational education suffered from decreased enrollments. Since China began to implement economic and educational reforms in the early 1980s, there has been growing demand for trained personnel with applicable skills in the Chinese society (Yang, 2003/2005).

While vocational training was initially given priority over the education of children, a broad network of schools was eventually established at all levels. The system was characterized by a high degree of administrative decentralization and local flexibility. In rural areas, vocational education was introduced with the full cooperation of local residents and structured so as to meet their needs and schedules (Kaplan et al., 1979). Most schools undertook as minimum goals a standard of functional literacy, basic arithmetic skills and practical instruction in skills applicable to the local economy.

In the area of vocational curriculum, the Ministry of Education issued lists of authorized primary and secondary texts; guidelines were issued that cautioned against narrow-minded utilitarianism or empiricism that refuses theoretical learning (Kaplan et al., 1979). As Yu and Xu (1988) put it, the development of curriculum and specialties is closely related to the development of economy, science and technology in the larger context (p. 13). All courses of study and training methods were to reflect these central directives and were, furthermore, to be submitted for approval by the ministry.

Although there are some differences between Western vocational education and Chinese vocational education, the Chinese "double-track" system is not unfamiliar to Western vocational education instructors. In this system, "little treasure pagoda" schools are maintained as full-time, state-aided institutions preparing students for advanced studies and, ultimately, professional careers. The remainder of the system focuses on training industrial and agricultural workers.

Although multiple philosophical traditions, including Confucianism, Marxism and Maoism have influenced education in China, Chinese vocational education does not appear to reflect a dominant philosophy. No empirical study has been conducted to determine what philosophy drives the teaching activities implemented by Chinese vocational education instructors. China has been doing business with the United States since the early 1980s. Has the notion of competency-based education been brought to China as a result of China's open door policy? Has American behaviorism influenced vocational education in China like Confucianism, Marxism and Maoism? If so, to what extent have Chinese vocational education instructors adopted and adapted American performance-based education? A comparison of teaching philosophies between Chinese vocational education instructors and American vocational education instructors will definitely shed some light on the above questions.

METHODOLOGY

Design

The study used a quantitative survey design. A researcher-designed questionnaire was administered to a sample of vocational education instructors teaching at institutions of higher education in China and the United States. The survey instrument was designed to elicit the instructors' preferences for teaching methods or modes of instruction that are consistently associated with six clearly defined philosophical orientations. Thus, instructors' scores could be interpreted as reflecting the instructors' philosophical preferences.

Sample

A survey of 64 vocational education instructors at five vocational agricultural universities representing the northeast, the northwest, the southeast, the southwest and the central regions of China was conducted. These vocational agricultural universities enroll thousands of students per year, and their instructors shoulder a heavy load of teaching responsibilities. These vocational education instructors are bona fide vocational education instructors, fulfilling the goal of educating and training industrial and agricultural workers for China's rapid economic development. The vocational education instructors teaching in these vocational agricultural universities range in age from 29 to 65. They are full time faculty at these institutions of higher learning but are also employed at other universities as part time faculty. Most of these instructors choose to work part-time at other universities to supplement the low pay they receive from their home institutions.

The same survey was administered to 64 vocational education instructors at five land grant universities representing the South and Midwest of the United States of America. These land grant universities all have departments of vocational education where such vocational education leaders as Roberts (1971) and Miller (1985) worked to shape the teaching philosophies of vocational education instructors in the West. For example, Roberts developed and classified teaching philosophies into organization, administration, and instruction (Bott et al., 2003; Roberts, 1965); Miller grouped the philosophies of vocational education into people, programs, and processes as a matter of convenience (Bott et al., 2003; Roberts, 1965). While the terms of these taxonomies differed, they are all closely related to the six prevalent Western philosophical perspectives: *liberal, progressive, behaviorist, humanistic, radical* and *analytical*. The influence of these two leaders is still felt today, and their philosophies of vocational education are still taught in the approximately 100 universities of vocational education in the United States.

Instrumentation

The researcher designed a survey instrument called the Philosophies of Vocational Education Scale (PVES) to determine what type of philosophy drove the teaching of these instructors in a given situation. The survey instrument design was based on Elias and Merriam's (1995, 2005) description of what instructors may do if they possess one of six philosophical orientations: *liberal, progressive, behaviorist, humanistic, radical* and *analytic*. The overall PVES score was comprised of six subscales measuring the six factors that reflect the above-mentioned philosophies in vocational education.

The survey utilized a Likert scale from five to zero with five being the highest (support for the philosophy implied in the factor name) and zero the lowest (support for a different philosophy). For this study, survey responses were used to identify the general philosophy of vocational education instructors in order to develop the base of data. The vocational instructors' mean scores on each of the six PVES factors were calculated using the Statistical Package for Social Sciences (SPSS-14.0 for Windows). The mean score of 2.5 represented the midpoint between 0 and 5.

High mean scores for factors represent support for the philosophy implied in the factor name. Low mean scores indicate support for a different philosophy. If a mean score nears the mean score (2.5), it may indicate support for the philosophy implied in the factor name; it may also indicate support for a different philosophy.

The researcher clearly defined the six factors in the PVES instrument as follows:

> In Factor 1, liberal vocational education is indicated by two positive items in the instrument. Those who support a liberal vocational education use lecture method as an efficient instructional strategy and develop students' intellect through reading, reflection, and production.
>
> Factor 2 is concerned with progressive vocational education. This factor is comprised of four positive items. Instructors who scored high in this factor organize, stimulate, instigate and evaluate the highly complex process of education. They provide the setting that is conducive to learning. While being a helper, guide, encourager, consultant and resource person, they also become a learner in the learning process.
>
> Factor 3 relates to behavioral vocational education and consists of two positive items. Instructors who supported this factor design an environment that elicits desired behavior for meeting educational goals and extinguishes behavior that is not desirable. These instructors are contingency managers, environmental controllers or behavioral engineers who plan in detail the conditions necessary to bring about desired behavior.

Factor 4 is made up of four positive items and one negative item. Instructors who score high on this factor prefer a humanistic approach to vocational education. Humanistic instructors implement group dynamics, group relations training, group process, sensitivity workshops, encounter groups, and self-directed learning.

Factor 5 is concerned with radical vocational education and contains three positive items and 1 negative item. Instructors who support this philosophy offer problem-posing education to students.

Factor 6 includes one negative item and one positive item. Instructors who score high on this factor seek to eliminate confusion with language and do not construct explanations about reality.

A total of 10 vocational education instructors in the department of vocational education in a land grant university in the Midwest of the United States and in a vocational agricultural university in northeast China, who were not included in the sample, completed the PVES in a pilot study to validate the instrument. Data gathered from the validation study were not included in the study but were used to determine whether revisions to the instrument were needed. The validation study was also used to test to clarity and comprehensibility of the questionnaire items. Validation study results indicated revisions to the instrument were not needed since the vocational education instructors in the validation study understood clearly the questions in the survey instrument. In sum, the questions used could be considered content valid. The alpha reliability coefficient for the instrument was 0.92.

The quantitative survey instrument for this study was e-mailed as an attached electronic file to vocational education instructors at participating universities of vocational education in China and in the United States.

Data Analysis

Data collected in this chapter were analyzed using SPSS (14.0 for Windows) software. Since the survey instrument called PVES (Philosophies of Vocational Education Scale) contains both positive items and negative items, different values were assigned to these items. For positive items, the following values were assigned: "Always" equals five, "almost always" equals four, "often" equals three, "seldom" equals two, "almost never" equals one and "never" equals zero. For negative items, the following values are assigned. "Always" equals zero, "almost always" equals one, "often" equals two, "seldom" equals three, "almost never" equals four and "never" equals five. Omitted items are assigned a neutral value of 2.5.

Analysis was conducted for each factor specified in the research question. For descriptive statistics, mean scores and standard deviations were reported for the vocational educators' responses. To provide a better picture of the population surveyed, the overall scale mean scores and standard deviations were also calculated. The findings were entered into tables and figures, and a narrative was developed to report the findings.

FINDINGS

This chapter was designed to identify the teaching philosophies identified in this studied as preferred by Chinese vocational education instructors in terms of six dominant philosophical systems: liberal, progressive, behaviorist, humanistic, radical and analytical. Using a Likert-type scale instrument, respondents were asked to indicate their preference for teaching methods or modes that consistently reflect the six specified philosophical orientations to education. Sixty-four Chinese vocational education instructors answered survey questions, using the researcher' survey instrument called PVES. Another 64 American vocational education instructors answered the same survey questions.

The following Tables summarize the survey results. The mean scores for these vocational educational instructors on each of the six factors are presented in separate tables. Each of the six factors contains several items that make up the instructor's general philosophy. The standard deviation scores for these vocational education instructors are also provided in the Tables.

Table 11.1 summarizes the vocational education instructors' responses for Factor One.

Table 11.1 indicates that vocational education instructors had high scores in the two variables that make up Factor 1. The results suggest that both Chinese and American vocational education instructors favored

Table 11.1.   Mean Responses: 64 Vocational Education Instructors From China and the United States

	M	SD	M	SD
Factor 1: Liberal Philosophy	*(China)*		*(United States)*	
1. I use the lecture method as an efficient instructional strategy.	3.73	0.50	3.00	1.41
19. I develop students' intellect through reading, reflection, and production.	3.68	0.89	4.00	1.00

Note: n = 64; N = 87.

liberal philosophy in their teaching. They tended to use the lecture method as an efficient instructional strategy and supported the notion of developing students' intellect through reading, reflection, and production. Table 11.2 summarizes the vocational education instructors' responses for Factor 2.

Table 11.2 shows that both Chinese and American vocational education instructors had high scores on the four variables that comprise Factor Two. These results indicate that these vocational education instructors applied progressive philosophy in their teaching. First, they provided a learning setting in which they became a co-learner, a helper, guide, encourager, consultant, and resource person. They also organized, stimulated, instigated, and evaluated the highly complex process of education.

Table 11.3 summarizes the vocational education instructors' responses for Factor 3.

Table 11.3 indicates that both Chinese and American vocational education instructors had high scores on the two variables in Factor Three, Behavioral Philosophy. The results show that vocational education instructors designed an environment that elicited desired behavior toward meeting educational goals and to extinguish behavior that was not desirable. They were contingency managers, environmental controllers or behavior engineers who planned in detail the conditions necessary to bring about desired behavior. These results indicate that Chinese vocational education instructors favored behavioral philosophy in their teaching.

Table 11.4 summarizes the vocational education instructors' responses for Factor 4.

Table 11.2.   Mean Responses: 64 Vocational Education Instructors From China and the United States

	M	SD	M	SD
Factor 2: Liberal Philosophy	*(China)*		*(United States)*	
3. I organize, stimulate, instigate, and evaluate the highly complex process of education.	3.64	0.82	3.65	1.18
6. I am a helper, guide, encourager, consultant, and resource instead of a transmitter, disciplinarian, judge, and authority.	4.02	0.62	4.22	1.18
7. I provide the setting that is conducive to learning.	3.89	0.77	4.30	1.08
8. I become a learner in the learning process.	3.85	0.82	4.30	1.08

Note: $n = 64$; $N = 87$.

Table 11.3.   Mean Responses: 64 Vocational Education Instructors From China and the United States

	M	SD	M	SD
Factor 3: Behavioral Philosophy	*(China)*		*(United States)*	
4. I design an environment that elicits desired behavior toward meeting educational goals and to extinguish behavior that is not desirable.	3.91	0.68	3.89	1.13
5. I am a contingency manager, an environmental controller, or behavioral engineer who plans in detail the conditions necessary to bring about desired behavior.	3.75	0.69	2.97	1.24

Note: n = 64; N = 87.

Thus Table 11.4 indicates that both Chinese and American vocational education instructors had high scores in four of the five variables that make up Factor 4. These results suggest that these vocational education instructors basically favored humanistic philosophy in their teaching except that they provided information to their students, which is something humanistic instructors do not do. The results show that these vocational education instructors were facilitators, helpers, and partners in the

Table 11.4.   Mean Responses: 64 Vocational Education Instructors From China and the United States

	M	SD	M	SD
Factor 4: Behavioral Philosophy	*(China)*		*(United States)*	
11. I design an environment that elicits desired behavior toward meeting educational goals and to extinguish behavior that is not desirable.	3.74	0.70	3.97	1.07
12. I am a contingency manager, an environmental controller, or behavioral engineer who plans in detail the conditions necessary to bring about desired behavior.	3.64	0.96	4.46	0.77
13. I provide information to my students.	1.19	0.97	0.49	0.77
14. I am a facilitator, helper, and partner in the learning process.	3.88	0.94	4.49	0.69
15. I create the conditions within which learning can take place.	3.88	0.96	4.30	0.91

Note: n = 64; N = 87.

learning process; they created the conditions within which learning could take place; they trusted students to assume responsibilities for their learning and respected and utilized the experiences and potentialities of students. Humanists do not provide information to students. However, these vocational education instructors provided information to their students.

Table 11.5 summarizes the vocational education instructors' responses for Factor 5. It demonstrates that both Chinese and American vocational education instructors had high scores in three of the four variables that comprise Factor 5. These results indicate that vocational education instructors generally applied radical philosophy in their teaching except that they determined the themes that served to organize the content of the dialogues, which is something radical instructors do not do.

Table 11.6 summarizes the vocational education instructors' responses for Factor 6. Table 11.6 indicates that both Chinese and American vocational education instructors did not favor analytic philosophy in their teaching. Although they eliminated language confusions, they constructed explanations about reality, which is not a practice of analytic instructors.

Table 11.7 summarizes the vocational education instructors' responses for overall scale means and standard deviations on the six factors.

Further examination of Table 11.7 demonstrates that both Chinese and American vocational education instructors had high scores on Factor 1, Factor 2 and Factor 3. This result suggests that Chinese and American vocational education instructors were liberal, progressive and behavioral in their instruction. They had relatively high scores on Factor 4 and Factor 5. Although these vocational education instructors had relatively high scores in Factor 4 and Factor 5, the low score one item from each of these

Table 11.5. Mean Responses: 64 Vocational Education Instructors From China and the United States

	M	SD	M	SD
Factor 5: Radical Philosophy	*(China)*		*(United States)*	
9. I offer a libertarian, dialogic, and problem-posing education.	3.87	0.58	3.27	1.07
10. I emphasize the importance of dialogue and equality between teacher and learners.	4.02	0.92	4.08	0.95
16. I am open to clarifications and modifications.	3.67	1.06	4.65	0.63
17. I determine the themes that serve to organize the content of the dialogues.	1.46	0.89	1.35	0.79

Note: n = 64; N = 87.

Table 11.6. Mean Responses: 64 Vocational Education Instructors From China and the United States

	M	SD	M	SD
Factor 5: Analytic Philosophy	(China)		(United States)	
2. I eliminate language confusions.	3.91	0.77	3.95	1.37
18. I emphasize the importance of dialogue and equality between teacher and learners.	1.57	0.87	1.54	1.37

Note: n = 64; N = 87.

two factors indicated that they were not humanistic or radical in their teaching. Their score on Factor 6 was low, indicating that these vocational education instructors were not analytic in their instruction.

DISCUSSION

The purpose of this chapter was to identify the general philosophies (i.e., *liberal, progressive, behavioral, humanistic, radical, or analytic*) practiced by Chinese vocational education instructors in light of the predominant "competency-based" education (behavioral philosophy) in American vocational education. The findings indicated that there were no significant differences in the teaching philosophies between Chinese vocational education instructors and American vocational education instructors ($p > 0.01$).

The study's findings showed that the Chinese vocational education instructors surveyed supported *liberal, progressive* and *behavioral*

Table 11.7. Mean Responses: 64 Vocational Education Instructors From China and the United States

	M	SD	M	SD	M	SD
Factors	(China)		(United States)		Differences	
1. Liberal Philosophy	3.71	0.70	3.50	1.21	0.21	-0.51
2. Progressive Philosophy	3.85	0.76	4.12	1.13	-0.27	-0.37
3. Behavioral Philosophy	3.83	0.69	3.43	1.19	0.4	-0.57
4. Humanistic Philosophy	3.27	0.91	3.54	0.84	-0.27	0.07
5. Radical Philosophy	3.26	0.86	3.34	0.86	-0.08	0
6. Analytic Philosophy	2.74	0.82	2.75	1.23	-0.01	-0.41

Note: n = 64; N = 87.

philosophies in their teaching. These were the same teaching philosophies preferred by American vocational education instructors. They used the lecture method as an efficient instructional strategy and supported the notion of developing students' intellect through reading, reflection, and production. They provided an environment in which they were co-learners, helpers, guides, encouragers, consultants, and resource persons. They organized, stimulated, instigated and evaluated the highly complex process of education. They designed a learning setting that elicited desired behavior toward meeting educational goals and to extinguish behavior that was not desirable.

The findings also indicated that both Chinese and American vocational education instructors were *humanistic* and *radical* in their instructions in that they trusted students to assume responsibilities for their learning and respected and utilized the experiences and potentialities of students. They offered a problem-posing education and they were open to clarifications and modifications. The findings demonstrated that they were not *analytic* in their teaching (China: $M = 3.91$, $M = 1.57$; United States: $M = 3.95$, $M = 1.54$). Although these vocational education instructors were basically *humanistic* and *radical*, there were situations in which they were not *humanistic* and *radical*.

It is not out of the ordinary to Western scholars that Chinese vocational education instructors apply liberal philosophy in their teaching because this finding corroborated Wang and Bott's (2004) research concerning the modes of teaching of Chinese educators. Wang and Bott found that Chinese educators in general have been clinging to a liberal philosophy in education that views instructors as having absolute authority over learners. Wang and Bott's research further indicated that Chinese vocational education instructors supported a teacher-centered mode of teaching, viewed lecturing as a superior method and considered themselves as providers of knowledge rather than facilitators.

Table 11.8.   Paired T-Tests for the 64 Vocational Education Instructors in China and in the United States

Factor	t - Value	p - Value
1. Liberal philosophy	0.39	.076
2. Progressive philosophy	-2.63**	0.08
3. Behavioral philosophy	1.05	0.48
4. Humanistic philosophy	-1.05*	0.35
5. Radical philosophy	-0.25	0.82
6. Analytic philosophy	-0.14	0.91

*$p > 0.05$; **$p > 0.01$

The current study also confirmed the Chinese educational belief that there is always a truth proposition (knowledge) or an accepted theory that can be disseminated through the agency of the teacher (as cited in Wang, 2007a, p. 114). This very belief is manifested in the liberal philosophy in education. Other scholars such as Paine (1992) explain that Chinese teaching philosophies are designed to help students master teaching materials, apply these teaching materials, and help the student master the basic function of each instructional segment (p. 189). To achieve this instructional goal in vocational education, memorization is viewed as an optimal method in teaching and learning in general.

Based on the literature review of Chinese vocational education, it appears that Mao and Marx's teachings have become the central directives in Chinese vocational education in that theories and practice must be united. Chinese vocational education instructors are opposed to the Western "narrow-minded utilitarianism or empiricism that refuses theoretical learning." This is probably why Westerners often see Chinese educators expound in minute detail on textbook materials in their classes to enhance theoretical learning. Chinese cooperative arrangements are not unfamiliar to Western vocational education instructors. The fact that Chinese vocational education instructors are progressive suggests that they value interaction between learners and the environment and that they value the function of helpers more than that of disciplinarians.

Although "competency-based" education (CBE) is typical American vocational education (behavioral philosophy), this mode of education is not unfamiliar to Chinese vocational education instructors. For example, since China opened its door to the outside world in the early 1980s, vocational education has had the concrete task of providing the people with the skills required for rapid economic development. Short training courses have been offered toward this end, and courses typically contain specific learning objectives. And it is natural that Chinese vocational education instructors use programmed instruction to achieve their teaching goals. Although Mao and Marx shaped Chinese education in general, China has a history of seeking Western influence in education. In 1922, Chinese education showed a marked shift from Japanese to U.S. influences (Kaplan et al., 1979, p. 219). John Dewey, the most prominent U.S. educator of the time, spent 26 months lecturing in China between 1919 and 1921. Dewey's progressive philosophy and Western behavioral philosophy may have spread throughout China as a result of his influence.

The fact that Chinese vocational education instructors are humanistic in their teaching should also not surprise Western scholars in vocational education because it was Confucius who advanced humanism first in China twenty-five centuries ago (Wang & King, 2007, p. 256). The writings of Confucius reveal abundant examples of humanism, and even

Western scholars such as Rogers (1969) and Knowles (1975) were heavily influenced by Confucian teachings. Humanists maintain that humans have unlimited potential for learning and that they are capable of self-direction in learning.

The confirmation of Chinese vocational education instructors' radical philosophy in teaching is somewhat surprising given Chinese educators' reputation for preferring spoon-feeding methods to problem-posing education (Wang, 2007b). Chinese educators are known for promoting rote learning instead of critical thinking in their teaching. However, since China opened its door to the outside world in the early 1980s, the Western democratic approach to teaching (e.g., dialogue, and discussion) has been experimented with and implemented on a trial basis.

Analytic instructors are not expected to construct explanations about reality. That Chinese vocational education instructors like constructing explanations about reality may reflect their preference for liberal philosophy over an analytical approach to education. Instructors with this liberal philosophy view themselves as unchallengeable authorities. Naturally, authorities should provide answers to "all" questions and problems, without any limitations whatsoever.

IMPLICATIONS

This chapter was designed to identify the general philosophies (i.e., *liberal, progressive, behavioral, humanistic, radical, or analytic*) practiced by Chinese vocational education instructors in comparison to the predominant "competency-based" education (behavioral philosophy) in American vocational education. Western scholars may have preconceived notions about the kinds of philosophies Chinese vocational education instructors may hold. However, the reality is that Chinese vocational education instructors have also adopted the Western "competency-based" education to effectively cultivate every type of constructive talent among the Chinese people. The lesson drawn from this study is that teaching philosophies preferred by Western educators are also applicable to Chinese educators regardless of the differences in social environments. Confucianism, like the teachings of Socrates and Plato, has influenced educators globally for generations. If one's teaching philosophy seeks only to promote "competency-based" education, learning objectives are unlimited. The fact that Chinese vocational education instructors are liberal, not analytic in their approach represents a perfect example of how educational objectives can shape teaching philosophies.

For example, in the area of vocational curriculum, the Ministry of Education issues lists of authorized primary and secondary texts. This policy leaves no room for Chinese vocational education instructors to pursue an analytic approach. Rather, they must conform to the liberal philosophy in teaching. At the same time, to restrict teaching philosophies to a particular social environment is becoming impractical, especially when the world is becoming a global village where teaching must foster "competency-based education." To label teaching philosophies as Western or Chinese is extremely problematic, especially when Western educators and Chinese educators borrow effective teaching philosophies from one another via educational ambassadors such as John Dewey and most current ones. Finally, to say which of the philosophies leads to better learning is probably impossible since each of us who teaches engages in not only a time-honored process but one that is quite unique to the immediate situation in which we are actually teaching (Jarvis, 2002, p. 29). No single philosophy of vocational education should dominate the field (Wang, 2007b, p. 149). The best way of making one's philosophy work for the best teaching/learning results is to adopt and adapt a philosophy according to one's specific teaching/learning situation that may involve a plethora of other factors such as learner needs, learner styles, learner experience and learner motivation.

The present chapter supports a fresh look at the prevalent philosophies through the lens of the Chinese and American vocational education instructors. The study implies that specific educational goals and objectives may shape educators' philosophy of teaching. Most importantly, the chapter has provided insight into vocational education and training, particularly as globalization brings different cultures together to learn from each other. It is the researcher's intent that by examining the acts of others we improve our own practice in teaching. Further research is needed, especially in the form of qualitative investigation, to understand the influences and motivations that lead Chinese and American vocational education instructors to hold certain philosophies in teaching.

REFERENCES

Bott, P. A., Slapar, F. M., & Wang, V. (2003). *History and philosophy of career and technical education*. Boston: Pearson.

Chen, T. H. (1981). *Chinese education since 1949: Academic and revolutionary models*. New York: Pergamon Press.

Cheng, Y., & Manning, P. (2003). Revolution in education: China and Cuba in global context, 1957-76. *Journal of World History, 14*(3), 359-391.

Dewey, J. (1961). *Democracy and education*. New York: Macmillan.

Elias, J. L., & Merriam, S. B. (1995). *Philosophical foundations of adult education*. Malabar, FL: Krieger.

Elias, J. L., & Merriam, S. B. (2005). *Philosophical foundations of adult education* (3rd ed.). Malabar, FL: Krieger.

Grubb, W. N. (1998, December). *Preparing for the information-based workplace: Pedagogical issues and institutional linkages.* Paper prepared for "Learning Now: An International Symposium on Skill for the Information Economy," Chapel Hill, NC, Dec. 13-15, 1999; and for "Labor Organizations and Labor Market Institutions in the New Economy: Lessons from Silicon Valley," San Jose, Jan. 29-30, 1999. Retrieved May 23, 2007 from http://mitsloan.mit.edu/iwer/pdf/tfgrubb.pdf

Jarvis, P. (2002). Teaching styles and teaching methods. In P. Jarvis (Ed.), *The theory & practice of teaching* (pp. 22-30). London: Kogan Page.

Kaplan, F. M., Sobin, J. M., & Andors, S. (1979). *Encyclopedia of China today.* New York: Harper & Row.

Knowles, M. S. (1975). *Self-directed learning.* New York: Association Press.

Knowles, M. S., Holton, E., & Swanson, A. (1998). *The adult learner.* Houston, TX: Gulf.

Knowles, M. S., Holton, E., & Swanson, A. (2005). *The adult learner* (6th ed.). Boston: Elsevier Butterworth Heinemann.

Mao, T. T. (1957). *Selected works of Mao Tse-tung: On the correct handling of contradictions among the people.* Retrieved February 24, 2005, from http://www.marxists.org/reference/archive/mao/selected-works/volume-5/mswv5_58.htm

Miller, M. D. (1985). *Principles and philosophy for vocational education.* Columbus, OH: Ohio State University.

Paine, L. (1992). Teaching and modernization in contemporary China. In R. Hayhoe (Ed.), *Education and modernization: The Chinese experience* (pp. 183-209). New York: Pergamon Press.

Roberts, R. W. (1965). *Vocational and practical arts education: History, development, and principles* (2nd ed). New York: Harper & Row.

Roberts, R. W. (1971). *Vocational and practical arts education: History, development, and principles* (3rd ed.). New York: Harper & Row.

Rogers, C. R. (1969). *Freedom to learn.* Columbus, OH: Merrill.

Skinner, B. F. (1968). *The technology of teaching.* New York: Appleton-Century-Crofts.

Wang, J. L., & Colletta, N. (1991). Chinese education problems, policies, and prospects. In I. Epstein (Ed.), *Chinese education problems, policies, and prospects* (pp. 145-162). New York: Garland.

Wang, V. C. X. (2007a). Chinese knowledge transmitters or western learning facilitators adult teaching methods compared. In K. P. King & V. C. X. Wang (Eds.), *Comparative adult education around the globe* (pp. 113-137). Hangzhou, China: Zhejiang University Press.

Wang, V. C. X. (2007b). How contextually adapted philosophies and the situational roles of adult educators affect learners' transformation and emancipation. In K. P. King & V. C. X. Wang (Eds.), *Comparative adult education around the globe* (pp. 139-150). Hangzhou, China: Zhejiang University Press.

Wang, V. C. X., & Bott, P. A. (2004). Modes of teaching of Chinese adult educators. *Perspectives: The New York Journal of Adult Learning, 2*(2), 32-51.

Wang, V. C. X., & King, K. P. (2007). Confucius and Mezirow—Understanding Mezirow's theory of reflectivity from Confucian perspectives: A model and perspective. In K. P. King & V. C. X. Wang (Eds.), *Comparative adult education around the globe* (pp. 253-275). Hangzhou, China: Zhejiang University Press.

Wang, V. C. X., & Redhead, C. K. (2004). Comparing the Russian, the Sloyd, and the arts and crafts movement training systems. *International Journal of Vocational Education and Training, 12*(1), 42-58.

Xinhua. (2006). *China to invest 14 billion Yuan to develop technical training.* Retrieved January 9, 2007, from http://www.zju.edu.cn/english/news/2006/news061115.htm

Yang, D. P. (2005). China's education in 2003: From growth to reform (J. Eagleton, Trans). *Chinese Education and Society, 38*(4), 11-45. (Original work published in 2003)

Yu, B., & Xu, H. Y. (1988). *Adult higher education: A case study on the workers' college in the People's Republic of China.* UNESCO: International Institute for Educational Planning.

CHAPTER 12

AUSTRALIA'S VOCATIONAL EDUCATION AND TRAINING

Kisilu Kitainge

INTRODUCTION

Education and training generally aim at preparing people for various roles and responsibilities in life. They target the development of the powers, capacities and inherent potentials of the learners. To achieve this, education and training processes depend on a systematically organized set of induction programs into the ways and activities of the society in which they take place. The society, on the other hand, is influenced by the world's global trends. For example, Haan (2001) reports that in the past two decades, important developments have taken place that can be assumed to have a major impact on the need for education and provision of training services. Besides, the processes of economic liberalization and globalization have changed the context in which enterprises operate and consequently the skills that are valued for effective performance. These changes in the global context have impacted all sectors, education and training included, and there have been many systems rearrangements to cater to these changes.

Innovations in Career and Technical Education: Strategic Approaches Towards Workforce Competencies Around the Globe, pp. 241–264
Copyright © 2008 by Information Age Publishing
All rights of reproduction in any form reserved.

While there have been many impacting forces on the world, technology has had a significant impact, cutting across all sectors of society (Chappell & Johnston, 2003). Education and training have not been spared in these global changes with the resultant need for rearrangement and modifications due to new and changing technology. Technology is now being used in the classroom more than at any other time. Training arrangements are being redesigned in the form of online learning, distance learning and education and training teleconferencing. The pace of these changes is also causing a serious need for system adjustments not only in education and training, but also in the workplace. The adoption of new technologies in the workplace demands that training should facilitate the learning of the appropriately aligned skills. These are the training requirements for the new global economy.

AUSTRALIA IN BRIEF

As shown in Figure 12.1, the Commonwealth of Australia covers an entire continent and its outlying islands. It comprises six states and two internal territories. These are New South Wales, Queensland, South Australia, Tasmania, Victoria, Western Australia, the Australian capital territory and the northern territory. It lies between the Indian and Pacific Oceans with about one-third of the mainland north of the Tropic of Capricorn. It is an Oceania continent between the Indian Ocean and the South Pacific Ocean at the geographic coordinates: 27 00 S, 133 00 E. There are about 21 million people in Australia, most of whom live live and work in the major cities and regional hubs of Sydney, Melbourne, Brisbane, Canberra, Perth and Darwin. Australia is the sixth largest nation in land area with about 8 million square kilometers. It encompasses a range of climatic conditions, from the tropical north to the temperate south. Much of the inland is arid, and the population is concentrated on the comparatively narrow coastal plains of the east, southeast and southwest. Separating the arid inland regions and the coastal plains in eastern Australia is the Great Dividing Range, which stretches from the north to the south of the continent (Department of Education Science and Training (DEST), 2000). The focus of this chapter is Australia's vocational education and training (VET) which exists within the context of the general education and training system.

The Commonwealth of Australia has a population of about 20.2 million people, most of whom live in the major coastal cities and regional centers. It has a prosperous Western-style capitalist economy (Ainley, Malley, & Lamb, 1997). The Commonwealth of Australia comprises six states and two territories. The administration of education and training in

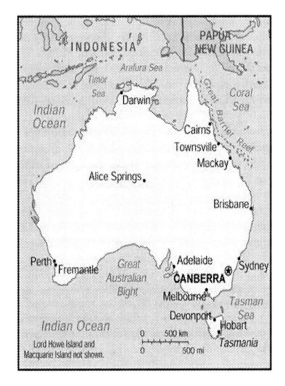

Source: Central Investigation Agency, 2007.

Figure 12.1.   Map of Australia.

Australia is a joint affair between the state and the commonwealth governments. The states control the lower tiers of education while the commonwealth coordinates the higher education sector.

Technical and further education (TAFE) institutes, and other registered training organizations (RTOs) including departments within universities, offer VET in Australia (DEST, 2000; Smith, 1998; Smith & Keating, 1997). VET policies and practices in Australia are elaborate and actively involve most of the significant stakeholders (Ainley et al., 1997; Australian National Training Authority (ANTA), 2002). VET in Australia in general has undergone several changes since the mid-1980s in the quest to try to make it responsive to workplace demands and changes in technology (Smith, 1998). These changes were also focused on making VET more flexible in order to increase the adaptability of the Australian workforce. The different states VET systems enable providers to operate and issue qualifications that are nationally recognized. The common mode of teaching and assessment is through training competency, derived from national training packages. These training packages specify the competencies that must be achieved (Smith, 1998). They also specify industry requirements for assessment and prescribe qualifications that result from successful completion. The learning is often described as self-paced, learner-centred and competency-based training (Smith & Keating, 2003).

The commonwealth, state, and territory governments determine the policy and regulatory frameworks for the VET system (DEST, 2000; Smith, 1998). It is the responsibility of the individual state governments to implement the National Training Framework (NTF). This ensures consistency and the national recognition of provider services. State and territory governments also provide the main source of the funds required for the system, while the learners in the system provide just a small proportion of the total. On Australian VET funding Haukka, Keating, and Lamb (2004) noted:

> Vocational education and training has a diverse funding base, relative to those of the other two major sectors. However, the State and Territory governments are the major sources of funding, (providing approximately 80%) with student fees and charges accounting for only 4.5% of recurrent revenue in 2002. (p. 10)

There are five key objectives outlined within the mission statement that guide the VET system. These are, to provide a VET sector capable of equipping Australians for the world of work; to enhance mobility in the labour market; to achieve equitable outcomes in vocational education and training; increase investment in training and maximize the value of public VET expenditure (ANTA, 2002; DEST, 2000).

The achievement of these five objectives in VET used to be emphasized and monitored by ANTA up to 2006 after which DEST took over. This close monitoring coupled with continued support for VET research, and the fact that there have been reforms since the 1980s (Smith, 1998) show that Australia's VET system is in constant review. As a result, VET in Australia serves as a role model since it is a leader in the implementation of industry-driven training and qualifications (DEST, 2000). Australia also has a well-defined structure based on training packages that are strongly endorsed by the designated industry. Alongside this is an established quality-training framework to underpin the quality assurance of the training system (Blom & Meyers, 2003). It also claims to be responding to the challenges of economic globalization and developing technologies (ANTA, 2002; Keating, Medrich, Volkoff, & Perry, 2002). In Australia, VET plays an important role in ensuring that industry and the communities have the skills and knowledge to compete in this changing environment. However, Blom and Meyers (2003) lament that the current VET system in Australia is mainly geared toward meeting the expectations of business and industry. They argue that it is often narrowly focused on equipping learners to function in the current work environment rather than concerning itself with preparing the learners for work in the future and the journey of lifelong learning. Such comments suggest that there is room for improvement.

EDUCATION AND TRAINING IN AUSTRALIA

Although there are debates and issues related to VET policies in the different Australian States, Australia has a well-developed education system with participation rates and secondary school completion rates among the highest in the world (DEST, 2000). The Australian VET system is based on strong connections between providers of training and industry sectors (Misko, 2001). Australian governments at all levels are continually reviewing and reforming education and training to address the issues that arise from social and economic change. In many cases, Australian models attract international attention and Australia is involved in co-operating with the development of educational programs in a number of overseas countries (Ainley, Malley, & Lamb, 1997; DEST, 2000; Goozee, 2001).

School education is the responsibility of the individual states and territories, although the influence of the federal government exists. The state education departments recruit and appoint teachers in the government schools, supply buildings, equipment, and materials, and provide discretionary funding for use by the schools (Ainley, Malley, & Lamb, 1997). There also exist some nongovernment schools most of which have some religious affiliation. Approximately 75% of the nongovernmental schools have religious affiliation. The Catholic Church is a strong force in this aspect. The state and the federal taxation revenues provide almost all the financial resources for the operation of the government schools.

There is no common school curriculum across the country, although almost all the students are exposed to a curriculum that provides for coverage of English language, mathematics, science, social studies, humanities, the creative and performing arts, physical education, and less frequently, a foreign language. The schools have considerable autonomy in deciding the curriculum detail, textbooks and the teaching methodology. However, at the senior secondary level, the curriculum is more likely to be specified in detail by the state authority responsible for examining and certifying the student achievement. The high retention rate in Australia is explained by the policy initiatives taken by the education authorities to improve education completion rates (Ainley, Malley, & Lamb, 1997).

The statutory responsibility for VET rests with the state and territory governments. Employers and unions are represented on the state training authorities and through the state industry training boards where they can more specifically influence training arrangements for an industry. A federal statutory authority, the Australian National Training Authority (ANTA) used to provide coordination of and support for policy initiatives in the area until 2006 when it was reattached to DEST. At the federal level, the Industry Training Advisory Boards (ITABs) develop training plans for industry. The ITABs, in consultation with the education experts decide on the learning competencies to be included in the curriculum. The government representatives also attend deliberation meetings.

In each state, institutes of technical and further education (TAFEs) are major providers of VET although there are some private providers. TAFE institutes provide a wide variety of courses including preemployment programs, apprenticeships, training and updating programs, paraprofessional and liberal adult education. TAFE is the most accessible part of the tertiary education sector. Participation in TAFE is characterized by both full and part time attendance and a wide age range among the participants.

One of the most important traditional components of VET in Australia is the apprenticeships system (Ainley, Malley, & Lamb, 1997; Smith, 1998; Smith & Keating, 1997). The duration of apprenticeship is 4 years during which the apprentice works for an employer and attends training for part of the time. Arrangements for attendance vary between industries and States, with some courses preferring block release from workplaces for the institute-based training. However, Ainley et al. (1997) highlight some of the problems of the apprenticeships. They are the extent of regulation, the limited flexibility, and linkage to traditional occupation, lack of response to modern technology and lack of access for women. Traineeships were introduced to provide a shorter and more flexible approach to entry-level training. They involve a 1-year program (some 2 years) with an employer incorporating on-the-job and off-the-job training.

HISTORICAL DEVELOPMENT OF VOCATIONAL EDUCATION AND TRAINING IN AUSTRALIA

Australian technical and vocational education and training (TVET) presently referred to as vocational education and training (VET) dates back to the colonial period of the late nineteenth century (Goozee, 2001). This type of education was generally referred to as technical education, and more recently as technical and further education (TAFE). The establishment of mechanics' institute, schools of mines and technical and working men's colleges to develop the skills of Australia's working population was the first instance of the growth of VET. For almost 100 years, training and institutions were largely concentrated around males working full time in a fairly narrow band of trade related industries (ANTA, 2003a; Goozee, 2001).

In the 1970s, it became clear that Australia's traditional manufacturing, mining, and agricultural industries had started to decline and new industries such as communications, finance, and other service industries were emerging. More women were entering or reentering the workforce and undertaking postsecondary education and training (Goozee, 2001). Technical education became known as technical and further education (TAFE) and started to receive substantial interest and funding from the federal government. These institutions were a mixture of government, business and community initiatives, and reflected the wide variety of interests in technical education. Industry, labor movements, and community all had interests. Murray-Smith (cited in Smith & Keating, 1997) laments the fact that these interests could not produce and sustain a broad vision of technical education that would combine both scientific and technical learning and a broader liberal education. The technical education take up was not as swift as expected.

The 1974 Kangan report on needs defined the mission of the TAFE system. This was a major development since it placed TAFE on the national agenda and provided an impetus for a national identity for TAFE (Goozee, 2001). Although this sector of education remained the responsibility of the states and territories, substantial federal government funding was injected into the system and several national bodies were established (Smith & Keating, 1997). TAFE had a national focus but still continued to develop very much in line with the needs of each state and territory.

Training began to change with more preparatory and prevocational training slowing growth in the traditional heartland of trade and technical training. In the 1980s the services industries continued to expand at the expense of the mining and construction industries. A number of reports pointed to the need for the training system to be driven by the needs of the individual and industry so that the economy as a whole could prosper (Goozee, 2001). As an example, the *Canberra Times* of August 4, 1987 printed an article headed, "TAFE Cuts Uneconomic." The article stated the government had made it clear that it wanted Australia's education system to be more closely tied to the needs of industry. The article also pointed out that some overseas nations, such as Sweden, Austria, and West Germany had shown the benefits of developing a multiskilled workforce and of extensive job retraining schemes that prepare workers in a declining industry to transform it to an industry with sound prospects. This article was prompted by another report, "Australia Reconstructed."

This Australia reconstructed report recommended that Australia could no longer depend upon farm and mine products for its expert income, but had to become competitive in manufactures.

By the late 1980s, demands for increased training to meet the changing needs of Australian society led to the Deveson Report of 1990 that argued for the private sector and industry playing a fundamental role in improving the quality and relevance of education and training (Smith & Keating, 2003). It was also in the discussion of this Deveson report, that a ministerial conference agreed on the implementation of competency based training (CBT), development of integrated curricula for on- and off-the job training, establishment of a national framework for recognition of training, the development of a national market for delivery of VET and establishment of integrated entry level training system (Goozee, 2001). The Devenson, Finn, and Carmichael reports looked at expanding training systems, increasing young people's participation in training and a consolidated national system (Smith & Keating, 1997). Consensus developed across Australia that substantial reform and a unified national effort was required. In 1992, all states, territories, and the commonwealth agreed to the establishment of ANTA and a cooperative federal system of vocational and training with strategic input by industry.

Before the implementation of the current VET system in the mid 1990s, technical and vocational education was developed by each State and Territory to meet the needs of business and industry within their jurisdictions (Billett et al., 1999; Goozee, 2001; Smith & Keating, 1997). No national system was fully in place. Most technical and vocational education was provided within the TAFE colleges and institutes with only a small number of private institutions. The institutions or relevant education authorities, often in conjunction, developed courses offered by technical and vocational education institutions with local employers or industry advisory bodies. Programs were accredited through the state or territory training/ recognition authorities (Goozee, 2001, Smith & Keating, 2003). The curriculum combined theoretical and practical components relevant to the subject area and level of education/training. In some cases, especially in more recent years, practical training in the workplace was included. Programs were based on the awards under the Register of Australian Tertiary Education (RATE), which included certificates in various streams, advanced certificate, associate diploma, and diploma (DEST, 2000).

The length of technical and vocational education programs leading to RATE awards was usually described in terms of the number of years or semesters of full-time study or part-time equivalent with two semesters per year. One year of full-time study represented around 40 weeks or 700 hours of class time including practical components. Substantial amounts of individual study outside of these hours were also required to meet the assessment requirements of the programs. Generally, the advanced certificate was 2 years full-time, the associate diploma 2 years full-time and the diploma 3 years full-time.

In 1994, the Fitzgerald report into implementation of the national system led to some current elements of today's VET system. These include concepts of best practice and user choice, states and territories taking responsibility for accreditation and standards endorsement, and a stronger and more coherent industry training advisory board. In the late 1990s new apprenticeships were introduced, the national training framework (NTF) was established, VET was introduced in schools and training packages were developed (DEST, 2000; Smith & Keating, 1997). In 2000 and beyond, the national VET system continues to respond to industry, and individual and community needs. It is focused on capturing the best advice possible from industry, meeting clients' needs, and clearer higher quality standards, all within a nationally consistent, quality VET system. In the rapid changing global work and social environment, improvement must be continuous and the VET system will continue to change to equip Australia and Australians for the future (ANTA, 2003a).

The drive to establish a national system of training came from three issues of the 1970s. First, was the concern about the adequacy of the structure of the skills and skills training within Australia to meet the then perceived challenges of internationally competitive markets and of the emerging new technologies (Goozee, 2001). Second, was the growing awareness (then) about the rising levels of poverty in Australia and the possible impact of education in providing access to jobs and income. Third, was the awareness in international terms that the Australian provision for school completion or further education other than the university was well below that of other developed countries (Ainley, Malley, & Lamb, 1997).

CURRENT VET SYSTEM IN AUSTRALIA

The commonwealth, state, and territory governments provide the policy and regulatory frameworks for the VET system. The Commonwealth Department of Employment, Science and Training (DEST) provides some funding for VET but the states and territories provide more (Smith, 1998). The governments implement the national training frameworks to enable consistency, and national recognition of provider services; however, Smith (1998) points out that the involvement of the commonwealth and state governments in VET has often created tensions as a result of nonagreement on the policies. In his opinion, the situation could be improved by involving the unions and other stakeholders in VET decision-making. The commonwealth and state governments provide the larger share of the funds required for the system, while the learners in the system only provide part of the rest. Specifically, the commonwealth government provides 22.2%, state and territory governments 56.7%, fees for service accounts for 11% while direct student fees accounts for 4.5% (Haukka et al., 2004; National Centre for Vocational Education and Research (NCVER), 2001b). Training for the majority of students (69.8%) is funded recurrently by government, while a growing proportion of students are participating on a fee for service basis at TAFE (ANTA, 2004).

The mode of training and approach to assessment and qualifications within the Australian VET system is competence based training (CBT). The definition of CBT as given by the vocational education, employment and training advisory committee in 1992 was that CBT is training that is geared toward the attainment and demonstration of skills to meet industry specified standards rather than to an individual's achievement relative to that of others in a group (NCVER, 2001a).

On its part, the Australian Chamber of Commerce and Industry cited in Smith and Keating (2003) define CBT as:

> A way of approaching vocational training that places primary emphasis on what a person can do as a result of training (the outcome) and as such represents a shift from the emphasis on the process involved in training (the inputs). It is concerned with training to industry specific standards rather than an individual achievement relative to others in a group. (p. 122)

From these definitions, the key points are that CBT focuses on industry specified standards and outcomes rather than inputs (Goozee, 2001; Smith & Keating, 2003). In this kind of training, the workplace competency standard and the benchmarks for workplace performance are used as a basis for determining enterprise agreements, recruitment policies, staff development and selection for promotion. The educational content is therefore related to the knowledge and skills required in workplaces (Chappell, Gonczi, & Hagar, 1995). The characteristics of this particular form of training are summarized as being based on competency standards focused on outcomes not inputs and involving industry, taking account of and recognizing prior learning. There is modularized self-paced assessment based on demonstration of skills in addition to the theoretical knowledge assessment (Billett et al., 1999; Smith & Keating, 1997). The result of assessment formally has only two levels of performance indication: competent/not competent.

CBT was introduced in the late 1980s as a part of wider economic policy measures to improve the skill levels of the Australian workforce. It was driven by the concern to improve the flexibility and adaptability of the workforce in order to make it more globally competitive, an initiative linked to the micro economic reforms aimed at improving aspects of work practice (Billett et al., 1999; Goozee, 2001; NCVER, 2001a). These reforms resulted from debates about Australia's declining economic standing and the negative international appraisals of the nation's performance in the VET sector (Billett et al., 1999). In addition, the reform was aimed at establishing new career structures for the Australian workforce (NCVER, 2001b). Among the many criticisms made of the training systems before the restructuring of VET that finally led to the introduction of CBT were:

1. VET arrangements for the emerging industries were inadequate

2. TAFE was not flexible enough to meet industry needs

3. Qualifications were frequently not portable across State boundaries

4. There were not enough linkages between education providers, such as between schools and TAFE

5. Apprenticeship training was old fashioned and too dependent on time served rather than skills gained

6. Training which took place within companies was not recognized elsewhere.

7. Training was not always accessible to people from minority or equity groups (Smith, 1998, p. 21).

To remedy these deficiencies in the VET sector, CBT was proposed as an avenue that could first quantify exactly what the industry needs were. Second, it was to solve the problems of the time based training whose final qualifications were distinction, credit, pass or fail. These two reforms were to be achieved by having the organization and administration of VET being closely linked to the needs of industry (Billett et al., 1999). The implementation of CBT was neither smooth nor rapid but the commitment by the VET participants, particularly the high profile industry representation and governments, has remained strong (NCVER, 2001b).

Gonczi (1999) outlines some of the advantages of competency based VET. The first advantage is that it provides a curriculum and training framework which links practice to theory in more coherent ways. Second, it has the potential to break the dichotomies of "knowledge that" (theoretical) and "knowledge how" (practical) which leads to some knowledge being branded inferior to others. Thirdly, CBT can provide a basis for approaches to teaching and learning which could enhance students' adaptability and flexibility over their lives. These advantages are on condition that CBT is holistic and integrated rather than the traditional form of CBT. Other implied characteristics of CBT that promote its advantages is that it is individualized learning that provides personal feedback to students with emphasis on the exit rather than the admission requirements, although it has a strong recognition of prior learning. It is also hailed for being modularized and systematic leading to increased student and program accountability (Smith & Keating, 2003).

THE APPRENTICESHIP TRAINING IN AUSTRALIA

> The environment for vocational education and training is changing, prompting the need for VET practitioners to extend existing skills and to develop new skills in teaching, learning and assessment. Changes in the VET environment include: skill shortages; new technology in industry; the structure of work; the needs of youth, the disadvantaged and mature-aged workers; competition between providers; and the expectations of industry and the community. (Mitchell, Chappell, Bateman, & Roy, 2006, p. 7)

In line with the view of Mitchell et al. (2006), the current VET system in Australia has developed within a wider context of changing economic and political philosophies. The preparation of people for employment is recognized as one in which the government has significant interest in, although the focus of interest has varied. For instance, Hawke, Bauchanan, Fraser, Curthoys, and Diesendorf (2000) report that the Australian government interest in VET in the early 1990s was primarily economic. This is because VET is regarded as a powerful tool for economic reform. Although a key feature throughout is the instrumental nature of the present interests in the government, today, VET is seen as a means of addressing broader social aims rather than being an end in itself. Some of the broader issues involved are unemployment, competition policy, industry skill shortage, and concerns about the aging workforce.

Nearly all training for trade occupations in Australia occurs through apprenticeship. Apprenticeship as a system of training has a history stretching back at least into the medieval times (Aldrich, 1999). It involved apprentices bound by indentures to a master for a term ranging from 5 to 9 years while they were initiated into the theory, practice and details of a particular trade. Some of the abiding features of the historical apprenticeships as stated by Clarke (1999) are first that it was and still is part of the development of wage labour. Second, it is based on the acquisition of skills through work experience, embedding it in the workplace and making it highly dependent on the individual master or firm. A third aspect of the apprenticeship is that it serves as a means of entry into the trade or industry. Fourth, the apprentice is destined to be a tradesperson distinguished from a labourer. This apprenticeship system is formulated, regulated and divided at a higher social level than merely the master, the workshop and the apprentice.

Today, apprenticeship is a system of employment and training involving a contract between an apprentice and an employer. The training component is undertaken in conjunction with a public TAFE institute or a privately run registered training organization (RTO). The training agreements are registered with the relevant state or territory training authority (DEST, 2000). As a system of training, apprenticeship involves a systematic combination of work and education, which normally takes one of the following forms:

1. On-the-job training is combined with prescribed technical education, usually in TAFE colleges
2. On-the-job training is combined with prescribed technical education and approved off-the-job training.
3. On-the-job training only

The general conditions of apprenticeship training are similar across the States and territories in Australia. The typical period of the apprenticeship is 4 years although the period can be reduced depending on the entry knowledge of the trainee. The legislation governing apprenticeship does not discriminate on the basis of sex (Smith & Keating, 1997) although apprentice wages vary depending upon the age, stage, and trade of the apprenticeship.

The current Australian apprenticeship is called "new apprenticeship" to differentiate it from the original system where most learning was done on a one to one basis in the workplace. Goozee (2001) stated:

> The stated aim of New Apprenticeship system was to make training, particularly entry-level training, an attractive business proposition for a much wider range of enterprises, thereby expanding employment and career opportunities, particularly for the young people and the increasing international competitiveness of Australian enterprises through enhancing workforce skills. (p. 95)

The new apprenticeship combines practical work with structured training to provide a nationally recognized qualification. Thus new apprenticeship is a flexible arrangement of combining work and vocational training. It is a result of a reform that occurred in 1996 that led to the establishment of the modern australian apprenticeship and traineeship system (MAATS). New apprenticeships involve a training agreement between an employer and an individual (referred to as a new apprentice), under which the employer provides employment and training so that the new apprentice will achieve an agreed competency level in a particular occupation or trade (DEST, 2000). This new apprenticeship is a system which delivers assistance to the job seekers, serving both the economic and social needs of the apprentice. It has new and more flexible forms of assistance, approaches to target groups and significant reforms to payments and incentive arrangements (Ainley, Malley, & Lamb, 1997; Goozee, 2001).

The important contextualized issues for this reform were the need for the MAATS to reflect and strengthen the enterprise-based training and deal with the neglect of the traditional apprentice system in meeting the emergent skill needs of small to medium enterprises. Other issues to be dealt with were the complexity and cost of the provision of off-the-job training by traditional training providers to enterprises and the decline in apprentice numbers. In addition, the MAATS aimed at dealing with the industrial control of the apprenticeship concept, which prevented the application of emerging occupations in areas such as the communications technologies. Finally this reform refocused the role of the State governments in the administration of training systems (Ainley, Malley, & Lamb, 1997).

Group training companies may also hire new apprentices. These group-training companies take primary responsibility for the employment and training arrangements but place the new apprentice with one or more host employers over the period of the apprenticeship. In group training arrangements the trainees are allocated to work within different businesses that offer the variety of tasks required by the training. The theoretical component of training may be offered within the group training registered training organization or may be subcontracted to a TAFE institute (ANTA, 2002; ATA, 2002; DEST, 2000).

1. The training options which new apprenticeships provide to young people within apprenticeship and traineeships have advantages in that they:

2. involve paid job opportunities combined with a mix of on and/or off-the-job training

3. lead to a nationally recognized and portable qualification that is valued in the labour market

4. link to higher qualifications to provide career opportunities

5. make apprenticeship and traineeships available on a part time basis in schools

6. provide jobs and career opportunities in a wider range of industries (Automotive Training Australia [ATA], 2002).

New apprenticeships are conducted using competency-based assessment hence students need not take the prescribed 4 years for apprenticeship and 1 year for the traineeship. The off-the-job training is offered at either a public TAFE institute or at a private RTO. These new apprenticeships build on the strengths of the previous system of apprenticeships but provide greater flexibility and relevance to the workplace. They operate through cooperation between the federal and state/territory governments and industry. New apprenticeships include both the general apprenticeships and traineeships (Goozee, 2001). Traineeships are a system where the trainees undertaking trade training are not necessarily employed in any workplace. It incorporates taking courses that are part of Certificate II in a given trade and VET in schools program (part of secondary schools programs). Once the traineeship is completed, the trainees are at an advantage in securing an employment contract with a workplace to continue the apprenticeship. Traineeships were an initiative of the government to encourage employers to offer more jobs to young Australians (Hawke et al., 2000).

Also participating in research and VET issues are the Industry training advisory bodies (ITABs), which provide links between industry and VET. They provide governments with advice from industry, develop industry-training plans, and develop and maintain training packages to meet the needs of industry. The national ITABs work closely with the networks of state and territory ITABs (DEST, 2000).

For instance, Automotive Training Australia (ATA), focusing solely on the automotive industry was established with the ITAB in 1990. It facilitates the training of a highly skilled workforce, which is consistently able to meet the professional, production, service and competitive practice of the ATA (Braddy, 2002). ATA is owned by the industry, the shareholders being the Federal Chamber of the Automotive Industry (FCAI), the Motor Trades Association of Australia (MTAA) and the Australian Council of Trade Unions (ACTU). Board members include FCAI, MTAA, The truck industry council, and the federation of automotive products manufacturers. Automotive Training Australia (ATA) runs a newsletter called *Inside the Rim* which highlights the major issues in the automotive industry. It also organizes an annual conference that brings together industry practitioners and automotive training experts.

POSSIBLE LESSONS BASED ON THE AUSTRALIAN VET CONTEXT

Learning at Work

Boud in the foreword to Billett (2001) argues that the view that learning only takes place in schools and colleges is inadequate. He argues that initially, the workplace was seen as a place to work, to produce goods or offer services. It was assumed that learning occurred before employment or as part of special training. However, the demands of the workplace have now become more complex and no amount of initial training can prepare a person for a lifetime.

From the illustration above, it is clear that there is a need to practice doing the real work after learning the theory. This notion is based on the understanding that learning and cognition are fundamentally contextual or situated and that understanding develops through learners engaging with the social and the cultural context as a result making performance and understanding one and the same thing (Gonczi, 1999). The doing of the task enables the trainees to internalize and perfect the skill and hence move from being novices toward becoming experts. While being guided by the experts at the workplace, the trainees will be able to learn more about the trade and the hidden or remote details, as Billett (2001) refers to them that can only be availed through work.

This view is in line with Dewey cited in Billett (2001, p. 132) advocating that the only way to learn about occupations was through occupations and making the most of immediate experiences and opportunities in this learning. This grants the advantage of moving toward developing the full potential of the individual by developing long-term outcomes. Dewey saw the object of learning as developing the capacity of the learner to engage in appropriate practice, which was seen by the individual as being related to the intentions in pursuit of the vocation. Dewey further regarded experience as the basis for constructing new meaning and learning how to interpret new situations (Stevenson, 2003). Some of the attributes of this meaning (Stevenson, 2003) thus constructed is related to the doing of the task and is connected across being living and working. Further, the construction of meaning is situated in practice.

In terms of meaning and doing (Stevenson, 2003), trainees are able to develop a concrete meaning rather than abstract, and specific rather than general. Stevenson (2003, p. 8) cites Dewey (1916) advocating that active doing is the cornerstone of developing meaning:

> The knowledge that comes first to persons, and that remains most deeply ingrained is knowledge of how to do [in this case we should have known how to change a clutch plate in practice]. When education [and training] fails to recognize that the primary or the initial subject matter always exists as a matter of an active doing, involving the use of body and the handling of material, the subject matter of instruction is isolated from the needs and purposes of the learner [trainee] and so becomes something to be memorized and reproduced upon demand.

In this case, doing the actual learned activity develops and enhances the meaning of the activity and the goals to be achieved. In support of the link between theory and practice, Garrick (1999) notes that learning is embedded in the realities of the work processes, systems and technologies; hence making one's experience becomes vital. Thus apprenticeships' training in the real life situation of the workplace scores some advantages.

The link between theory and practice has been the core to institute-based vocational education and training. It is with this view that institutes offer a theoretical background to the tasks that are performed at the workplace besides simulating these tasks. It is also noted that the fact that people learn best from concrete to the abstract, with guidance from experts (Billett, 1999; Garrick, 1999).

Link Between the Training Institutions and the Industry

This link between training and work has a big role in facilitating the smooth transition from school to work. It is a concept that has known support. For example Jung, Misko, Lee, Dawe, Hong, and Lee (2004) report that in the United States, the School to Work Act 1994 emphasizes the preparation for the transition and the strengthening of linkage between school and the world of work. Its key areas of concerns are school-based learning, work-based learning, and activities connecting the classroom and the workplace. The link enhances that required preparedness for the transition from the institute-based training (school) to the workplace. On this issue again, Jung et al. (2004) state:

> effective measures for the school-to work transition have important consequences for vocational education and training (VET) students, who generally move into employment earlier than those in general education track. Preparing these students to enter the world of work with the minimum psychological shock will help their initial adaptation to work. Moreover, when the students successfully complete effective school-to-work transition programs, they will have developed the skills that enable them to adapt to the workplace. (p. 14)

There is a need for updating their knowledge about workplace procedures, tasks and requirements. As a result, government should provide for training leave to update this knowledge. This update will enable them to link theory with practice so that they are able to handle the requirements for change and changes related to technology advances. Fullan (2001) emphasizes the need for this link by stating:

> It is important to acknowledge that the best insights into change process come from our association with practice. While Kurt Lewin was right stating, "There is nothing as practical as a good theory," it is equally true that "there is nothing as theoretical as good practice." (p. xiii)

From this statement, it is argued that good theory and practice should go hand in hand for the best results. To achieve this matching it is important that the programs and curricula are evaluated, reviewed, and updated with time and technology changes.

Curriculum Evaluation

There are seven main areas of curriculum that are evaluated regularly.

1. Content for relevance, quality and currency.
2. Delivery for quality in relation to the mode of delivery (self paced, distance learning, problem centred, inquiry or practical/theory).
3. Student achievement in relation to progress toward achieving the objectives.
4. Resources in terms of extent and quality.
5. Assessment and reporting for relevance, accuracy and fairness.
6. Student and industry demand and support for the course.
7. Enrollment and successful participation rates of all client groups.

These seven points are based on training relevance and the need for economic competitiveness in a global context. In this vein, Jung et al. (2004) points out:

> The Australian system for vocational education and training has undergone considerable reforms since the mid-1980s. The impetus for these changes was provided by the adoption of training reform agenda aimed at developing a more skilled workforce to improve economic competitiveness in global markets. ...The role of this training system was to train workers who were able to adapt to, and use, new technologies, and were able to work independently as well as collaboratively, in autonomous work groups to achieve business outcomes. (pp. 43-44)

These reforms were an attempt to enable students to make a smooth transition to the workplace and to develop the skills required by industry. The creation of a national system for VET also aimed to overcome the obstacles presented by separate but similar vocational education and training systems of the different Australian states, and also to improve the ability of students to transport their qualifications between the states. The adoption of competency-based training was central to these reforms.

These views highlight the issue that there is need for reviews into the VET systems to make them practical, useful to life after training and responsive to world market demands. While reviewing the programs is important, it is also important to continue to update the training facilities in order to maintain the relevance of the program. This issue is related to the importance of trainees' familiarity with the handling of equipment, machines and tools at the workplace.

On the issue of curriculum change, Walkington (2002, p.133) states:

> Today's faculty leaders and managers in higher education [VET included] can no longer facilitate curriculum development as they used to in the past. Strategic planning and operational decisions must reflect the changing nature of society, the world of work and education. This does not mean just reacting to changes in other paces, but to be proactive in predicting and responding to future needs of all stakeholders in higher education. (p. 133)

Technical and Generic Skills

Related to the views expressed above Walkington (2002) further suggests that there is a need to incorporate technical skills besides the generic skills into an integrated approach of teaching and training. The main attributes that are suggested in the curriculum design issues are the considerations of the "why," "how" and "when" questions in the development of an integrated training system. Although these comments were primarily devoted to higher education and training, they well suit the arguments advanced in this VET study for promoting responsive automotive training to the changing demands of the workplace.

> Life skills are seen as those that promote better lives. They help people cope with growing uncertainty and rapid change. Such skills are believed by many to already be possessed by individuals and communities but are seen as being in need of further development. The particular set of life skills relevant to any setting must reflect the contextualized needs of the relevant individuals, communities and nations. Another aspect of the cluster of meanings surrounding life skills is that they are related to lifelong learning. Hence, they are developed throughout life and in various settings. (McGrath, 2003, p. 7).

Education and training in the era of changing technology should promote acquisition of life skills. Mostly, these are skills related to work. However, McGrath (2003) points out that different people view life skills differently. He contends that there is considerable variation in understandings of the notions of life skills and work skills, as well as disagreement about the relationship between the two concepts. He notes, (McGrath, 2003):

> On the one hand, it is argued that such [life] skills are holistic and so should be seen as relevant to the whole of life. On the other, it is pointed out that work, employment and income are so central to life that the most important of life skills are those that are also work skills. ...In such a view it makes no sense to separate preparation for work from preparation for citizenship. (p. 7)

With such a strong case for linking training and work, it is only imperative that the workplace should provide for some form of learning so that the workers continually develop their skills. The best place to learn about specific skills required for work should also be the workplace. While training institutions should promote the general skills that cut across workplaces, it is only at the workplace that the context based skills are learned. This is because skills reflect a range of contextual factors (McGrath, 2003).

KEY ISSUES RELATED TO VET IN AUSTRALIA

These issues are related to the key message in Mitchell et al. (2006, p. 6) that:

1. The VET sector is distinguished by complexity and opportunity. Many critical issues were identified by stakeholders under the banner of these two terms but, for the majority of VET stakeholders, quality is the most critical issue in teaching, learning and assessment.

2. The concept of quality provokes different responses from VET stakeholders. Some stakeholders focus on managing quality systems and quality indicators, while others focus on creating cultures to stimulate continuous improvement. Ideally, both perspectives are needed.

3. VET practitioners need to extend their existing skills to meet the challenges of the new VET environment, which includes a range of learning styles, new assessment practices, diversity of clients (from industry to individual students) with a diversity of requirements (such as customized service), and enhanced technologies. They need the time and space to do this.

4. VET practitioners will need to adopt a variety of methodologies to develop these new skills. Work-based learning takes into account new thinking about adult learning and learning organizations and can involve coaching, mentoring, industry release, and work shadowing as well as participating in networks, communities of practice and professional conversations. It has been shown to be successful

in supporting the achievement of high-quality teaching, learning and assessment.

5. All VET stakeholders will need to adopt innovative approaches to their various roles. For individuals, critical success factors include their adopting new work roles, such as learning manager or facilitator. VET organizations need to develop an agile, flexible, creative, and innovative culture balanced, but not dominated, by the need to comply with systemic quality requirements.

6. Partnerships and networks support the achievement of high-quality teaching, learning and assessment by encouraging the exchange of information, ideas, techniques, and approaches between VET practitioners, their clients and industry representatives.

Critical issues in terms of the skills and resources needed by contemporary VET practitioners include:

1. Many VET practitioners need improved skills in implementing training packages, despite their widespread availability in the sector, in some cases, for the past 7 or 8 years.

2. VET practitioners need skills that enable them to take advantage of the new digital technologies as they become available.

3. VET practitioners need skills and resources to provide effective support for learning that occurs in the workplace.

4. Finally VET practitioners need an increased awareness of the broad spectrum of types of learning and the varied contexts. New skills are also needed to provide assessment services, for example, to conduct assessment in the workplace, to provide recognition, and to assess generic skills.

CONCLUSION

As the context in which vocational education and training (VET) operates changes, a new notion of VET practitioner is emerging, one whose role is to meet the increasing expectations of industry clients and individual students. The new VET practitioner does not rely on the old certainties such as preset curriculum and classroom instruction, but develops attributes, attitudes, ideas and techniques to meet the needs of clients. This new practitioner should look outwards at market needs and seeks to meet those needs. The attributes of the new VET practitioner reflect a new amalgam mix of sound educational practice on the one hand, and contemporary business strategies on the other. This mix is understandable, given that VET practitioners are being encouraged to work more closely with industry and work enterprises.

REFERENCES

Ainley, J., Malley, J., & Lamb, S. (1997). *Thematic review of transition from Initial education to working life: Australia background report.* Canberra: Australian Council of Educational Research.

Aldrich, R. (1999). The apprentice in history. In P. Ainley, & H. Rainbird (Eds.), *Apprenticeships: Towards a new paradigm of learning* (pp. 14-24). London: Kogan Page.

Australian National Training Authority. (2002). *Training packages: Successes, issues and challenges in implementation.* Retrieved May 12, 2003, from www.anta.gov.au

Australian National Training Authority. (2003). *A bridge to the future: Australia's national strategy for vocational education and training 1998-2003.* Retrieved November 20, 2003, from http://www.anta.gov.au

Australian National Training Authority. (2004). *Annual national report of the Australian vocational education and training system.* Brisbane: Author.

Automotive Training Australia (ATA). (2002). *New apprenticeship information.* Retrieved October 28, 2002, from www.automotivetraining.org.au/

Billett, S. (2001). *Learning in the work place: Strategies for effective practice* (1st ed.). Crows Nest NSW: Allen & Unwin.

Billett, S., McKavanagh, C., Beven, F., Angus, L., Seddon, T., Gough, J., et al. (1999). *The CBT decade: Teaching for flexibility and adaptability.* Leabrook: National Centre for Vocational Education Research.

Blom, K., & Meyers, D. (2003). *Quality indicators in vocational education and training: International perspectives.* Adelaide: Australian National Training Authority.

Braddy, J. (2002). *Training for profit: Conference 2002.* Retrieved October 28, 2002, from http://www.motor.net.au/?url=/ata

Canberra Times. (1987, Aug. 4) TAFE cuts uneconomical. Canberra Rural Press Ltd. Retrieved August 8, 2007 from http://canberra.yourguide.com.au

Chappell, C., & Johnston, R. (2003). *Changing work: Changing roles of vocational education and training teachers and trainers.* Leabrook, Australia: National Centre for Vocational Education Research.

Chappell, C., Gonczi, A., & Hagar, P. (1995). Competency based education. In G. Foley (Ed.), *Understanding adult education and training* (pp. 175-187). Sydney: Allen & Unwin.

Central Investigation Agency. (2007). *The world fact book.* Retrieved February 2, 2007, from http://www.odci.gov/cia/publications/factbook/print/au.htm

Clarke, L. (1999). The changing structure and significance of apprenticeships with special reference to construction. In P. Ainley & K. Rainbird (Eds.), *Apprenticeships: Towards a new paradigm of learning* (pp. 25-41). London: Kogan Page.

Department of Education Science and Training. (2000). *Country education profile for Australia.* Retrieved October 8, 2000, from http://www.dest.gov.au/sectors/school_education/publications_resources/profiles.htm

Dewey, J. (1916). *Democracy and education.* New York: Free Press.

Fullan, M. (2001). *The new meaning of educational change* (3rd ed.). New York: Teachers College Press.

Garrick, J. (1999). The dominant discourses of learning at work. In D. Boud & J. Garrick (Eds.), *Understanding learning at work* (pp. 216-231). London: Routeledge.

Gonczi, A. (1999). Competency based learning: A dubious past-an assured future? In D. Boud & J. Garrick (Eds.), *Understanding learning at work* (pp. 180-196). London: Routledge.

Goozee, G. (2001). *The development of TAFE in Australia* (3rd ed.). Leabrook: National Centre for Vocational Education Research Ltd.

Haan, H. C. (2001). *Training for work in the informal sector: New evidence from Eastern and Southern Africa.* Turin, Italy: World Bank.

Haukka, S., Keating, J., & Lamb, S. (2004). *Alternative mechanisms to encourage individual contributions to vocational education and training.* Adelaide: National Centre for Vocational Education Research.

Hawke, G., Bauchanan, J., Fraser, M., Curthoys, A., & Diesendorf, M. (2000). *Pictures of the future.* Sydney: University of Technology Sydney RCVET.

Jung, T. H., Misko, J., Lee, K., Dawe, S., Hong, S. Y., & Lee, K.C. (2004). *Effective measure for school-to- work transition in the vocational education system. Lessons from Australia and Korea.* Adelaide: National Centre for Vocational Education Research.

Keating, J., Medrich, E., Volkoff, V., & Perry, J. (2002). *Review of research: Comparative study of vocational education and training systems: National VET systems across three regions under pressure of change.* Leabrook: National Centre for Vocational Education Research. Melbourne: Australian Education Council.

McGrath, S. (2003). Life and work skills and their contribution to education and training debates. In S. McGrath (Ed.), *Debates in skills development: Skills for life and work* (pp.7-13). Bonn, Germany: International Labour Organisation.

Misko, J. (2001). *Developing industry linkages.* Leabrook: National Centre for Vocational Education Research.

Mitchell, J., Chappell, C., Bateman, A., & Roy, S. (2006). *Quality is the key: Critical issues in teaching, learning and assessment in vocational education and training.* Australian Government, Adelaide: National Centre for Vocational Education and Technology.

National Centre for Vocational Education and Research. (2001a). *Australian Apprenticeships: Research at a glance.* Adelaide: National Centre for Vocational Education Research Ltd.

National Centre for Vocational Education and Research. (2001b). *Australian apprenticeships: Facts, fiction and future.* Leabrook, Kensington Park: National Centre for Vocational Education Research.

Smith, A. (1998). *Training and development in Australia* (2nd ed.). Sydney: Butterworths.

Smith, E., & Keating, J. (1997). *Making sense of training reform and competency based training* (1st ed.). Wentworth: Social Science Press.

Smith, E., & Keating, J. (2003). *From training reforms to training packages*. Tuggerah, NSW: Social Sciences Press.

Stevenson, J. (2003). Expertise for the workplace. In J. Stevenson (Ed.), *Developing vocational expertise* (pp. 3-25). Crows Nest: Allen & Unwin.

Walkington, J. (2002). A process for curriculum change in engineering education. *European Journal of Engineering Education, 27*(2), 133-148.

GLOSSARY AND RESOURCES

The following terms may be encountered throughout the chapters. The definitions provided should inform their use in context. Before you read the book, you may want to take a brief look at these terms. Or you may wish to refer to these terms whenever you need clarification on a specific term while reading the book. However, it is necessary for our readers and learners to know how the name of career and technical education came into being. It is also important to know that in many instances, career and technical education cannot replace "vocational education," even though career and technical education may sound better to the ears.

First vocational education emerged in the form of "manual training." James P. Haney (Lang, 1898), in an address to the 1903 meeting of the National Education Association (NEA), suggested the term "manual arts" (Bennett, 1917) be used instead of "manual training" (Ham, 1900) as a means of placing emphasis on artistic elements of manual activity. Just a year later, in 1904, Charles R. Richards of Teachers College, Columbia University, suggested, in an editorial in the October 1904 issue of *Manual Training Magazine* that the term "industrial arts" be used instead of "manual training" or "manual arts" as more descriptive of this changing point of view. This also gave rise to the Industrial Arts (IA) Movement. Trade and industrial vocational education emerged as a major education program with the passage of the Smith-Hughes Act of 1917 (Douglas, 1921, p. 293). As many industrial arts teachers attempted to change their course offerings in the 1980s, Industrial arts was eliminated and many traditional areas were added. The new name that replaced IA was technology education in the 1980s (Dyrenfurth & Blandow, 1994). As teachers, learners and practitioners entered the 1990s, they felt that the term "vocational education" reflects the image of the skilled trades person. This image may not appeal to a number of high school students. Hence career and technical education emerged to replace vocational education. It must be pointed out that, in many instances, the term vocational education is still used because it appears to be irreplaceable.

Accreditation: A systematic process of evaluation whereby a team of peers evaluates an educational institution and recognizes it for a specific time period. Certification that an institution's programs and activities meet selected standards necessary to accomplish the role, scope and mission of the institution.

Adult Education: One broad definition from UNESCO: Education programs below the college level for persons over the age of sixteen who have completed or left high school or have already entered the labor market or who are unemployed. Adult education also refers to any organized and sustained communication designed to bring about learning in adults, excluding education following directly after initially primary and secondary education, and excluding vocational education. Or it refers to adults who are engaged in learning to develop their abilities, enrich their knowledge, improve their technical or professional qualifications, or turn them in a new direction and bring about changes in their attitudes or behavior in the two fold perspective of full personal development and participation in balanced, independent, social, economic, and cultural development. This definition was provided by UNESCO (Also see Jarvis's 2002 *International Dictionary of Adult and Continuing Education*).

Adult Home Economics Occupational Programs: Short or long term programs which are preparatory or supplemental in nature and which are offered day or evening. Courses/Programs for out-of-school youth and adult who want to learn new skills or upgrade skills which lead to (1) immediate employment, (2) change of employment, and (3) job advancement.

Advisory Committee: A group of persons, usually outside the education profession, selected for the purpose of offering advice and counsel to the school regarding the vocational program, with particular attention to keeping the program practical and attuned to community needs.

Apprentice: A worker who is learning a recognized occupation in accordance with a written apprentice-training contract between the student and employer, which provides for a given period of planned work experience through employment on the job, supplemented by appropriate related information, and with other specified provisions of the arrangement. The minimum age of an apprentice is 16 years of age, but most programs will not accept applicants under 18.

Apprenticeship: Traditionally, the idea of apprenticeship has been associated with the process of skill formation within a craft and industrial production, and to a lesser extent, within certain professions. In a situative perspective of learning, the idea of apprenticeship is used to conceptualize both the process of learning and the practices, tools and resources that support the learning. It may be viewed as a general theory of learning that might link learning at work and learning in classrooms rather than being only distinct contexts within distinct outcomes.

Apprenticeship Training Program: A program registered with the U.S. Department of Labor or the State Apprenticeship Agency in accordance with the Act of August 16, 1937, known as the National Apprenticeship Act, which is conducted or sponsored by an employer, a group of employers, or a joint apprenticeship committee representing both employers and a union, and which contains all terms and conditions for the qualifications, recruitment, selection, and training of apprentices.

Appropriation: Money set aside by a, legislature when a budget is approved. This could be money set aside to satisfy an authorization of an act, which was passed previously.

Area Vocational-Technical School or Area Vocational School: A facility that offers vocational technical instruction for a district or a number of districts. An institution formed in 1964 in the United States to deliver skill training. These are included in two categories

1. Type I Area Vocational School—any vocational education school which is organized and approved by the state board of education and operated under the control of an elected board of education of a school district or a board of trustees of a community college.

2. Type II Area Vocational-Technical School—any vocational education school which was designated a Type II school and having a governing body called the board of control constituted as provided by agreement of the districts participating therein.

Articulation: (A) The process of arranging the instructional programs of a school system to provide a closely interlocking, continuous, and consistent educational environment for students as they progress through the system. (B) The degree of continuity, consistency and interdependency of the offerings of a school system or between school systems.

Australian National Training Authority (ANTA): It is the Australian government's body that coordinated research and other issues in vocational education and training (VET). This body was reattached to the Department of Education, Science and Training (DEST) from October 2004. Following the prime minister's announcement on Friday October, 22, 2004 the responsibilities and functions of the Australian National Training Authority (ANTA) have now been transferred to the Department of Education, Science and Training (DEST).

Australian Vocational Education and Training Research Association (AVETRA): This is a body that conducts VET research in Australia. It looks at VET research at all levels. It also organizes an annual conference where VET practitioners meet to share issues related to research and current trends in the sector. It draws its membership from Universities, Technical and Further Education (TAFE) colleges, nongovernmental registered training organizations (RTOs) and other research bodies. It is also defined as a body that coordinates VET research in Australia. AVETRA is Australia's only national, independent association for research in vocational education and training, brings together research stakeholders and researchers from the TAFE, university, industry and government sectors.

Authorization Act: An act that authorizes a legislative body to expend a certain amount of money for stated activities.

Automotive Training Australia (ATA): It is a body that coordinates curriculum issues for the automotive training for the industry. It approves and coordinates revision and review of the teaching standards and materials. It also approves new programs for the automotive training in Australia.

Business Education: A program of education which equips the student with marketable skills, knowledge, and attitudes needed for initial employment and advancement in business occupations clusters. The business curriculum includes stenographic subjects (typing and shorthand), bookkeeping, clerical practices, office machines, word processing, and desktop publishing. *General Business Education* provides the student with information and competencies, which are needed by all, in managing personal business affairs and in using the services of the business world.

Business Entrepreneurs: Individuals in our society who are creative and innovative and are able to initiate new business ventures by adding value to the ventures by creating news ideas, new markets, and services and new products.

Career Education: An educational concept which enables an individual to be better prepared for planning a career. This concept, which bridges all grade levels K-12, consists of three phases— Career Awareness, Career Orientation, and Career Exploration.

Career and Technical Education: Organized educational programs which are directly related to the preparation of individuals for paid or unpaid employment or for additional preparation for a career which does not require a baccalaureate or advanced degree.

Career and Technical Education Program: An instructional program with a planned series of educational experiences designed to prepare individuals for job entry or job advancement in an occupational field.

Certificate: A document which gives recognition to students for successful completion of competencies, a program of studies, course, class, or cocurricular activity, or for graduation from a school; for example, a diploma, or other formal paper, promotion to the next school, and awarding of units of value.

Clerical Practice: A business subject dealing with the various duties of office workers other than stenographic, for example, typing, filing, keeping records, handling office forms, and using duplicating, computing, word processing, desktop publishing, and other office machines.

Combination Cooperative Vocational Education Program (CCVEP): A cooperative education program in the United States that provides an opportunity for schools in small communities to provide general and direct related career and technical classroom training combined with on-the-job training in a variety of occupations to enable students to develop occupational knowledge, skills, and attitudes. The program is appropriate for communities of less than 5,000 or a 9-12 enrollment of 400 or fewer students.

Community College: A public 2-year postsecondary degree granting institution approved and accredited by the state board of education that may award certificates and degrees for comprehensive instructional programs in general, liberal, practical arts, career, and vocational education and transfer programs to institutions of higher education.

Competency: An ability or capability demanded in the successful performance of a specific act or behavior. It is regarded as being a measurable skill.

Competency Based Training (CBT): CBT is training that is geared toward the attainment and demonstration of skills to meet industry specified standards rather than to an individual's achievement relative to that of others in a group. It is a way of approaching vocational training that places primary emphasis on what a person can do as a result of training (the outcome) and as such represents a shift from the emphasis on the process involved in training (the inputs). It is concerned with training to industry specific standards rather than an individual achievement relative to others in a group.

Consumer and Homemaking Education Program: Consists of instructional programs, services, and activities at all educational levels for the occupations of homemaking including: (1) comprehensive homemaking, (2) child development and guidance, (3) clothing and textiles, (4) consumer education, (5) family health, (6) family living and parenthood education, (7) food and nutrition, (8) home management, (9) housing and furnishings, and (10) other.

Continuing Education: Learning activities that occur beyond formal job preparatory training programs. The learning activities are most often associated with competencies or skills identified by employers, trade associations, licensing or certification agencies for the specific purpose of upgrading or recertification of employees.

Cooperative Education: A program for persons who are enrolled in a school and who, through a cooperative arrangement between the school and employer, receive part-time vocational instruction in the school and on-the-job training through part-time employment

Cooperative Industrial Training: An instructional program at the secondary level which is designed to prepare persons who wish to enter what are commonly called trade and industrial occupations. This is a cooperative program.

Coordinator: A member of the school staff responsible for administering the school program and resolving all problems that arise between school regulations and on-the-job activities of the employed student in a cooperative education program. The coordinator acts as a liaison between the school and the employer in cooperative education programs or other part-time job training.

Counseling: The process of helping an individual through interviews and other individual relationships to solve personal problems and improve personal planning. Counseling implies a situation involving two persons in which one known as the counselor gives a certain kind of assistance to the other—the counselee. Counseling is engaged in for the purpose of:

- Assisting the individual in the interpretation of personal data
- Helping the individual in the identification of major vocational, educational, and personal problems.
- Assisting the individual in the planning of possible solutions to the problems identified.
- Helping the individual make a start toward carrying out personal plans.
- Providing assistance in necessary modifications of personal plans.

Department of Education, Science and Training (DEST): This is the government department that handles all education and training matters for the commonwealth of Australia.

Displaced Homemaker: (A) Persons who have been homemakers, but who now, because of dissolution of a marriage, must seek employment, and (B) Persons whom are single heads of households and who lack adequate job skills.

Displaced Homemakers Centers: First was established on the campus at Mills College, Oakland, California in May 1976, to assist women who were divorced, separated, or no longer eligible for aid for dependent children. They provide counseling, job training, and assistance in finding employment.

Distributive Education: In the context of career and technical education (CTE), distributive education is considered as an instructional program on the secondary level to prepare persons who wish to enter, or have already entered the field of distribution. This is a cooperative education program.

Diversified Cooperative Training: A trade and industrial program that combines supervised and preplanned employment in selected skill development at a training station. Instruction includes in-school related technical subject matter and regular high school subjects required for graduation plus on-the-job training in job skills. The objective of the course of instruction is preparation for employment in an occupation of the individual's choice.

Diversified Health Occupations: A health occupations program which combines an in-school and a cooperative program of instruction during a 2-year period offering training in diversified health occupational areas.

Diversified Occupations Program: A high school course in which students are given supervised work experiences in any one of a variety of occupations combined with related classroom instruction. This type of program is especially suited to communities where the need for workers in any one occupation is too limited to justify separate courses for each trade. The diversified occupations program is usually under the direction of the trade and industrial education division.

Educational Guidance: The systematic categorization of an individual's abilities and aptitudes in order to assist the individual in choosing correct educational courses or avenues of study. It implies a concerned and appropriate judgment as well as a skilled assessment of a person's needs and capabilities. The ultimate aim of educational guidance is recognized as the development in individuals of insight that will enable them eventually to undertake sensible directions for their own affairs.

Entrepreneurs: People who actively and continuously seek out new ways and approaches to solve current problems, avert impending threats, or seize upon emerging possibilities in the institutions and organizations for which they work.

Entrepreneurial Spirit: The spirit of adventure and the willingness to take initiative to try new things, new ideas, and to take risk. Entrepreneurial spirit can also be defined as a combination of ambition, the need to create, the taste for risk, the refusal of failure, unyielding work, and dedication.

Family and Consumer Sciences (Home Economics) Education: A program of instruction, which assists boys and girls and men and women, to understand and solve problems in personal, home, and family living. The subject matter areas comprising the field of family and consumer sciences include: Child development and family relationships, foods and nutrition, clothing and textiles, family economics and home management, housing and home furnishing and home equipment, and family health. The term *home economics* is the outdated term used to designate this educational field. Programs at the community college and university levels prepare students for such professional services as homemaking teacher, dietitian, nutritionist, nursery school teacher, and institutional manager.

(FHA) [Now called Family, Career and Community Leaders of America (FCCLA)]: A student organization composed of students that are enrolled in the home economics program. The activities are an integral part of the Home Economics program.

Guidance: The process of guiding a person in educational pursuits as well as in choosing a career. The concept of guidance is essentially democratic in that the assumptions underlying its theory and practice are, first, that individuals have the right to shape their own destiny and second, that the relatively mature and experienced members of the community are responsible for ensuring that each person's choice shall serve both the individual's interests as well as those of the society to which the individual belongs. It is the function of those who guide to orient the individual toward those opportunities afforded by the environment, which can guarantee the fulfillment of personal needs and aspirations.

Health Careers: An awareness and exploratory program offered at the secondary level. This program allows the students an opportunity to explore a variety of health careers while analyzing their own interests, aptitudes, and aspirations in light of a realistic view of a health career goal, by becoming aware of the type of work to be performed and the scholastic standards required to achieve the goal.

Health Occupations: A program of instruction which assists the student in preparing for job entry into various health fields. These programs require clinical experiences as a portion of the instruction.

Health Occupations Education: A training program at the post secondary level that provides planned instruction in liberal arts, biological science, physical science and occupational theory along with articulated clinical experiences. The programs prepare individuals for occupations that render direct patient service. These programs prepare individuals for careers below the professional level.

High-Technology: The state-of-the-art computer, microelectronic, hydraulic, pneumatic, nuclear, robotic, telecommunication, and other technologies being used to enhance productivity in manufacturing, commercial, and similar economic activity and to improve the provision of health care.

Home Economics Cooperative Education (HECE): A cooperative education program that prepares individuals for occupational home economics occupations. Basic home economics and related knowledge are taught in the secondary institutions and the skills are taught on-the-job by employees of the cooperating business or industry.

Home Economics Related Occupations (HERO): A student organization for the occupational and cooperative home economics programs that function at local, district, state, and national levels. The chapters focus on vocational understanding, leadership development, civic responsibility and social awareness. The activities are conducted as an integral part of the training program.

Homemaker: An individual who is an adult caring for the home and family primarily without remuneration. This situation quite often results in the individual having diminished current marketable skills.

Homemaking Education: Education which is centered on home activities and relationships, designed to enable girls and boys and men and women to assume the responsibilities of making a home or improve home and family living.

Industrial Arts Education: A program of general education which pertains to the awareness and exploration of information or skills pertaining to industry. The program assists the students in preparing for vocational skills and making them better consumers. This program is usually referred to today as technology education.

Industrial Education: A generic term applying to all types of education related to industry, including general industrial education, (Industrial Arts or Technology Education), Vocational Industrial Education (Trade and Industrial Education), and Technical Industrial Education (training of persons between the professional and skilled workers).

Jamaica Movement for the Advancement of Literacy (JAMAL): The purpose was to wipe out illiteracy in Jamaica by offering programs that incorporate the teaching of life-coping skills to enable persons to function in society.

Learning: Learning reflects the academic specialisms from which the study is conducted. It refers to the process of acquiring knowledge, skills, attitudes, values, beliefs, emotions, senses. Learning is different from education. Learning emphasizes the person in whom the change occurs or is expected to occur whereas education is an activity undertaken or initiated by one or more agents that is designed to effect change in the knowledge, skill, and attitudes of individuals, groups, or communities.

Local Education Agency (LEA): A board of education or other legally constituted local school authority having administrative control and direction of a public political subdivision of a state; or any other public educational institution or agency having administrative control and direction of a vocational education program.

Lyceum: Self-help adult education organizations, in which members were both learners and teachers. Josiah Holbrook started the lyceum movement in Massachusetts in 1826. The associations, normally town-based, were usually for working people. They were formed for mutual improvement through the acquisition of useful knowledge by lecture, discussion or any other appropriate method. The movement grew to such an extent that there were over 3,500 lyceums in different towns within a decade of the start of the movement. By 1850, the national movement had disintegrated, although individual lyceums continued to function. The lyceum was originally called the Society for Mutual Education and it then became known as the Society for the Improvement of Schools and Diffusion of Useful Knowledge.

Marketing Education: A cooperative education program offered on the postsecondary level for those who wish to prepare to enter or have already entered the marketing field.

Ministry of Education, Youth and Culture (MOEYC): It provides a system which secures quality education and training for all persons in Jamaica and achieves integration of educational and cultural resources in order to optimize individual and national development.

Morrill Act: The Federal Act in the United States of 1862 and 1880 that made land and funds available for the creation of the land grant colleges.

National Center for Vocational Education and Research (NCVER): The National Centre for Vocational Education Research (NCVER) is not-for-profit company in Australia owned by the federal, state and territory ministers responsible for training. It is unique in Australia's education system. It is responsible for collecting, managing, analysing, evaluating and communicating research and statistics about vocational education and training (VET).

National Training Agency (NTA): This refers to the government organization designated to monitor, coordinate, and promote technical and vocational education and training. It also facilitates and promotes the development of a competent workforce through lifelong learning, labor market research, national occupational standards and quality assurance of the technical, vocational education and training system.

Occupational Home Economics Program: A home economics program that utilizes home economics knowledge and skills needed for preparing males, females, youth and adults, to secure and maintain employment at the entry and/or advanced levels. These instructional programs comprise the group related subject matter areas, programs, courses, or classes of instruction designed and organized for the purpose of enabling the learners to acquire knowledge and develop understandings, attitudes, values, and skills relevant to meet the specific and unique requirements of the occupations.

Philosophy: Philosophy is normally viewed as one of the following: (1) A body of philosophical principles, especially, the body of principles underlying a given branch of learning, or major discipline, a religious system, a human activity or the like; (2) Has three central concerns: the nature of reality, truth, and value; (3) A statement of philosophy is an articulation of fundamental assumptions about reality, truth and value.

Postsecondary Education: All learning activities undertaken after completing secondary education, with the exception of adult basic education and education in the secondary curriculum. It is also a generic term for higher education or tertiary education.

Practical Arts Education: A type of functional education predominately manipulative in nature which provides learning experiences in leisure-time interests, consumer knowledge, creative expression, family living, manual skills, technological development, and similar outcomes of value to all. It includes those phases of agriculture, business education, fine arts, homemaking, and industrial arts in which occupational efficiency in not a major goal.

Prevocational Program: A program designed to introduce participants to broad vocational areas and to the tools, materials, and processes used in each. Industrial arts, general agriculture, and general business are examples of such programs.

Private Industry Council (PIC): In the United States a council established for each service delivery area (SDA) under the Job Training Partnership Act (JTPA) to provide policy guidance and oversight. The council is composed of representatives from business, industry, labor, education, economic development agencies, community-based organizations, rehabilitation agencies, and the public employment service. These boards are known as workforce development boards under the current legislation.

Registered Training Organization (RTO): RTO is a term used to refer to any authorized institution that offers VET training in Australia. All Government TAFE colleges and nongovernmental institutions that offer recognized VET qualifications fall under this general term of RTOs.

Reimbursable Vocational Program: In the United States any vocational program which is conducted in accordance with the provisions of the State Plan for vocational education and is thus eligible to receive federal vocational education funds.

School Leavers Training Opportunities Programs: A fully funded alternative training opportunities program in Australia to help young people to prepare for vocational education.

Secondary Education: A form of initial education organized by day schools for children of about 12 years and older, some with a vocational strand and others with a more general education approach. Often, the remedial education is directed toward providing opportunities for adults to undertake or repeat this period of their education.

Service Delivery Area (SDA): A designation in the United States of a state or political subdivision of the state designated by the governor, for the purpose of program planning, operation, and allocation of funds for job training through the Job Training Partnership Act. An SDA promotes effective delivery of job training services, is consistent with labor market areas, and areas in which related services are provided under other state or federal programs.

Skill: The ability to perform correctly and effectively in action-based situations. It also refers to a psychomotor action.

Smith-Hughes Act: 1917, U.S. Act that made federal funds available for education in agriculture, home economics, industry, and commerce; it also created the Federal Board for Vocational Education.

Social Entrepreneurs: Individuals in our society who are creative and innovative and are able to initiate and sustain new possibilities in health, education, environment, and not for profit organizations.

State Council on Vocational Education: A council appointed by the State Board of Education composed of thirteen individuals established in accordance with the Carl Perkins Vocational Education Act of 1984 for the purpose of assisting with planning, evaluating and improving vocational education.

State Department of Education: The state agency under the direct control of the state board of education which has the responsibility of administrating federal and state laws, rules, and regulations as they pertain to public schools.

State Education Agency (SEA): This is defined as (a) the state board of education; or (b) other agency or office primarily responsible for the state supervision of public elementary and secondary schools; or (c) if there is no such office or agency, an office or agency designated by the governor or by state law.

State Plan: The document submitted by the State Board of Vocational Education to the U.S. Office of Education describing the state's proposed vocational education program. This includes policies to be followed by the state in maintaining, extending, and improving existing programs to meet the intent of the Vocational Education Acts. This plan is prerequisite to receiving federal funds under the acts.

Technical and Further Education (TAFE): TAFE institutes is the Australian abbreviation for Technical and Further Education institutes. They form the backbone of the Australian VET and are highly regarded as an alternative pathway to achieving academic excellence. They provide for the pathways required to achieve industry recognized qualifications in addition to qualification for further education.

Technical Education: Education to earn a living in an occupation in which success is dependent largely upon technical information and understanding of mathematics and the laws of science and technology as applied to modern design, distribution, production and service.

Technical Vocational Education and Training (TVET): It prepares learners for careers that are based in manual or practical activities, traditionally nonacademic and directly related to a specific trade, occupation or vocation, hence the term, in which the learner participates. This is also defined as the UNESCO's accepted reference for vocational education and training. It has a wider coverage than the traditional VET.

Technician: A worker on a level between the skilled person in the field and the professional in the field. The technical knowledge of this person permits them to perform many duties formerly assigned to the professional. Technicians usually perform the functions of technical occupations, which are necessary but are not carried on by the skilled person or the professional. These persons are usually graduates of a 2 year or less program in a community college, technical institute or career, and technical schools.

Technologist: A worker on a level between the skilled person in the field and the professional in the field. The technical knowledge of these persons permits them to perform many of the duties formerly assigned to the professional. Technologists usually perform the functions of technical occupations, which are necessary but are not carried out by the skilled person or the professional. These persons are graduates of technology programs in 4-year institutions. Most technologists have completed a baccalaureate degree.

Technology Education: Programs, often in middle school and high school where students become aware of and explore the various technologies associated with an information and "high tech" society. Instruction usually is individualized and modularized so that a number of different technologies can be studied on an individual, scheduled basis. The activity-oriented problem solving approach emphasizes process over product. The activities result in technological awareness, psychomotor development; and awareness of the development, impact, potential, and careers related to technology. This is the favored term in the modern school for what in the past was called industrial arts.

Theorem: A proposition that can be proven from accepted premises; a law or principle.

Tertiary Education: Tertiary education is offered in a variety of public and private institutions that differ in history, mission, philosophy, programs and structure. It provides undergraduate and post graduate programs. It is used mainly to refer to post-secondary education. While it does not refer specifically to adult education, adult students are regarded as part of the potential clientele of most tertiary colleges. It includes higher education and further education.

Trade and Industrial Education: Instruction which is planned for the purpose of developing basic manipulative skills, safety judgment, technical knowledge, and related occupational information for the purpose of fitting young persons for initial employment in industrial occupations and to upgrade or retrain workers employed in industry.

Training: A planned and systematic sequence of instruction under supervision, designed to impart skills, knowledge, information and attitudes. Training is often contrasted to education and used with reference to vocational education. It usually refers to shaping learners' behavior and habits. Training is also defined as a planned and systematic effort to modify or develop knowledge, skills or attitude through learning experiences. Training sometimes refers to teaching techniques, such as demonstration.

UNESCO (United Nations Educational, Scientific and Cultural Organizations): It was founded in 1946 to further all its objectives throughout the world. It is based in Paris, France. It contributes to peace and security in the world by promoting collaboration among nations through education, science, culture, and communication. UNESCO works to create conditions for genuine dialogue based upon respect for shared values and the dignity of each civilization and culture.

United States Agency for International Development (USAID): It refers to an independent government agency that conducts foreign assistance and humanitarian aid to advance the political and economic interests of the United States.

Upward Mobility: Social movement upwards, for example, from working to middle class in the United States.

Vocation: Previously it meant a calling to one's work, many times having a spiritual connector or connotation. Now it means an occupation or what one does for a living.

Vocational Education: Organized educational programs that are directly related to the preparation of individuals for paid or unpaid employment or for additional preparation for a career requiring less than a baccalaureate degree. This term is used interchangeably with career and technical education.

Vocational Education Program: An instructional program with a planned series of educational experiences designed to prepare individuals for job entry or job advancement in an occupational field.

Vocational Education and Training (VET): This term is beginning to be associated with competency-based education in order to broaden the perspectives on occupational preparation. In chapter 12, this is defined as the kind of training that is focused to some extent to a career after formal training. In this research, VET is viewed as a pathway to the acquisition of job related training and advancement into the general education and training.

Vocational Guidance: The process of assessing an individual's abilities and aptitudes, to assist in making better career choices. The use of cumulative records, the results of standardized objective test of ability, attainment and aptitude, questionnaires, attitude scales, inventories, and interviews designed to assess the candidate's interests and preference, which provide the evidence on which guidance can be based. Also, the provision of occupational information, which may be used to make career choices.

Vocational Student Organizations: Organizations for individuals enrolled in vocational education programs which engage in activities as an integral part of the instructional program. Participation in the organization assists the students in developing leadership skills and permits them to compete on the state and national levels in affective, cognitive, and psychomotor areas.

Vocational-Technical Education: An older term indicating training intended to prepare the student to earn a living in an occupation in which success is dependent largely upon technical information and an understanding of the laws of science and technology as applied to modern design, production distribution, and services.

Work: A physical or mental effort directed toward some end or purpose. This may be a paycheck or it could be the joy and satisfaction of doing something worthwhile. See extended discussion in chapter 6 in the evaluation of work ethic.

Work-Study: In the United States, it refers to undergraduate students or high school students taking work for their universities or schools while they are studying.

PROFESSIONAL RESOURCES

The following Web sites provide pertinent information about student organizations within career and technical education:

Agriculture Education Student Organization:

The National FFA Organization http://www.ffa.org/about_ffa/index.html

Business Education Student Organizations:

Business Professionals of America http://www.bpanet.org/About/
Future Business Leaders of America—Phi Beta Lambda http://www.fbla-pbl.org/
History of International Association of Administrative Professionals http://www.iaap-hq.org/CONNECTIONS%20newsletter/Images/History_of_IAAP.htm
California DECA http://www.cadeca.org/

Health Occupations Education Student Organization:

HOSA: Health Occupations Students of America http://www.hosa.org/whatis.html

Family and Consumer Science Student Organization:

American Association of Family and Consumer Sciences http://www.aafcs.org/

Vocational Industrial Education (VIE) Student Organization:

Skills U.S. Massachusetts http://www.maskillsusa.org/

Technology Education Student Organization:

Technology Student Association http://www.tsaweb.org/
International Technology Education Association http://www.
iteaconnect.org/

The Largest Association for Career and Technical Education in the United States:

The Association for Career and Technical Education (ACTE) http://
www.acteonline.org/

REFERENCES

Bennett, C. A. (1917). *The manual arts.* Peoria, IL: The Manual Arts Press.

Douglas, P. H. (1921). *American apprenticeship and industrial education.* New York: Columbia University.

Dyrenfurth, M. J., & Blandow, D. (Eds.). (1994). *Technology education in school and industry: Emerging didactics for human resource development.* New York: Springer.

Ham, C. H. (1900). *Mind and hand manual training: The chief factor in education.* New York: American Book.

Lang, O. H. (Ed.). (1898). *Educational creeds of the nineteenth century.* New York: E. L. Kellogg.

ABOUT THE AUTHORS

THE EDITORS

Kathleen P. King, EdD, is professor of adult education and human resource development at Fordham University's Graduate School of Education in New York City. King's major areas of research have been transformative learning, professional development, distance learning, and instructional technology. Her experience in adult learning has spanned these fields in diverse organizations including community based organizations, business, higher education, career and technical education and numerous partnerships. Most recent endeavors continue to explore and develop learning innovations and opportunities to address equity, access and international issues. She is the author of 10 books and numerous articles. Dr. King is the editor in chief of *Perspectives, The New York journal of Adult Learning* and research board member for several national and international academic journals. In addition to receiving numerous academic and professional awards in the field of adult learning, her coedited book about distance education, *Harnessing Innovations Technologies in Higher Education,* received the Frandson Book Award from the University Continuing Education Association in 2007. And she has received numerous other international and national awards for her leadership, research and innovation in adult learning, adult education and distance learning. Dr. King was included as one of 50 adult educators highlighted *North American Adult Educators: Phyllis M. Cunningham Archive of Quintessential Autobiographies for the 21st Century* published by Discovery House in 2007 and she was recently nominated for The International Adult and Continuing Education Hall of Fame. Dr. King may be reached at kpking@ fordham.edu

Victor C. X. Wang, EdD, is assistant professor and credential coordinator at California State University, Long Beach where he teaches courses in career and technical education, adult education and curriculum development in the electronic classroom and the traditional classroom. He holds four graduate degrees in vocational and adult education obtained from American institutes of higher learning. He is the author of dozens of articles in national and international journals, book chapters, and books dealing with vocational education, adult learning, training, transformative learning, curriculum development for adult learners and distance education, and an editorial board member for prestigious journals. He is the recipient of numerous academic honors and awards, including two outstanding teaching awards and two research awards. He has published books in China and in the United States. Prior to working for universities in the United States, he taught for different universities in China. Dr. Wang may be reached at cwang@csulb.edu

THE CONTRIBUTORS

Ernest Brewer, EdD, is professor and principal investigator/director of pre-college enrichment programs at The University of Tennessee, Knoxville. He is the editor of *International Journal of Vocational Education and Training*. He is the author of numerous articles and books in career and technical education and has received numerous academic honors and awards. He is a successful grant writer and grant administrator and has brought millions of dollars to the university. Dr. Brewer's current research interests, which are frequently intertwined, include job satisfaction, occupational stress, and job burnout. In his current capacity as a professor, he chairs masters and doctoral committees at the university. Dr. Brewer may be reached at ewbrewer@utk.edu

Kisilu Kitainge holds a PhD, in technology education from RMIT University Australia, a MPhil. in educational psychology and a BEd in Technology education Moi University, Kenya. He is a lecturer in technology education. He is an author of numerous journal articles and a recipient of numerous grants. Dr. Kitainge can be reached at kitainge@yahoo.com

Fredrick M. Nafukho holds a PhD in human resource development from Louisiana State University, where he was a Fulbright Fellow 1996-1998, an MEd economics of education, and BEd business education and economics from Kenyatta University. He is associate professor in the Department of Educational Administration & Human Resource Development, College of Education & Human Development at Texas A&M University, College Station, Texas. Prior to joining Texas A&M University, he was associate professor of adult education and human resource development, University of Arkansas. He was also a senior lecturer and head of the Department of Educational Administration, Planning & Curriculum Development, Moi University Kenya. He is the recipient of numerous grants and the author of over 60 articles, book chapters, and two books.

Henry O'Lawrence holds a PhD in workforce education and development from Penn State University. He has been a research specialist in quantitative analysis. His research areas cover workforce education, community college leadership, training, adult learning and distance education. He has published refereed articles in the above areas in national and international journals. He is associate professor of workforce and adult education and department Chair at California State University, Long Beach where he teaches courses in workforce education and development and research methods in the electronic classroom and the traditional classroom. He is a popular presenter at numerous national and international conferences on career and technical education. Dr. O'Lawrence may be reached at holawren@csulb.edu

Gregory Charles Petty, PhD, is professor at the University of Tennessee, Knoxville. For the past 2 decades, he has focused on the study of the occupational work ethic, that is, the scientific exploration of behavioral factors and motivation of workers. His unique and original research has led to the design of a psychometric instrument, the occupational work ethic inventory, OWEI ((c) Petty, 1992) to determine an individual's occupational work ethic. He teaches undergraduate and graduate courses in health and safety. His primary research areas are work ethic for a healthy life, behavioral issues for safety and health including occupational stress and psychometric measures of performance, attitude, and self efficacy. He has contributed to and/or written various grants funded by the Department of Health and the Department of Labor and has been a consultant to private industry for organizational behavior and management. His academic work includes directing 24 doctoral dissertations and 20 master's theses; publishing 43 peer reviewed publications and 53 scholarly refereed papers at national conferences. Dr. Petty may be reached at gpetty@utk.edu

Carol Koerner Redhead took her graduate studies at Cal State Long Beach in vocational education, human development, and gerontology.

She was a student of distinction and graduated with honors. Presently, Carol works in the retail horticulture field, designs and maintains landscapes, teaches vocational education students, and also teaches at the elementary and middle school levels. By drawing on her wide experience in both the wholesale and retail aspects of ornamental horticulture, as well as her expertise in the field of horticulture therapy, and coupled with her experience in the design and implementation of many early childhood education programs, Carol has been able to bring to students of all ages the practical and theoretical learning in which they may find a career or a fulfillment of self-interest. Carol Redhead may be reached at carolredhd@att.net.

INDEX

Printed in the United States
97052LV00001B/13/A